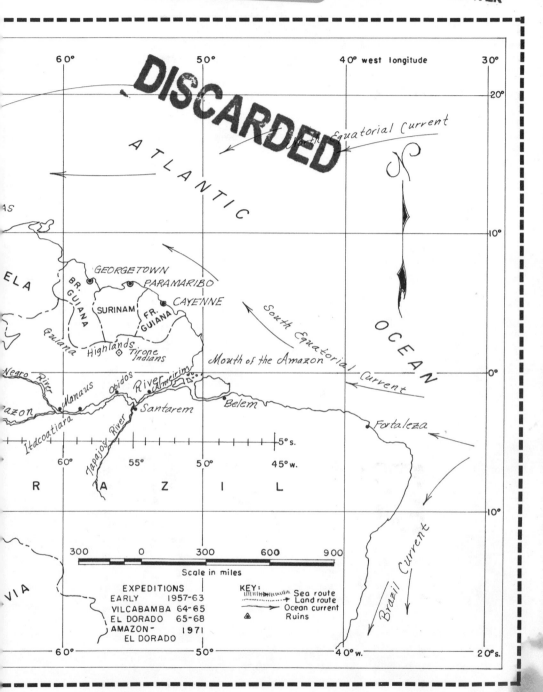

60°   50°   40° west longitude   30°

20°

ATLANTIC

North Equatorial Current

10°

GEORGETOWN
BR. GUIANA   PARAMARIBO
SURINAM   CAYENNE
FR. GUIANA
Guiana Highlands   Tirone Indians   South Equatorial Current
OCEAN

Negro River   Mouth of the Amazon   Current   0°
Manaus   Obidos   River   Almeirim
Itdcoatiara   Tapajos River   Santarem   Belem
Amazon   Fortaleza
5°s.

60°   55°   50°   45°w.

R   A   Z   I   L   10°

Brazil Current

300   0   300   600   900
Scale in miles

EXPEDITIONS   KEY:
EARLY   1957-63   ·········· Sea route
VILCABAMBA 64-65   ——→ Land route
EL DORADO   65-68   ——→ Ocean current
AMAZON-   1971   △ Ruins
EL DORADO

60°   50°   40°w.   20°s.

VIA

PROJECT "X"

The Search for the Secrets of Immortality

by Gene Savoy ❦

Illustrations by Nicholas A. Nush

THE BOBBS-MERRILL COMPANY, INC.
Indianapolis / New York

By Gene Savoy

The Cosolargy Papers
Antisuyo—The Search for the Lost Cities of the Amazon
On the Trail of the Feathered Serpent
The Child Christ
The Decoded New Testament
Prophecies to the Americas (2 Vols.)
The Image and the Word

With James C. Geoghegan

The Essaie Transcripts

All photographs used in the text are by the author unless otherwise credited.

Published by the Bobbs-Merrill Company, Inc.
Indianapolis   New York

Designed by Ingrid Beckman
Manufactured in the United States of America
First printing

Library of Congress Cataloging in Publication Data

Savoy, Gene.
  Project X.
  1. Occult sciences. 2. Savoy, Gene.
  I. Nush, Nicholas A.   II. Title.
BF1999.S3423   001.9   76-44670
ISBN 0-672-52181-4

To Anna Van,
who encouraged me to write this book

CONTENTS

Author's Note and Acknowledgment v
Warning viii

First Transition–TIME

1 The Fountain That Regenerates the Aged 3
2 At the Sun Temples 14
3 The Enigma of Man's Origins 20

Second Transition–CONSCIOUSNESS

4 Project "X" 39
5 Beyond the Sun 45
6 The Disappearance of Societies 62
7 The Solar Ages of the Earth 65
8 The Sun of Intelligence 74

Third Transition–BEING

9 The Great Discovery 85
10 The Reality of Immortality 96
11 The Illusion of Death 104
12 Dual Images 114
13 Mind / Time / Space Control 120
14 Introduction of Solar Energy into the Brain 139
15 Fusion of Heaven and Earth 152
16 Energy Fields 164
17 Time / Space Entities 171
18 Brain Images 174
19 Objects from Outer / Inner Space 188
20 Light Alchemy 202
21 Cosmic / Solar Energy Intelligence Factors 218

Fourth Transition–FORM

22 The Golden Man 227
23 In the Lands of the Amazons 236
24 A New Solar Genetics 242
25 Transformation of Man into the X Variation 256
Bibliography 267
Index 273

WARNING

The techniques described in this book are not intended to be employed by the reader and must not be employed by the reader.

While direct viewing of the sun is described in this book, the reader should not attempt to view the sun. Viewing of the sun is hazardous and causes blindness.

Neither the author nor the publisher can assume any responsibility whatsoever for any harm that may result from the use or application by the reader of the techniques described in the following pages.

AUTHOR'S NOTE AND ACKNOWLEDGMENT

The research project that prompted the writing of this manuscript is still being carried on. The discoveries may eventually provide new horizons in science and are certain to influence philosophy, psychology and religion. The experiments themselves have been kept secret for many years and for good reason. Some of the techniques involved can seriously affect the human brain and the other parts of the nervous system, so much so that I have deleted certain details.

In recounting the story of Project "X" and the transcripts, I received invaluable assistance from many colleagues and research assistants, some of whom have been collaborating with me for nearly two decades. They encouraged me to tell the story as completely as possible, without sparing scientific details for the sake of the lay reader. These aides helped me work through original transcripts, amounting to more than four thousand typewritten manuscript pages, composing twenty-four volumes, a total of over a million words.

For their review of the manuscripts and their selections of relevant portions and for valuable technical and editorial corrections and suggestions, I thank Elena Baugh and my wife Sylvia. For help with the recordings and tapes I thank Ellen Seaman. I also wish to thank all the members of The Academy for Advancement in the Religious Arts, Sciences and Technologies of Cosolargy for their assistance and help with research.

This rather technical story stresses advanced metaphysical and philosophical concepts as well as some complex scientific issues. I have tried to explain these ideas, issues and techniques so as not to confuse the reader. However, since the transcripts go beyond the three dimensions of our physical world and the written word cannot always make them clear, I have used a certain symbology similar to mathematical equations and medical formulas.

Many prominent persons were involved in this remarkable exploration of self. Since some of them wished to remain anonymous, their names have been changed by me. However, in most cases, real names have been used.

While this story is a true narrative, it happened over a six-year period. Even so, I have tried to re-create the tension and drama we all felt when these startling events occurred.

Gene Savoy
Reno, Nevada
October 21, 1976

First Transition

TIME

1

The Fountain That Regenerates the Aged

Monte Cunga, Peru

July 7, 1970—The explorer stared hard at the face of his wristwatch. The second hand was running unusually fast. Although it was noon by the sun, the chronometer registered seven o'clock, a seven-hour gain during the previous twenty-four.

I was the explorer, and I knew my watch was reliable. It had been checked only days before in Lima by a Swiss firm that assured me it was in perfect running order. It had been running fast for weeks, which had prompted me to have it examined in the first place.

While I thought I knew why my watch was racing, I had wanted to make certain that my facts were correct: it only gained time when I wore it.

I tucked the watch back under my sheepskin and pulled on my left glove, shivering momentarily against the cold air that swept down from the towering heights off to the west. July was the coldest month in the Andes; and the mule train had labored 5,000 feet up the craggy trail since sunrise. Near the pass at the 13,000-foot level, clouds were forming and flecks of snow were beginning to appear. A strong wind tore at my clothes. So I took the extra wool poncho from behind the saddle, slung it over my shoulders, and tucked the ends under my leather boots against the stirrups.

The poncho smelled of animal sweat. And no wonder: the neck and shoulders of my mule were wreathed in white foam. Wisps of steam rose from its body, and its flared nostrils puffed clouds of vapor into the cold air. I grabbed my hat as a sudden gust threatened to blow it away.

My own body was drenched in perspiration, too, but that came from a raging fever that my thermometer said was close to 107° F. The fever had held me in its grip for five days now. While fevers were no stranger to me, and I had grown accustomed to their discomfort during the many years I had been hunting the forgotten remains of the ancient civilizations in the Amazon jungles, this fever was more tenacious, more critical than any I had ever had. I knew it wasn't yellow fever, because I had been vaccinated against it. I had also been taking my anti-malaria pills regularly. I knew the cause of the fever perfectly well, yet I was still stunned when my hair began to fall out by the handful and my skin and fingernails started to flake and peel away.

I told myself I should have known that a person cannot fight against death without risking death. That was the chance I was taking with my experiments, and I had to accept the results, whatever they might be. I could not have known how near to death I was to come or how close my work of nearly two decades would come to perishing with me in the hours ahead.

Despite my illness, I was determined to reach a complex of hidden sun temples situated on the crests of the forested peaks. I had attempted unsuccessfully to reach them before, and now that I was so close, I had to keep going. It was crucial to me that I reach them.

These temples seemed more important than all the sites I had reclaimed over the last fourteen years, and I had forty cities on my roster of discoveries. Among them was the legendary lost city the Incas, called Vilcabamba, that had eluded explorers for some four centuries. Its discovery had gained me international fame and recognition.

To the archaeological community, I, Gene Savoy, was an enigma. Because I was self-trained, archaeologists could not understand why I kept looking for ruins without stratigraphic documentation by trained and competent specialists. To them I was a visionary and a mystic. They simply could not understand what drove me.

All right, I had found cities of ancient peoples where none had been thought to exist. My ideas on man's origins in the Americas challenged long-accepted theories.

In my lectures before scientific bodies I presented my findings simply for what they were: evidence that high civilizations had occupied the eastern slopes of the Andes and, more important, that their cultures were highly advanced in the arts and sciences of medicine, astronomy and metaphysics. A major part of my theory was that their religions were every bit as sophisticated as those of the supposed Old World. I also believed that these American cultures had preserved knowledge that went back thousands of years. I speculated that America was really the Old World and that it may have sustained civilizations of the very earliest races. Such ideas were strongly resisted by so-called scholars, and my work was ignored by these academics. Some specialists with connections had even gone so far as to try to discredit my work.

Knowing I was not the first explorer of new ideas to meet with resistance, I reacted by dedicating all my time to explorations and research. I had no desire to quibble with the so-called men of science who could not have known I was charting new spiritual territory. How could they understand that my findings went beyond archaeology, anthropology and a materialistic and mechanistic science? If the world was to catch up to my discoveries, I believed I must turn away from the criticism, or become cynical and embittered.

Fortunately, I had developed a considerable following: dedicated men and women who believed in my work to the extent that they assisted me financially and offered to help with research. My investigations were fascinating, and it's easy to understand why they attracted loyal supporters. But to help the reader grasp what I was actually accomplishing, I'd need to explain my ideas carefully.

Albert Einstein postulated in his special theory of relativity (applying to matter in motion) that an object attaining a velocity near the speed of light would diminish in size in the direction of

motion. A human—for instance, a crewman aboard a hypotheti-
cal spacecraft—attaining such a velocity would also contract in
size. All physiological processes would slow down. All clocks
aboard the spaceship, including the timepieces worn by the crew
members, would lose time. Because of the relativity principle, the
crew members would also experience a slowing down of the aging
process.

The same effect would be produced if a watch were transported
to the sun. Any material object attaining the actual speed of light
would be transformed into energy; the equation $E = mc^2$
demonstrates that there is never any real loss of mass-energy in
the universe, only change.

As a university student I had been drawn to a study of Einstein's ideas on relativity, when I was attempting to find an answer to the idea of transient energies postulated by the French
Jesuit scientist-philosopher Pierre Teilhard de Chardin when
explaining the nature of cosmic ether. On the other hand, I
postulated a fifth dimension of existence, a higher reality
beyond the physical world to which man had access, and that
time and energy could somehow be manipulated in such a way
as to penetrate it.

I had left the university and had studied privately for seven
years before departing for South America in 1957. There, I
believed, I would find the answers among the ruins of ancient
civilizations which had produced sun priests with a vast but now
lost knowledge of the uses of energy, especially solar energy.

While all of Einstein's ideas regarding spacecraft were theory at
the time he formulated them, crew members of space vehicles
could not expect to attain velocities near the speed of light
(186,000 miles per second or about 670 million miles per hour).

After 15 years of research and experiment, I had actually
demonstrated Einstein's theory on the physiological level. I had
succeeded in slowing down my watch to some degree, and there
was evidence suggesting that my physiological processes were
equally slowed down by my practicing of techniques inherent in
what I had named "The System." It was the ancient writings of
Spaniards who had recorded many wondrous tales during the
conquest of the Americas that had stirred my imagination. I was

especially interested in the stories of Indians who had lived to a great age.

The Florida of the Inca by Garcilaso de la Vega described the adventures of Juan Ponce de Leon, who set out to look for the island of Bimini or Buyoca, where it was rumored among the Indians that there was a fountain which rejuvenated the aged and converted old men into youths. Unfortunately, Ponce de Leon's expedition was ended before he could reach his goal. He perished from wounds inflicted by the natives of Florida, and the secret never came to light.

Antonio Pigafetta's manuscript on the voyage of Ferdinand Magellan told me about inhabitants of Verzin (Brazil) who lived to ages of 125 to 140. Repeatedly, the Spanish explorers described long-lived Indians along the Amazon—women who were said to be 150 years of age, yet had the appearance of forty. Convinced that these accounts were reliable, I decided to discover the secret of this reputed long life.

Stories of the Inca king Huayna Capac provided one of my earliest clues to the puzzle. The Inca looked straight into the sun with the naked eye, although admonished not to do so by a sun priest standing near him. It was forbidden for anyone except the priests at the sun temples to look into the sun. Legend tells us the Inca continued to gaze at the brilliant orb and contemplate its nature.

Why had he looked at the sun? And more important, why was it forbidden? I felt that the prohibition itself was a strong clue, because the act involved light—or solar energy—and the human eye, a direct pathway to the brain and nervous system.

How was the Inca able to look at the sun without harm to his eyes? Some Yogins of India stare at the sun, but eventually they go blind. Why was the Inca not blinded? The story intrigued and baffled me.

A medical doctor and professor of physics at the University of Leipzig, Gustav Theodor Fechner, had stared at the sun in 1848 as a means of producing afterimages in the retina. He was blinded, but he claimed that prayer and meditation had restored his eyesight three years later. Remarkably, the good doctor said that as a result, he possessed a new kind of expanded sight. He said he could see a "field" around living things such as plants.

His book *Life After Death* and an earlier work "Comparative Anatomy of the Angels" recounted his new-found ability to see spiritual forms around plants. Although these and later books shocked his colleagues, they were very popular with the general public. Fechner's experiences had altered his attitude toward life. He wrote that the true freedom of any creature can only be found in the soul, whose awakening enables the individual to see life as it really is, not just as it appears.

There appeared to me to be a link between the act of the Inca Huayna Capac and Fechner. The Inca had contemplated the sun because of a natural interest—probably because he had seen the sun priests performing the sacred act. He might have wondered why the sun made a regulated course through the sky in a predetermined manner, which indicated the sun was under the influence of a higher power, just as the subjects who obeyed his wishes were under his influence.

Fechner may have been drawn to look at the sun from a scientific point of view, but not understanding the proper method, he suffered the penalty of blindness. My idea was that by introducing sunlight into the brain and nervous system via the eyes one became to some degree extraterrestrial. Not only could one project oneself into the universe, but one might bring these cosmic energies down to man. I thought the mere act itself would tend to speed up an electromagnetic field surrounding living organisms.

It was only a theory based on the ideas of Einstein, who had pointed out that the heart (and I imagine the same thing would hold true for the electromagnetic fields enveloping the human organism) could be compared to a clock. Hence the heartbeat of a person traveling at a velocity close to that of light would be slowed down, along with respiration and all other physiological processes, including the electro-phenomena of the nervous system. I believed that as a result of the very act of introducing solar energy into the powerful electric fields via the eyes and optic pathway, the organism would change its mass into energy by the ejection of beta particles from the nuclei as in radioactive substances, and the organism would possibly take on the characteristics of light or radiation. Einstein had postulated that a clock transported to the sun would run at a slightly slower rate than on earth. Therefore I was using the sense of vision to transport myself to the sun. Plato had said centuries ago, "The true lover of knowledge is always striving after being. . . . He will not rest at those multitudinous phenomena whose existence is appearance only. . . . The prison house is the world of sight." I was using sight to escape the confines of the earth and in a manner of speaking transporting part of my being to the sun.

In 1945 I began looking at the sun. I first viewed a solar eclipse with the use of smoked-glass filters and by forming tiny apertures with my fingers and looking through them. It was not until 1955 that I learned the secret of how to look directly into the sun with the naked eye for brief periods without harm. But I was seeking more profound results. Two years later, when I journeyed to Peru to explore for sun temples, I was convinced that the old sun priests of the Americas had possessed secret sciences of the sun in relation to man.

Something had gone wrong. The procedure had started to reverse itself, and at an alarming rate. My watch was now gaining time, which suggested, in theory, that I was now aging. Hours passed. At five o'clock in the afternoon the caravan approached a wooded plot where it was to spend the night. The animals, sensing their day's work was done, broke into a trot and stopped in front of an adobe cabaña thatched with grass.

The Indian muleteers, who had been trotting alongside the noisy pack train, tethered the animals one by one at the crude hitching post and started unloading them. While this was going on, the head man sent two helpers out to gather firewood, and when this was done he personally attended to me and helped me into the hut. Soon a fire was going and before long there was hot coffee laced with sugar, served in wooden bowls.

Soon after this I curled up in my sleeping bag on the floor. The other men hurriedly ate their thick llama soup and for an hour afterwards chewed coca leaves. Then they rolled up in their wool ponchos and went to sleep without making a sound.

Antonio, head man and my old friend, threw his poncho over my tired form. He and I had explored together for four years, and I was touched as I watched the light from the fire dancing over his face. The light and his skin seemed to blend into a single radiant glow. Antonio was puzzled. What was it that drove me, someone from a faraway land, to explore this, his country? I had spent money, far more than I should have, on guides, mules and provisions in order to examine the remains of Antonio's ancestors—old stone remains that shouldn't have interested any-one with good sense.

At first the head man had accepted the good pay for his services and the mules, thinking there might be some hidden motive. He had learned, as had the porters and machetemen, who were always suspicious of strangers who came into their land, that I never looked for treasure or disturbed the temple sites in any way. My sole purpose was to photograph them, make quick sketches and record them in my journals. Mostly, I was satisfied to have the ruins cleared of the thick mantle of jungle growth that hid them from untrained eyes, then sit for hours in the buildings, usually at the larger sites built of the better-cut stones, and gaze into the sun.

How could I do this when the light was so bright? Some of the men had tried to imitate me by turning their eyes toward the fiery disk, only to be forced by its brilliance to look away. Not even Antonio could look at the sun. Anyway, why should a man want to do so? It seemed senseless to Antonio and the other men. Was I simply mad?

Some might have thought so. But not Antonio. He may have grown to love me, yet he didn't hope to understand me. Like most Peruvians of the uplands, he had learned early as a youth to accept things he did not understand. Antonio was well into his middle fifties, past the prime of life, and I was ten years his junior, though one wouldn't have thought so by looking at us, for he appeared much younger. Even so, I was accepted by the Indians of the highlands as a *viejo,* an old one, who was respected and admired as if I were one of them.

Antonio sat before the fire for a long time, looking into my fevered face. I had aged considerably these past few days, and now I looked drawn and tired. Around midnight Antonio finally fell asleep with his chin buried in his chest.

Antonio did not see, nor did any of the other Peruvians, the scene that took place around three that morning. A brilliant light awakened me, and as I opened my eyes, I saw a golden face. At first I thought it was a hallucination brought on by my fever, but then I realized it was a luminous form composed of some matter every bit as real as any other, though the figure was from some other world of space and time. The face looked at me but said absolutely nothing. Then I noticed my own hands were glowing like the radium dial of my watch.

If I stared at the form closely, it began to fade, but then appeared brighter than before when I stopped. The form seemed more radiant and took on sharper lines when my eyes were not focused. Then I could retain the image for a long time.

The form's diamondlike eyes were set in a face that seemed to be made of polished gold. Not one word was spoken. The form appeared to be trying to communicate, and in fact it was, though not through the spoken word. The eyes, those brilliant eyes glowing like crystals, were communicating a message to me. As I looked into them I was shocked to recognize something familiar. The reality stunned me. The eyes were my own, the face was mine, and both were made of a substance unknown to me.

As suddenly as it had appeared—as if waiting to make an exit until I had discovered who it was—the form vanished. I sat up in my bedroll, hoping it would return, but it did not. I searched my mind for an answer, while staring at my arms, which still glowed eerily. After an hour, I went back to sleep, puzzled and mystified.

A cock crowed in the predawn. One by one the men rose from the dirt floor. One of them lit a fire and another went out to fetch water for morning oatmeal and chocolate. As I always did before sunrise, I pulled on my boots, wrapped myself in my poncho and went out to meet the coming sun. It had been a ritual for many years now, and though I wasn't yet myself, I didn't want to miss it. After walking down to a running stream, I washed my face, drying myself with a large handkerchief from my hip pocket.

Slowly, I walked up a slight incline, my legs heavy and weak from the fever. Finding a rock outcropping, I sat down on the cold stone, using my poncho as a blanket. My watch read 9 o'clock, and should have shown a few minutes after 5 o'clock. At that point 20 hours had been gained. What would occur if the watch gained a full 24 hours?

In theory I would then begin aging rapidly. I wondered where I had gone wrong. I put the questions out of my mind as I prepared myself to receive the first rays of the morning sun. The meaning of last night's occurrence and the events that had preceded it haunted me. I felt the answer lay in continuing what I had started.

Then, composing myself, I slowly began modifying my level of being. It had taken me years to master the technique. It was not meditation, through which one goes silently within, stilling the mind and senses as in the Yoga practice. On the contrary, I had learned to reach beyond the boundaries of self, projecting myself into all life around me. Retreat was not part of my method; it was more an expansion of self. I had learned the technique from the Indians of the interior.

Long ago I had recognized that the people of the Andes had been far more advanced in the arts of metaphysics than their counterparts in the far-flung Himalayas. Not much had survived, but I had found enough, preserved by oral tradition among the primitive tribesmen, to interpret a good deal more and to formulate a system of self-transformation that had been used for centuries by masters of the arts.

When I had attained the state desired, I sat motionless, ready to receive the benevolent rays of the solar star. The hymn of nature surrounded me, a soft concert of sounds—songbirds saluting the coming sun, the music of rushing water, wind in the trees, a gentle rustling of animal movements, a multitude of insects humming to life before taking flight or moving about the underbrush. Amid this hushed symphony the sun broke over the mountain, spilling its warmth over the green meadows and thick forests.

In the center of the display of nature, I sat quietly facing the light, my eyes fixed on the central point that blesses the planet with heat and light. For an hour I looked at the sun, absorbing the strong light into my eyes and thus into my brain and nervous system.

Then I returned to the hut. When the men had rounded up and loaded the pack animals, our mule train moved out again deeper into the high jungles that grew luxuriantly at these altitudes: nearly 10,000 feet above sea level. We took a trail known to Antonio, whose concern for me seemed to increase by the hour.

My physical appearance had been so altered by my illness that Antonio hardly recognized me. I wasn't eating, and I appeared detached from my surroundings, following along behind the rest of the caravan, lost in a world of my own.

Antonio's portly figure trotted alongside me, keeping an eye on my leaning posture, for fear I might fall off the mule. Antonio had seen me looking at the sun earlier and had no doubt noted the radiant glow that had enveloped me on the rock, when the birds had come in large numbers to circle above. But he didn't like the dark circles under my eyes. From his concern over me I realized that Antonio had the feeling that this was to be our last expedition together.

2

At the Sun Temples

Heights Above Balsas, Peru

July 8, 1970 — For nearly six hours the string of mules and cargo bearers had labored through the thick forest. At midday they emerged from the dense growth onto an open plateau.

Dismounting with some effort, I drew my machete from its scabbard and motioned for Antonio to join me with the cutters. Deliberately we moved away from the main party, cutting our way through the heavy vines and jungle growth towards the heights. There were big ruins at the crest, according to what some Indian had told us.

Some two hours later we reached a summit ridge thick with forest and approached a mound of vegetation, where we sat down to rest. One of the men tore several sheets of green moss off the side of the mound, exposing a wall of stone blocks. At this he grunted his satisfaction, sat down on the floor of the jungle and stuffed his mouth with coca leaves.

"Shall we clear the site?" asked Antonio, spitting on a rock and drawing his blade from its leather sheath. The other men began honing their machetes on selected rocks. We had reached the first temple buildings. Although my legs felt like lead weights and my head was pounding from the effort of the climb and the altitude, I told them to go ahead. Swaying on my feet, head swimming, I forced myself around the wall, while the men started cutting vegetation.

Moving by sheer will power now, I passed enclosures tenoned with benevolent-looking sculptured stones, made in the image of human faces, up to a platformlike level several hundred feet above the party below. Every muscle in my body ached. At one point I staggered, my knees folding like hinges, and I slumped against a huge boulder to catch my breath. Fatigued and gasping, I sat there staring at the valley far below.

The ancient builders had selected an excellent spot for their temples—inaccessible to those not familiar with the stone pathway that spiraled up the rugged jungle cliffs. I knew the buildings were part of a chain of structures stretching for many miles along the summits, north and south, east and west. They may even have been the remains of the largest and most complex series of ancient structures ever erected by man. There were hundreds upon hundreds of circular buildings, up to fifty feet in diameter, built atop stone terraces that had turned natural mountains into pyramid-like heights far greater than anything found in Egypt. Their architectural beauty was graced with geometric, animal and human designs made from elemental units placed together like parts of a mosaic.

Protecting these wondrous cities of the upper Amazon with their temples, aqueducts, canals and fountains, the whole linked by a network of stone roads, was like a sacred trust to me. I no longer shared their whereabouts with others, electing instead to wander among the silent citadels, absorbing their beauty. To me they were my cities to care for, to safeguard. To have spoken of them publicly seemed like a kind of blasphemy and might have contributed to their being pillaged by tomb robbers after treasure, or by archaeologists licensed to steal museum pieces from the resting places of the dead.

All too often walls were toppled, tombs exposed and sometimes the forest burned off to clear the buildings, leaving them naked to the first rains. More than one of my beloved cities had been damaged beyond repair by such treatment. Desecration of the burial sites of the dead was to me the foulest of deeds, and the wanton destruction of these majestic cities was a crime against the human race. No, I would never again reveal the whereabouts of my cities.

Oh, it was glorious here—restful, peaceful after the hard climb. The strength was returning to my limbs, and I began to breathe normally. On the other side of the valley, visible through the hanging vines and ferns, no more than six hundred feet away, were the remains of a white monument. I could see the broken stonework lying about a grassy pampa, although most of it was submerged in vegetation.

I had searched for these complex ruins for months, and now that I had found them, there was no need to examine all the sites and clear each building. In any case, that would require months of work, and I did not have any months to spare. In fact, each temple layout with its terraced platform, round buildings, sculptures and rich architectural ornamentation, staircases, stelae and sculptured work was already etched on my mind.

Every site followed a uniform pattern of orientation to the sun and other celestial bodies. With their discovery the picture was becoming complete, because it wasn't so much what I found in the old cities, but what I felt there that contributed to my knowledge of these ancient people. My sensitivity had evolved to the point where I could just absorb energies, impressions and information psychically out of the living stone and out of the force fields of the cities built up over the centuries by those who had occupied these sites. The process appeared to operate in much the same way as infrared film captures the heat of bodies or objects even after they have moved away from a spot.

Now that my mind had cleared, it returned to the golden image that had appeared the night before. I was sure it had not been a hallucination. I had actually sensed the presence, felt the touch of its energy field. The image's eyes were alive and they had communicated something to me.

Hallucinations could be produced by narcotic plants like the coca leaf, *ayahuasca, chuchuhuasi* and other vision-producing plants and barks, whose uses had been taught to me by the *brujas* and *curanderos* of the interior. After taking a prescribed dose a person would swear he was flying through the air, penetrating the depths of the earth, carrying on a supposedly intelligible conversation with demonlike forms, phantoms, witches and the like, and all the while actually be lying perfectly still in bed and imagining the whole thing by means of the psyche. Moreover, the experiences and even the conversations could be fairly well predicted before they happened by the witch doctor administering the dose.

Different reactions could be altered by diet and other means known to the *brujas* and *curanderos,* who had preserved a tradition that went back many centuries. Long before, I had put aside these concoctions as dangerous to the stability and health of the mind and emotions, and I had serious doubts about the value of the kind of research being conducted by anthropologists who had in recent years become interested in the shamanism of the American witch doctors.

The peyote mushroom, chewed by the Mexicans, and the *huilca* seed, made into a powder called *cohoba* and sniffed into the nostrils through a tube by the Peruvians, induce a trancelike state that may have been useful to the trained Inca priest or doctor and possibly to the witch doctors in primitive regions, who employed a system of supernatural divination during their communication with invisible powers and used the drugs to cure the ill. But in the hands of the curious who wish to "take a trip," the degenerative effects of these drugs to the brain and nervous system are well known. When in the presence of all magical powers, one needs a strong belief in God to resist being taken over by the unconscious. No, my night visitor was no hallucination. I definitely knew the difference.

"Still running fast," I almost said aloud, glancing at my watch. Leaning my head back against the rock, I closed my eyes, wondering about the significance of the golden image and where I had gone wrong. While I was deep in contemplation, the rays of the sun penetrated the foliage canopy and fell on my eyelids. Instinctively, I opened my eyes and looked into the sun. At that instant, a ringing sound penetrated the depth of my being, and I could not move. Every nerve fought to control my form, but I was unable to call out or even blink my eyes; yet my mind remained perfectly alert. Then I was totally paralyzed, having lost control over my body entirely. I was unaware that the second hand of my watch had begun to speed up. A pulse of energy coursed through my being.

Suddenly, the golden image reappeared, this time out of the

sun itself. I became aware that I had stopped breathing, that I could no longer hear my heart beating. I felt suspended in space and time. The eyes of the golden image gazed into the center of my being and when its form drew closer, I felt myself wanting to merge with its radiance.

Was this to be my final transition? Was I transcending the earth to a higher dimension of reality? Perhaps this was what it was like to die. If that was true, at least there was no pain in the exit from the world; I felt no fear either, only the sensation of being unable to move my body. Was it catalepsy? My mind was clear; there seemed to be no loss of sensibility. It couldn't be an epileptic attack, for my body was unconvulsed and I was not in a trancelike state. These and other thoughts rushed through my mind, which seemed clearer than ever before in my life.

Only this incredible clarity kept me from surrendering to the form and to the urge to detach myself from my material body, which was slowly becoming transparent, like crystal, vibrating and oscillating like a spinning top. My eyes saw a world in transition, and it too was vibrant, crystalline. I could see through the trees and rocks to a world of another space and time. It wasn't all clear, but I was sufficiently aware of its existence to know that the material world was a kind of illusion, that there was more to it than anyone had ever suspected; actual force fields enveloped the material forms, and who was to say which was the true form? In that moment of suspended time I realized I was looking at my own true form and a new-found consciousness from somewhere deep within my being understood the meaning of life.

The whole mystery of life's purpose and direction was clear. Never had I experienced such a state of pure exhilaration. I saw, by some vision external to my physical form, my body resting against the rock, eyes open, staring into the sun. It was as if I were looking down at another being separate from my awakened consciousness. Then, like the pendulum of a clock, my reality swung back to my body and became aware of what was taking place. The rational mind took over, as if fighting for its own existence. Again I was looking at the golden figure before me. Now there was no fear or awe, but an understanding that the two forms, though of two sets of dimensions, were yet one, only occupying distinct places in time and being. For mounting seconds everything blurred; then with a great gasp I felt the breath return to my body. My heart began to pound like a pile driver.

The golden form had vanished with the return of my perceptory senses. Again I was part of the world and in control of my material body. Had I not returned when I did, I'm sure I would have passed out of the world forever.

When I had recovered from the shock of this experience, I stood up and slowly made my way back down the trail to the waiting men. I was stronger now, and my steps came quicker.

"Señor," shouted Antonio, "we have cleared the largest building. Are we to clear the others tomorrow, since it is so late?" Antonio approached, throwing glances over his shoulders to a stone building cleared of vegetation. It shone white in the dim light.

"No, Antonio, that won't be necessary." I clapped a friendly hand on my companion's shoulder, saying, "The expedition is over." Antonio gave me a puzzled look, but said nothing. He could see that my fever was gone, and this in itself gladdened him. He acknowledged my statement with a nod, and together we walked down the mountainside in the lengthening shadows, with the porters close behind.

3

The Enigma of Man's Origins

The Pajatén, Peru

August 14, 1970—Five weeks had passed since my transition in the northern jungles. Shortly after the experience, I had come back to Lima, and my health improved rapidly. Part of the reason for the improvement had been the reversal of the time gain of my watch. Now it was losing time daily.

Yesterday, Thursday, I had taken stock of my findings: a careful daily record had been kept since leaving the expedition. Shortly before sunrise, I sat down at my desk and pushed a chair up to the electric typewriter. Reading my watch carefully, I jotted down the apparent time and checked this against the clock-time on the wall, which I also noted. Satisfied that the two figures were accurate, I quickly began to type:

TRANSCRIPT

August 13

RECORD OF TIME VARIATIONS EACH 24 HOURS†

Month and Year	Day	My Watch Time	True Time	Difference
July	10	6:30 A.M.	9:45 A.M.	Loss: 3 hrs. 15 min.
1970	11	3:35 A.M.	9:45 A.M.	Loss: 6 hrs. 10 min.

12	6:10 A.M.	11:55 A.M.	Loss: 5 hrs. 45 min.
13	8:56 A.M.	11:56 A.M.	Loss: 3 hrs. 0 min.*
14	7:28 A.M.	10:38 A.M.	Loss: 3 hrs. 10 min.
15	6:30 A.M.	10:25 A.M.	Loss: 3 hrs. 55 min.
16	5:30 A.M.	9:30 A.M.	Loss: 4 hrs. 0 min.*
17	6:50 A.M.	10:10 A.M.	Loss: 3 hrs. 20 min.
18	5:40 A.M.	10:55 A.M.	Loss: 5 hrs. 15 min.
midnight 18	3:00 P.M.	12:00 P.M.	Loss: 9 hrs. 0 min.*

Hard work day. Concentration and creative writing. Watch and clock showing true time synchronized at midnight upon retiring.

19	6:42 A.M.	8:36 A.M.	Loss: 1 hr. 54 min.
20	5:00 A.M.	11:00 A.M.	Loss: 6 hrs. 0 min.*
21	4:34 A.M.	10:35 A.M.	Loss: 6 hrs. 1 min.
22	4:45 A.M.	11:17 A.M.	Loss: 6 hrs. 32 min.
23	3:25 A.M.	11:25 A.M.	Loss: 8 hrs. 0 min.*
24	5:41 A.M.	11:41 A.M.	Loss: 6 hrs. 0 min.*
25	5:29 A.M.	10:29 A.M.	Loss: 5 hrs. 0 min.*
26	5:25 A.M.	11:25 A.M.	Loss: 6 hrs. 0 min.*

Removed watch morning of July 26 and did not wear it during the day or upon retiring.

27	5:37 A.M.	5:37 A.M.	NO TIME DIFFERENCE
28	8:37 A.M.	11:33 A.M.	Loss: 2 hrs. 56 min.
29	6:38 A.M.	9:38 A.M.	Loss: 3 hrs. 0 min.*
30	8:45 P.M.	8:30 A.M.	Loss: 11 hrs. 45 min.
31	8:05 A.M.	11:00 A.M.	Loss: 2 hrs. 55 min.

Total Loss: 112 hrs. 53 min.

*I am puzzled by the recurrence of the even-hour time difference.

†Observations were made throughout the day, but the total time difference was generally recorded each morning.

TRANSCRIPT

August 13

Month and Year	Day	My Watch Time	True Time	Difference
August 1970	1	8:15 P.M.	1:42 A.M.	Loss: 5 hrs. 27 min.

My watch and clock synchronized at 1:42 A.M. true time. Spent day concentrating and doing creative writing.

| | 1 | 2:57 A.M. | 9:50 A.M. | Loss: 6 hrs. 53 min. |

Concentrated while asleep. Total time lost from morning of July 31 is 12 hrs. 20 min.

	2	2:22 A.M.	6:25 A.M.	Loss: 4 hrs. 1 min.
	3	3:22 A.M.	8:22 A.M.	Loss: 5 hrs. 0 min.*
	4	11:59 P.M.	7:14 A.M.	Loss: 7 hrs. 15 min.
	5	1:23 A.M.	5:23 A.M.	Loss: 4 hrs. 0 min.*
	6	2:18 A.M.	7:18 A.M.	Loss: 5 hrs. 0 min.*
	7	4:01 A.M.	8:03 A.M.	Loss: 4 hrs. 2 min.
	8	1:17 A.M.	6:14 A.M.	Loss: 4 hrs. 57 min.

Four hours lost during day while working. 57 minutes lost during night of restful sleep.

	9	1:16 A.M.	6:17 A.M.	Loss: 5 hrs. 1 min.
	10	1:55 A.M.	5:55 A.M.	Loss: 4 hrs. 0 min.*
	11	7:29 P.M.	7:29 A.M.	Loss: 12 hrs. 0 min.*

Worked until 3:00 A.M. true time of August 12.

	12	6:11 P.M.	5:17 A.M.	Loss: 11 hrs. 6 min.
				Total Loss: 78 hrs. 42 min.

Total time lost in 34 days or 716 hours is 191 hours 35 minutes, or 26.7%.

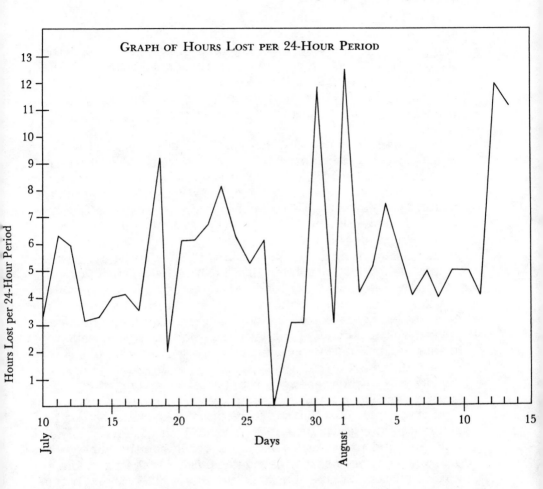

GRAPH OF HOURS LOST PER 24-HOUR PERIOD

NOTE:

I have made three important observations: (i) The watch is now losing time. The watch loses less time during the night while I am asleep, and the loss is greater during mental activity—especially while I am writing. (ii) The watch has to be worn on my person in order to lose (or gain) time. (iii) The above indicates that the electrical field around my body is somehow involved.

I am aware that an electromagnetic field similar to the magnetic field of the earth itself exists around the human organism. I can understand how this field could affect a watch because with clocks there's no static friction. That the electromagnetic field around the human body can be altered by changes in mental activity and the emotions, I know from my research. The mind and the emotions appear to generate energy which alters the field. It also appears that the techniques I have mastered of absorbing solar energy into the brain and nervous system via the eyes in some way intensify the electromagnetic field around my person. I am fascinated by the prospect of this abundance of energy and its effect upon my timepiece.

I have also observed that if my watch is allowed to run down, it immediately begins running again once I place it on my wrist. The energy of my body and of its field causes the watch mechanism to begin moving. Moreover, I can cause the watch to begin running merely by looking upon it. In some way that glance causes the watch to run. This experiment indicates the eyes actually radiate energy and furthermore that the radiated energy of the eyes can be influenced by the mental or emotional state. Thus, energy is a carrier of intelligence or information which I call IF (information factors).

That the watch slows down or speeds up according to the mental or emotional state of the person wearing it brings up the question of time and energy. It seems to me that time and energy are intimately related. The abundance of energy in the field and its modification by mental or emotional energy actually causes the watch to gain or lose time. Gaining time, when the second hand of the watch rotates rapidly, suggests that energy is being lost. Loss of time, when the second hand slows down, suggests a greater abundance of energy.

Einstein speculated that the properties of space could be influenced by a gravitational field. Though his ideas are not generally understood, he arrived at the conclusion that time intervals also vary with the gravitational field. He theorized that a clock transported to the sun would run at a slightly slower rhythm than on earth, just as a radiating solar atom would emit light of a slightly lower frequency than an atom of the same element on earth. This could be explained by the fact that the sun has a higher or more accelerated gravitational field than the earth. I have reasoned that my wrist watch has been affected by the gravitational field surrounding my person—a field that has been accelerated.

My watch has lost as much as twelve hours in a twenty-four-hour period. How can this be explained? In theory, the time loss of my watch suggests that I as a timekeeper am growing old less rapidly. Of course this slow-down is only relative. Nonetheless, the fact that I have done this on the physiological level, without having to attain a velocity near that of the speed of light or having to transport myself to the sun, is a revolutionary finding. Indeed, I have, in a manner of speaking, brought the sun and its energy down to my own being.

Though the experiments excite me, I am aware of the fact that I am only beginning to understand the idea of human immortality and of how time, energy and the human cognitive and emotional faculties are involved. The experience with the luminous or shining figure observed weeks ago suggests to me that there is far more to human life than our present-day science knows or admits. It appears to me that the approach of Darwin to the theory of human evolution, with its stress on the idea that natural causes are responsible for natural phenomena and that man evolved from lower animals or, more specifically, from "something very like an ape," is way off the mark.

I stopped typing, reread the pages I had copied, and checked the figures against my notes. Writing and recording data reminded me of how much I had learned and experienced since the expedition—and of how much there was to learn and to experience.

As I was about to review my notes once more, the telephone rang. I picked up the receiver and heard my personal secretary say, "Good morning. It's 6:15. You have fifteen minutes before the car arrives. See you at 6:30. Chau."

Hastily I shaved, showered, dressed and locked the leather bags containing my exploring gear. I reset my watch to true time, 6:30 A.M., and took the elevator down to the ground floor of the apartment building, where a long black limousine was waiting in the street. Sylvia Ontaneda was in the back seat. After the driver had put the bags in the trunk, I told him to drive us to the airport. Then I climbed in, greeting Sylvia warmly. She took my hand and kissed me on the cheek.

"Hi." Her melodious voice was full of excitement in anticipation of the trip ahead. She had worked with me for three years now and had been a tremendous help. A journalist, twenty-two years old, with an excellent memory and a sharp, keen mind for facts, she was as beautiful as she was efficient. She was taller than most Peruvian women, with long dark hair cascading down her shoulders. Because of her olive skin, most people took her to be Polynesian. Actually, she was Spanish-Arabian, born and raised in Peru. She was wearing form-fitting tan slacks, and a white blouse under a safari jacket with a red silk kerchief about her thin, Nefertiti-like neck. A wide-brimmed hat decorated with a leather band and tropical-bird feathers rested on her lap. I returned her kiss and slumped back into the seat.

"Well, how does it feel to be going on an expedition?" I asked, turning my head towards her. Her dark eyes met mine. "I really never thought you would keep your promise," she said. Months before I had told Sylvia I would take her with me to visit the Amazon territory and show her one of my lost cities, once it was safe to do so. She had read so much about my discoveries that she wanted to see one for herself. It seemed natural for me to ask her, since this might be our last opportunity to explore together, at least in Peru, for some time.

I had decided to take a year off in Mexico for a badly needed rest and to use some of this time to collate my notes, which had reached voluminous proportions, into meaningful texts. Besides, I was far behind in sending reports to members of the research group, and the move would give me a chance to catch up. I had asked Sylvia, along with others from the United States, to join me in Mexico. By this time I had become accustomed to her and dependent upon her reliability. I knew I would never be able to replace her and, too, I had grown very fond of her. When she accepted my invitation, I was delighted.

The limousine pulled up to Faucett Airlines, and we quickly checked the baggage and caught the 7:20 flight to Trujillo. From there we took a commercial flight over the snow-capped Andes and down into the Amazon basin to Tarapoto. I had radioed ahead and a small charter plane was waiting there. Thirty-three minutes later we landed at Juanjui, a quiet jungle community on the banks of the Huallaga, which empties into the Amazon further down. We taxied over the bumpy, grassy airstrip to a Bell helicopter that had just settled down.

Out stepped a tall, blond, blue-eyed pilot. He ducked under the whirling blades and ran over to open the door of the small airplane. The pilot cut the motors.

"Señor Savoy?" said the helicopter pilot putting out his hand.

"Si," I replied, shaking his hand. "Señor Trauten?"

The Peruvian, of unmistakable German extraction, answered in the affirmative and introduced himself to Sylvia. Then he helped unload the plane, which taxied away on its return to Tarapoto. The three of us stood talking under the hot tropical sky. I had chartered the helicopter to fly us up river over the Cordillera Central and then to the remains of an ancient city I had first explored and mapped five years before. I wanted Sylvia to see its magnificent citadel of stonework, built centuries ago by the Chacha people, of whom little was known.

A race of white men, the Viracochas, had erected their temple-cities atop a string of peaks, stretching for one hundred miles, at an average altitude of 9500 feet above sea level. They had centered their cities near caves, the Lodgings of the Dawn or the Place of the Birth of their ancestors, who they believed had first emerged from caves to civilize ancient Peru. Their rivals—the Incas—had conquered them. I had found scores of old Viracocha cities and temples and had explored deep into their caves and tunnels. This city, which I had named Gran Pajatén, was the one I had chosen to show Sylvia, mostly because it was one of the better known of my finds, one that had received international publicity following my first exploration of it in 1965.

Fortunately, a helicopter pad which made it accessible from the air had been cleared during its later study and excavation. I wanted Sylvia to experience the thrill of flying over the jungle and actually landing in the heart of an ancient city. That very day Trauten had lowered a cutter with a machete onto the pad, which, although it had been cleared four years previously, had become overgrown by the jungle. The machete man had cleared an area large enough to accommodate the helicopter when it returned hours later to land. Then, with Trauten's help, the cutter had cleared the pad sufficiently to allow the helicopter to land safely with Sylvia and me.

Trauten agreed to fly us to the ruined city at daybreak. Soon a youth piled our baggage on top of a rickety bicycle-like carriage and pedaled on ahead to the hotel, while the three of us walked casually into town. That night, in a small café overlooking the Huallaga, we dined on fresh fish taken from the river.

We talked about the project for hours—long into the night.

At first light I awakened, showered and dressed, then walked down a flight of stairs to call Sylvia. She was just finishing her makeup when I knocked on her door. Together we walked up the dusty street to the restaurant where we met Trauten. After eating a breakfast of fried eggs, toast and coffee, and having our thermos bottles filled with hot coffee, and fresh water put into the canisters, we returned to the hotel to pick up my cameras, film and some light gear containing food for the day, plus emergency rations, maps, compass and medicine kit.

I gave Sylvia an extra machete from my rucksack, knotted the nylon rope at the top and slung it over one shoulder with a casual flair. "All right, young lady explorer," I said, watching her buckle the machete around her thin waist, "let's be on our way." Taking her hand, I led her out of the hotel to the street, where Trauten and the youth with the bicycle carriage were waiting with our baggage. With the porter pedaling alongside, we made our way back to the airstrip, past banana groves and tropical flowers, with the sounds of macaws and songbirds filling our ears.

"This is going to be exciting," Sylvia said.

At the strip, our gear was arranged on the racks on either side of the helicopter bubble and lashed down with nylon line. Then we climbed aboard, and after the usual preliminaries Trauten lifted off. Reaching a sufficient altitude, he turned north and flew over the sleeping community of thatched roofs.

When we had crossed over Juanjui and reached the first canopy of trees, Trauten turned southwest 205° on the compass. A magnificent sight greeted us as we floated over the jungle. The sun had come up behind us, turning the forest into a patchwork of vibrant greens. The Huallaga, stretching below like a huge, winding highway, caught the first rays of sunlight on its surface, making a dazzling display. Soon we came to the Pachicilla, tributary of the Apisoncho off to the south, and after a short time we crossed the Huayabamba river. For three-quarters of an hour we climbed steadily past hanging forests and cascading waterfalls that emptied their foamy, sparkling water down hundreds of yards to the Apisoncho river below. When we had reached 19,000 feet, we pulled on our jackets in the cold air—a sudden change from the humid, hot weather of Juanjui. Soaring past rocky heights of purple and brown stone, the helicopter came upon a huge white limestone cliff clustered with hanging vines. It loomed out of the jungle like a gigantic iceberg. Taking a northerly course, we swept past the natural monument, banked east over two forked streams, circled back and hovered over the floor of the jungle, which was itself 10,000 feet above sea level. We spotted a clearing five hundred feet below us, and we slowly descended. In a few seconds we settled to earth at the ruins.

Trauten cut the motors, and as the big rotor whirled slowly to a stop, we unbuckled our seat belts and stepped into the stillness only a virgin jungle produces. Though we were but 62 air miles from Juanjui, the towering city, rising out of the jungle like an island, was in reality very remote from civilization. Five years before, it had taken my expedition the better part of a week to cut a way to it through the dense jungle. Today, barely an hour of flight had brought us there.

"This is the most wonderful experience of my life. I never thought anything could be so beautiful." Like so many others, Sylvia had read my reports of these cities of the inner Amazon, but to see for herself the awe-inspiring majesty of the works of ancient man in this near-primeval setting was quite another thing. "Incredible," she said. "Who would believe it?"

We strapped on our machetes and hacked a trail to the upper sections of the city, which were hidden by the growth. We walked through tight streets flanked by circular buildings, past sculptured winged figures of stone peering from the shadows like men frozen in time. An hour later we reached the largest building. There, Sylvia and Trauten sat down to rest on a stairway, but I refused to sit.

I walked to the edge of the terrace and surveyed the scene. There was the roar of the Pajatén hundreds of feet below. Everything about the place was familiar—the cliffs, the mountain heights. Then I remembered how it had been when the site was virgin. The city had been covered by a mantle of tropical growth so dense one could easily get lost between buildings. It was a maze of trees, vines and moss, teeming with insects. Days of work were needed just to make out its dimensions. Now the site was dry, topped by recent growth. The large trees that helped protect the city had been felled, underbrush cleared and burned by the archaeologists who had come in to map and study it. Once they had completed their mission, they abandoned this beautiful place to the first rains, which had toppled the exposed walls. Several sculptures had been yanked out and taken to Lima.

I felt literally sickened by the sight, regretting that I had announced its location to the press. To search any longer for more ancient cities in Peru—and goodness knows my maps were marked with other areas that needed exploration—was now meaningless, especially in the light of my new discoveries. Now, my sights were set on exploring new dimensions of reality and my inner self. How eager I was to spend more time learning just how the absorption of solar energy and its influence on the brain and nervous system—and on the electric fields around the human organism—worked upon the timepieces and, above all, to understand more about my "new light being." I needed time to think and to experiment. Exploring had given me this opportunity. But this was no longer true in Peru.

I seemed to have a tiger by the tail: difficulties with officials, the military and political figures, and the pressures of the press. No, it was time to move on to more fertile areas. As it was, I could hardly bring myself to look at the ruined city. Perturbed, regretting I had returned, I walked back to my companions. For an hour we walked among the ruins, but I was lost in thought.

When the sun was high in its arc, we lifted off the clearing, flew over the forested peaks, dropping down to the river past the northwest section of the white cliff. We soared past tombs—stone buildings, ornamented with designs and painted red and white, that contained the remains of the dead lords of the city—hung up on the face of the cliff like huge wasp's nests. Observing them through the bubble of plastic, I couldn't help thinking about the fact that the dead there had once been alive, much as Trauten, Sylvia and I, but now they were nothing but dust locked up in stone sepulchers. This thought accompanied me all the way back to Juanjui. I said very little.

Tired and grimy from the day's exploration, we went to our rooms for a cool shower and a change of clothing, then met in the dining room for a light lunch of fruit, cheese and wine. Afterwards, Sylvia and I walked around the village, then hired a dugout canoe equipped with outboard motor for a cruise up the river. From the outside, the jungle can be beautiful, and we both enjoyed the trip. The cool air felt good against our skin, darkening now under the bright sun. Myriad butterflies wafted over the calm water as we skimmed along. Fish jumped, too, and sometimes, as our course took us close to the shoreline, we skittered past bamboo huts and waved at little children who had come out to stare blank-eyed at us. At five o'clock we docked the dugout and walked back to the hotel, agreeing to meet at six for afternoon tea.

Sylvia waited until 6:20 in the lounge, and when I did not appear, she went up to my room. She knocked lightly, but there was no answer. Finding the door unlocked, she turned the knob and stuck in her head. She focused her eyes in the dim light and saw me sitting on the floor facing the setting sun. I was dressed in my tropicals sitting on bended knees with my hands, palms upwards, outstretched to the sun. She saw that I was reflecting and started to close the door.

I moved my head slightly and said, "Come in, Sylvia." She replied in a whisper, "I am sorry to bother. It was late, and I thought you might have lost track of time again." She knew about my work, having typed many of my notes and research papers. She had even begun to practice some of the techniques on her own.

She had been offered two scholarships, but had turned them down in order to continue working for me. Her reasons were quite simple: she found my work very exciting and, most of all, new. Its newness appealed to her very much. She closed the door quietly behind her and walked across the room, sitting on the floor near the open balcony doors, through which the sun streamed into the room. No words were exchanged between us for several minutes. Sylvia was content to sit there quietly observing my eyes reflecting the light of the sun. I held her utterly spellbound until the sun sank behind the blue cordilleras. Then I looked at her and asked, "What do you know about Darwin's theory of evolution?"

"Only what I have read," she replied. "He said that life evolved by natural selection through continuous development from simple to complex forms, that species evolved and survived according to their adaptation to the environment."

"Very good," I said. "But what about man's origins?"

"About the same, I guess. The idea seems to be accepted by most scientists that evolution doesn't make much sense unless Darwin's ideas regarding man's origins are true. Personally, I can't accept that man evolved from some kind of forerunner like the ape."

"What makes you say that?"

"Because Darwin's ideas are dominated by a material reality, they don't take into consideration any idea of the spirit. I mean any metaphysical approach to origins holds no place in Darwin's ideas. The supernatural was abandoned as untestable."

"Then you accept the Biblical creation concept?"

"Not entirely. I simply wonder how, if man evolved from lower animals, do we explain man's intellect and spirituality? There is much more to man than the physical, wouldn't you say?"

"Yes, I would—" I said, stretching my legs out in front of me and leaning back on my arms. "The survival of the fittest seems to hold true for animal life, as does the divergence of species. I believe Alfred Wallace, who spent years in the Amazon and who was the co-discoverer of the theory of natural selection, had a more advanced idea of the origin of species—he stressed that other forces were instrumental in the survival of man."

"What forces?" Sylvia asked.

"I would say spiritual forces. I think Wallace accepted the idea of a pre-existent archetype, a spiritual man who was responsible for man's origins."

"I don't understand what you mean."

"To put it concisely, there was, at one time, a spiritual man who occupied a spiritual world. This man and his world generated our physical world of reality."

"Where is this world now?" Sylvia replied, with a startled look.

"It still exists, though it may be imperceptible to man, or if you prefer, to the animal man of Darwin, who depends solely upon the brain and five senses."

"How do you know this? I mean, can you prove it?"

My mouth formed into a slight smile. "Because I've experienced it, seen and felt it—enough to know that man's origins can never be explained by a study of natural phenomena, of the material universe alone. Just because science abolished the spirit doesn't mean it doesn't exist. By stressing mental processes produced by the brain and senses, science has reduced man to little more than an animal, justifying all that Darwin wrote about evolution—man as a chance product without any goal, a sophisticated animal, if you prefer. Once you emphasize the spirit, those thought processes that came before the development of the brain, you enter a whole new world. It explains how ancient man, reduced to a primitive state by environmental changes, was able to rise above the surrounding conditions to an advanced, civilized being who produced great cities, temples, agricultural works, astronomy, medicine and high religions, almost overnight."

"But how was he able to accomplish this?"

"By the discovery of the spirit. Perhaps it was given by a Moses, a Plato, a Jesus or, in the case of these cities here in the Amazon, by a religious teacher called Viracocha by the Peruvians, and Quetzalcoatl by the Mexicans, who introduced them to a hidden system or science of the spirit. In other words, they had the key to man's true nature, one that could put them in contact with the stars, with God; because the most primitive savage existing in the jungle can, by application of such a system, elevate himself to genius, a near replica of the first spiritual man.

"You see, man has all the necessary equipment, dormant faculties, just waiting to be developed. This fact in itself invalidates Darwin's ideas of natural selection when applied to higher man. It happened right here in the jungle centuries ago. The builders of these great cities may have been existing as neolithic man, when suddenly a teacher burst upon them, teaching the arts of civilization. You saw today a city dedicated to him, and temples bearing his likeness in stone."

"What happened to the people; why were the cities abandoned?"

"Well, that's anyone's guess. With the coming of the Spaniards the civilization here perished; of course, it was in decay long before the conquest. Perhaps the people forgot their spiritual heritage and went over to the ways of the material world, which stressed commerce, competitiveness, waste and all the rest that leads to eventual enslavement of people and continual war. This is a kind of destruction, for whenever the material is emphasized over the spiritual, a kind of degeneration sets in, inevitably destroying any civilization, no matter how great. It happened to Rome and could very well happen to America, or Russia. That is why we have reached a stage where I believe it necessary, for our time, to alter radically our concepts of existence.

"Modern man must move away from materialism in science, religion and on all social levels, if he is to survive with dignity. Our task should be not to solve the bodily needs to the exclusion of the spiritual needs, but to nourish both, for they are interrelated. Of all living things, man alone has access to a world beyond our time-space continuum of physical reality.

"With this knowledge comes a new understanding of life, an understanding which can make men less aggressive and more tolerant of one another. Life can never have real meaning to men who understand only material things or material needs. The sooner man realizes he has access to a spiritual world, that he has faculties that function in this world just as the brain and the body function in the material world, the sooner he will accept that his true nature is greater than anything that science, with its stress on natural phenomena, can imagine."

Sylvia silently pondered my words.

As if anticipating her thoughts, I said, "I realize what I have told you sounds idealistic and impractical. But let me assure you that it is a very practical business, if I may use that word. If man originated from a pre-existent spiritual world—let us call it a highly advanced ultra-dimensional world—then it is quite possible the force field around the human organism, excluding the heat field produced by the physical body, is a spiritual or ultra-dimensional body beyond our concept of space and time.

"This would mean that this body is eternal, just as the spiritual or ultra-dimensional world is eternal. Didn't Christ speak of such a body, such a world?" Sylvia nodded her head in assent.

"The experience up north taught me something very important," I said. "I learned that time is relative, and man is not limited to his physical body. He is ultra-dimensional, spiritual—that is, he has access to other worlds of reality and existence. In order to reach this level of being, he requires energy, for the more a living being develops, the more varied its capacities, the greater its requirements of energy.

"Metabolism of food, oxygen and water provides the organism with energy sufficient for its biological functions. But it is a fact that intellectual activity requires very little of this kind of energy. I have discovered that absorption of sunlight provides creative energy not only to the mind, but to a higher level of being—a spiritual consciousness—the activation of which takes man beyond the limits of a third-dimensional space-time continuum."

"And this is all made possible simply by looking at the sun?" Sylvia asked.

"Well, that's only part of it—there is much more to it than meets the eye, if you'll pardon the pun."

"Pun?" She didn't remember what the word meant. Although her command of the English language was quite good—she had studied English as a child and later had been an exchange student in Kansas, graduating from Salina High—some words escaped her.

"Oh, I was only making a play on words. That's what a pun is. I meant to say that looking at the sun is only part of the technique."

"I understand." Then she studied my face intently, as she often did when concerned about something. "If I understand your notes correctly, the fact that your watch was running fast in Chachapoyas was indicative of some kind of speeding up of your force fields, that they were vibrating quicker, or oscillating at a more rapid rate, if I remember the word correctly. And this caused the transition, when you were in two worlds or sets of dimensions at the same time."

"That's right."

"But this was the opposite of what you were striving to achieve. I mean, by gaining time, you were living at an accelerated rate." She searched my eyes carefully before asking the next question. "Wouldn't this mean that you might have died prematurely, before the normal life span?"

"In theory, yes. But only on the physical level, as we understand it." The reply startled her.

"I don't understand."

"Well, there is a great deal we don't understand about life, its origins and meaning—and especially what happens to people when they die. After all, death is only relative. By that I mean we all die sometime, if not today, then tomorrow. If I had died up north it wouldn't necessarily have meant I, as an individual, would have died. I simply would have vacated the body to another dimension of space and time. The body would have died then as a result of my absence. After all, I nourish and sustain the body. It doesn't nourish and sustain me."

"Then you don't believe we die with loss of the physical body?"

"Not any more."

"Then you don't care whether you live or die?"

"I wouldn't say that. I enjoy life here. I am content to live and work, make my contribution, so long as there is meaning to it all. But I have no desire to live as an animal, struggling only for physical existence, killing others in order to survive. If that's all that life means, then there's no point to it all. My God! There has to be dignity for man—intellectually and spiritually."

The young woman gazed fondly at me. She couldn't imagine herself doing any other kind of work now. The outside world was boring, uninteresting, now that she had been exposed to the research. But she cared for me and had been concerned about my appearance and loss of weight upon my return from the most recent expedition.

"But you have no assurance your watch won't begin gaining time again if you continue with the techniques?" Now her voice was grave.

"The ancient wise men of India called the path taken by the initiates in their quest for God the 'razor's edge,' for each risked being cut if they faltered or hesitated. You see, Sylvia, I am standing barefoot on the edge of a razor. I can't turn back now . . ."

"But can you be sure you have the answer? I mean, if you have another transition, you might not come back."

"When the golden image appears again, I'll be ready."

Second Transition

CONSCIOUSNESS

4

Project "X"

Mexico City, Mexico

April 3, 1971—After moving to Mexico in October, I established myself with a staff of six research fellows, including Sylvia, on the entire twenty-third floor of a fashionable hotel complex near a large park away from the bustle of the inner city. There I went to work in earnest, compiling my notes into text form and inaugurating what came to be known simply as Project "X." My companions all shared a common belief: they were working on a new frontier that was unique and challenging. Volunteers all, they had dropped everything when my letter arrived, inviting them to share in my investigations.

After years of being exposed to a system of techniques via correspondence, they jumped at the opportunity to become actively involved and, leaving jobs, businesses and professions, hurried to Mexico. Once there, they were put to work typing notes, answering correspondence and sharing in the experiments. It was the hope of participation that brought them—actually to become engaged in my research and to apply what I had reported on in my previous letters had fascinated them.

At the first meeting, the question of the secret techniques came up. As to whether they would be allowed to practice them, I answered, "Why do you think I asked you here? What has been discovered is the property of everyone, not just me." Then I suggested that all of them keep daily time records, checking their watches upon arising and before retiring. Cryptically I explained that this was the first step. As for me, I was going on to the next phase of the research, which, I cautioned, was a penetration into unknown dimensions. Whatever the outcome, I extracted from them a pledge to carry on the Project in unity should I be forced to withdraw for some reason.

While this beginning carried ominous overtones, each agreed when I emphasized that the pioneering of a new philosophical approach to the understanding of life and its origins was more important than any individual. I also promised to keep them abreast of my own experiences and to give them regular reports on the new techniques I was applying.

Since arriving in Mexico, I had thought often about the golden image. There was no scientific explanation for it; therefore, I was forced to look beyond science for an answer. I was still convinced it was not a hallucination caused by my fever. An actual form had appeared. But was it part of the material universe as man knows it, or was it a specter? I had rejected both of these explanations. The form was too vibrant, too radiant with energy to be traced to either source.

My notes of March 16th reflect my feelings on the matter:

TRANSCRIPT

March 16

8 A.M.

All life requires energy if it is to emerge, continue living, reproduce and survive. The secret of life and its origins lies in the atom; all life is composed of atoms. Atoms in one state or another form the stars, planets, oceans and atmospheres—and all living forms therein. Since all living things evolved under the influence of sunlight, it appears that solar radiation is the key to man's origins. I am not so interested in when or where life evolved, but why life originated.

The answer to man's origins might be found in the stars or, more precisely, in our parent sun. The solar system, like the rest of the universe, appears to be 90% hydrogen and 9% helium. The human body is 88.5% hydrogen and oxygen (63% and 25.5% respectively). It is also a point of interest that oxygen is one of the most important elements in the ionization of gases in interstellar space and is responsible for or affects the nuclear synthesis of the heavier elements. Hydrogen is the most abundant in interstellar space, followed by helium and then by carbon, nitrogen and oxygen, all three of which, like hydrogen, are vital to human life. All the elements essential to life are in the upper half of the periodic table—we are curiously related to the solar system and the universe not only by composition, but also by increasing order of complexity of form. A comparison of the major elements follows:

COMPOSITION OF UNIVERSE %		COMPOSITION OF HUMAN BODY %
Hydrogen	90	63
Helium	9.1	0
Oxygen	0.057	25.5
Carbon	0.021	9.5
Nitrogen	0.042	1.4

9 P. M.

NOTE—If God is an abstract, mathematical term or symbol that describes and includes the ALL, then creation, the dance of life, is a grand cosmic recycling process. Nothing is gained, nothing is lost, at least as far as we can discern from our point of view in the 3-dimensional world of matter. If the building blocks, the elements of the material universe, are as limited in number and related in structure as we believe them to be, then is it not the process itself that constitutes the mystery? Can the process or processes be impossible to understand if we humans are as chemically related to the universe as we seem?

I expounded upon these ideas in my notes of March 19th:

TRANSCRIPT

March 19

If the processes of God are inherent or automatically operative in the incredible order and beauty of creation in form and matter, are not these processes an intelligence inherent in matter? And if so, do not our related atoms share in the intelligence of their counterparts in the solar system and universe?

It seems to me that solar energy is encoded with IF (information or intelligence factors) that, once received by the individual organism, are processed by the brain and other parts of the nervous system. Thus, radiant solar energy is responsible not only for life, but also for thought on our planet.

The absorption of solar energy through the eyes and thence into the nervous system links man directly with the sun. Moreover, such absorption of solar radiation, with its inherent IF, feeds and nourishes the nervous system with radiant energy and with cosmic intelligence or cosmic information brought in from outside the environment of the planet. Therefore, through these techniques, man is projected into space—and the energy and intelligence of the universe brought into direct contact with man.

The relationship between the eye and the sun determines and divides living creatures. Development of eye outwards from the brain in vertebrates, as opposed to inwards from the skin in invertebrates, is significant both biologically and symbolically. This development allows the production of clearer inner pictures, as in a camera, which can be impressed as an engram upon the brain and later reproduced from memory, as if by remembered sunlight, in both the waking and sleeping states.

The relationship between eye and sun is markedly different between day and night creatures. The difference is both chemical and structural.

Man probably enjoys the greatest range of color perception of all creatures. Has color perception increased within man's recorded history?

Solar energy, waves of different frequencies, is interpreted by the nervous system as color, through intelligent communication. The communication is not only contained within the human organism (eye to brain), but is extended outside the organism via the eyes, creating a relationship between man and the light source, the sun, through energy. If energy is the medium of communication, then it must also be the medium of information.

Human eyes developed little capacity for vision in the long-wave infrared range. Why? Infrared light has greater capacity for penetrating physical matter (as in infrared photography). Since sight is the most highly developed human sense, why did it not develop more keenly in this range? Why does eyesight improve with exposure to higher-frequency, shorter-wave ultraviolet light, as Dr. W. H. Bates found to be true in his research with sunlight and the eyes?

March 20

I have discovered that energy absorbed in the proper dosage into the nervous system through the medium of eyesight has a tendency to flood the field surrounding the human organism. The field, and consequently the body itself, becomes saturated with infrared radiations, often resulting in high fevers such as that I experienced in Peru. The secret lies in reflecting or emitting the energy outward through a technique which brings about a balance or polarization. If this is not done in a satisfactory manner, the heat continues to build up, resulting in severe headaches and body tensions, and tends to cause variant forms of nature to manifest themselves in one's vision.

Our research suggests that long and systematic exposure to sunlight not only enhances the sensitivity of the photoreceptors (rods and cones) in the retina, but somehow brings forth new ones able to register a creative energy contained within sunlight, which introduces new images into the medullary area of the brain and stimulates or brings about a higher consciousness. In our work we found that the pineal gland, located in the center of the brain, appeared to respond to the spectral characteristics of solar radiation, effecting biochemical changes. This appears to result in the development of a "third eye," which, unlike ordinary eyesight, produces a "vision" of its own.

Summary: The human organism can be made, by proper exposure to sunlight, to handle larger than normal amounts of radiation, resulting in a hypersensitivity that causes a heightened sense of conscious, visual awareness.

Energy from the sun holds the secret of life. Since the sun is composed of 90% hydrogen, and man is composed of 63% hydrogen, the relationship between man and the sun is not to be doubted. A survey of studies of the origin of the solar system by such scientists as A. G. W. Cameron, Fred L. Whipple and Donald H. Menzel indicates that when the sun was young the pressure of radiation expelled a large part of its original material out into space, leaving the planets behind.

If the earth is condensed from the primordial material of the sun, perhaps our origins might be traced to a pre-existent solar being (a light being), the archetype of man, Adam or the first man. This could explain man's evolution from a being of energy to a being of matter: a descent.

Was it not Plato who said, "Lower things will be found again in higher things—though in another form"?

Solar beings of light! Could they exist in the sun? Do such thoughts border on science fiction, or is there a basis of truth in this? If heaven exists, if that other world spoken of by Christ is real, then it must hold some position in the scheme of things. Christ often spoke of light in His sermons. Light/heat/radiation can be converted into matter, forming the material universe. Indeed, absorption of solar energy by our planet results in a net gain of matter. Astrophysicists theorize that someday the earth will be converted again into light/heat/radiation when our parent sun dies out. The universe, being in a state of continual change, is transformed from light to matter and back again. Is it logical to assume that solar beings, like angels, fly upon wings of light and manifest themselves to man within the vision of his inner eye?

My research into solar techniques has led me to believe (through experience) that human consciousness possesses a built-in point of contact with solar worlds. The human mind is indeed enlightened and illuminated by contact with the sun . . . the apparent source of our origin.

Yet, within the light that illumines the human mind exists a supreme consciousness, some force or power transmitted to us which may not fall within the category of electromagnetic radiation.

The visible sun is but a bridge to something higher!

5

Beyond the Sun

Teotihuacan, Valley of Mexico

September 6, 1971—As the faint light of the coming dawn reflected off my face, I sat quietly on the cold stone facing the eastern horizon, while other members of the Project sat clustered about me. We had all climbed the narrow steps of the Pyramid of the Sun to its summit 216 feet above the darkened valley.

We had come to look at the sun. The pre-dawn stillness was interrupted by songbirds saluting the burning circle of the sun as it peeped over the mountain crests. Not a word was spoken, each of us dwelling upon his or her innermost thoughts. For some time now, it had been a daily routine for us to gather in the pre-dawn darkness at Teotihuacan, to greet the solar disk in silence until it had come over the surrounding peaks. Each had been instructed to contemplate his respective thoughts and then to discuss them afterwards. In this way we learned together in community.

When we had finished with the technique, Bill Dailey spoke: "Very fulfilling. My comprehension of things is beginning to unfold, my mental awareness seems to have intensified." As he spoke, he looked over the dead city and took a deep breath.

A photogrammetrist, Dailey was a quiet, mentally alert man with a quick wit. At 39, he was a thinker who liked to live within himself. He had arrived in Mexico from Oregon to join me, his half-brother and senior by four and a half years. Not only was Bill a participant in the Project, but he was cartographer to the expeditions. The dullness of his work had persuaded him to take a year's leave of absence to assist me. He found the whole concept of the research intriguing.

"The sun has a humbling effect. No matter what man achieves, it is nothing compared to the sun. I am learning the meaning of reverence . . . and possibly how to find an answer to what lies beyond. Surely the people who built this city must have known about the uses of the sun." Then he became silent, directing his gaze straight at the sun. His evaluation was correct, because all the monuments of this ancient city, known in the Nahuatl language as the "City of the God," were oriented to the sun; indeed, the very pyramid upon which we sat pointed towards the spot where the sun sinks beneath the horizon at the end of its passage through the zenith. One could almost say the city, like the hub of a gigantic wheel, was geared to follow the course of the sun at various times, marking in stone the periodic death and resurrection of the sun and other heavenly bodies; evidence that an exact science was known to these mysterious people.

Like the many Nahuatl initiates, who had once climbed the pyramid to absorb the redeeming fire of the sun into their eyes and spirits, our group had gathered to attain the illumination and inner vision that comes to those who desire to be converted into light. Some of them may have heard in the stillness the Nahuatl neophyte's hymn to Xipe Totec (Lord of Liberation), directing man's spirituality: ". . . fire has set me free. Perhaps I shall vanish . . . and be destroyed, I, the tender corn shoot. My heart is green like a precious jewel, but I shall yet see the gold and shall rejoice. . . ."

Milenko Tomich must have heard the hymn, because he said softly: "I often think that when I transmit energy to the sun, I might be taken up into the light, body and soul." Rawboned, sinewy, over six feet tall, Tomich was 50 and an English professor. Dedicated to Yoga, the piano and the pursuit of knowledge, he had corresponded with me for three years.

Next to Tomich was Harry Hawkins, middle-aged, looking older than his fifty-two years. He was one of those successful businessmen who exercised too little, ate and drank too much. He also knew and understood too little. As Hawkins ran the fingers of his right hand through a patch of long, graying hair, he examined Tomich with sharp, keen eyes that revealed the strain of success in the business world. He had come to Mexico to learn from me about psychic energy and its uses, especially the unknown forms of energy and how they influenced extrasensory perception (ESP), paranormal phenomena (PSI) and psychokineses (PK). Trained in the pseudoscience of radiesthesia (sensitivity of matter to radiations), Hawkins was mainly interested in the body's energies and its force fields, as well as its sensitivity to radiation.

"Thought can affect the person thinking the thought," said Hawkins. "With the sun's energy you can and do concentrate and conduct more energy than you would ordinarily. You link up with the sun, and your thought patterns alter the wave front of the living force fields around your body. When you receive energy from the sun, you also transmit energy to the sun. This transaction creates a change in both you and the sun." His usually crisp voice was slurred as he uttered the words out of the corner of his mouth, as he always did when he was excited. "Here at the top of the pyramid, where the capstone used to be, there is a concentration of energy. You sit in the midst of energy forms. Like a piece of iron filing attracted to a magnet you could, theoretically anyway, be attracted to the sun"—he snapped the thumb and forefinger of his left hand—"just like that!"

Hawkins looked at Tomich as he said, "With absorption of energy, weight is lost. With weight loss, the living force fields around the body are altered. This means levitation and even dematerialization are quite possible. Instead of being material . . . well, you'd become light . . . or energy."

"What would happen to the material body?" Tomich asked. "Would it turn into pure energy?"

"Probably disappear," replied Hawkins.

"Hawkins has a point," I said, taking my eyes away from the sun. "All living things are surrounded by electric force fields."

With a nod, Tomich acknowledged what he had learned from the research papers and experiments we had conducted together.

"The fields determine the life of the organism, not the other way around," I said. "In view of this, if a person's field were to undergo change, through some form of metamorphosis, that is, the organizing field around the body would collapse or simply disappear, the body would remain behind, and the 'new' field, should it be transported to the sun, as Hawkins has suggested, would then organize a completely new form."

Sylvia, usually eager to enter any conversation, but not before she understood the matter under discussion, had held back. But with my mention of a "new form" she spoke up. "What do you mean by the field going to the sun and then generating a new form? What kind of form?"

"Well, we shouldn't confuse the simple electric fields associated with the human organism in general and the brain in particular with the pre-existing field of a higher or more refined light body and any spiritual consciousness. The spiritual field would have to undergo some drastic change before it could influence the electrical field of the body. In other words, the spiritual field might transfer itself to the sun, but the physical body would not transmigrate there. Upon the spiritual field's merger with the sun, the electric field of the human organism would collapse, leaving behind a disorganized and inert mass of flesh and bone. With no field to support it, it would simply die. The new field, transformed, would then generate an entirely new type of being. The basic research of Dr. Gustaf Stromberg teaches us this, if we analyze it in the religious sense."

"Wasn't Stromberg an astronomer renowned for his research at Mount Wilson Observatory?" someone asked.

"Yes, he was," I replied, "a most esteemed Swedish scientist who was philosophically motivated. His ideas sprang from some inner light that had little to do with his scientific training. Strangely, his work was acclaimed by other scientists."

"Was this acceptance because of his credentials as a scientist or because of his unique ideas?" Sylvia asked.

"Probably both," I answered.

"What would the scientific community think of our research project?" asked Tomich. "We aren't scientists, at least not astronomers, physicists, geneticists, medical doctors—the kinds of specialists one would expect to be doing this kind of research."

"That's true," I said, "but many of our associates represent those and other scientific specializations you didn't mention."

"But is our research accredited scientifically?" Tomich continued.

"Science is as varied as it is boundless," I answered. "It is not the property of any one school or institution. For example, when I delivered a lecture at the New York Explorers Club in late 1968, my findings were strongly challenged by an eminent authority and a group of scientists. I was told that my discoveries, regardless of their extent, had no scientific value because I did not have a degree. Of course, this was not the opinion of the majority of members, and only goes to show how a few can influence pioneers. My detractors had overlooked the very significant fact that it was the discoveries themselves—monuments, temples, cities—and what they could tell us of ancient man in the Americas that were important. Whether the remains were uncovered by a recognized authority shouldn't have mattered. After all, there is room in archaeology for everyone who loves it. If we allow only the experts to interpret the findings and give up our right to study and express our opinions—then archaeology will remain limited and confined forever to a few. The task of archaeology is the recovery, description and interpretation of artifacts, inscriptions and monuments. My specialty was the recovery of monuments in places no one else cared to look. While my books express my views, I was perfectly willing to allow other specialists to express their opinions. Science is open to everyone. If controlled, it is like despotism, because it destroys the spirit of freedom that true science should always enjoy. Some scientists have a contempt for everything they cannot comprehend. With skepticism, they attempt to destroy what does not fall within their understanding."

"Science is as old as humanity," Sylvia said. "Modern science spans just two centuries, with half the scientists that have ever lived alive today. Gene's attitude is more universal. I know some archaeologists who are afraid to express their opinions for fear of criticism and ridicule by established authorities."

"Right," I said. "During the explorations we discovered artifacts that could not be understood by orthodox archaeology, which explains why we had to branch out and develop new approaches to the understanding of these buildings."

"Then your explorations are not governed solely by science?" asked Tomich.

"Should they be?" I retorted.

Since no one replied, I answered my own question.

"The truths of the universe are well veiled. The attitude of the scientist with a degree is usually dictated by his training; he stays inside the framework of his training. The same might be said of the trained clergyman. His attitude is largely the result of his theological training. He has been told what to preach and what to think. That ends his creativity before it gets started. Which may explain why religions haven't changed for centuries.

"The Project and its research don't fall within the framework of natural science any more than they fall within the framework of orthodox religion. Yet, the Project is representative of pure science and pure religion. Let me explain. Secular science, like orthodox religion, is often naive about the great secrets of man's existence and the true nature of the universe. It is believed that a high school education, four years of college and possibly a master's, Ph.D. or Doctor of Divinity degree are all that are required to prepare an individual for an understanding of the secrets of the cosmos. One doesn't gain access to other worlds simply by reading books, or by simplistic belief in ideas. The very nature of academic training often limits one's ability to understand the spiritual universe we are pursuing in the Project, because it stresses sense data and the power of reason.

"Yet, some rational anthropologists, psychologists and philosophers believe they have the credentials to investigate mystic religion, even when the very nature of their disciplines is objective, thus making them unable to fathom the transcendental nature of the spirit. Secular scientists see the sun as a celestial object; mystics say the sun is a cosmic intelligence, a living force. If, because of its credentials alone, secular science continues to dominate the minds of men and to claim sovereignty over mystic religion, then the dawning of a new dark age is not far away. Man may be able to live without science, but not without mystic religion."

"I don't understand," said Hawkins.

"Well, Anaxagoras was banished from Athens in the fifth century B.C. because he said the sun was not the divine sun-god Helios, but just an incandescent celestial sphere."

Hawkins challenged me with this question: "Well, isn't the sun a fiery mass of burning gas?"

"Most laymen believe so, but the fact is, physics teaches that there is a continuous process of hydrogen changing into helium, with a resultant increase in the weight of the nucleus and the loss of a neutrino: an instance of energy without mass moving at incredible speed. Now back to Anaxagoras. He sought a scientific explanation of the solar system. He thought the sun was a blazing mass of metal, larger than the Peloponnese. His atomic theory was based on the idea that the planets were fragments of rock torn from the earth and ignited by the force or speed of their rotation. Anaxagoras challenged the established ideas of the priests, who taught that the sun was a divine manifestation of supreme intelligence and that Helios was a mediator between the visible and invisible worlds. They believed that a superintelligence could be found in sunlight and that this intelligence or logos within the light could transform the initiate and endow him with pure reason. Therefore the sun was not only an incandescent orb, but also a radiant catalyst of cosmic intelligence in the sky. Their colleges or academies of learning emphasized this concept. Therefore Anaxagoras's interpretation of the sun challenged the religious concept accepted as gospel. That was heresy. Other scientific thinkers broke away from the mystic view of the sun. Aristarchus of Samos in the third century B.C. observed that the earth revolved around the sun, making the journey in the course of a year. He also measured the distances of the sun and the moon from the earth, though his calculations were wrong. Hipparchus of Nicaea initiated trigonometry about 140 B.C. and put the matter of measuring the movements of celestial bodies on a geometrical basis. Ptolemy later corrected many of these measurements.

"These and other thinkers laid the groundwork for the modern secular scientific thinking that seeks a materialistic interpretation of the universe and rejects a mystic and religious one. They put their faith in the power of human intellect and human reason. They took the geometry of the priests and applied it to practical ends, something that was forbidden in the mystical schools, which taught that the visible world of sense-perception, where human intellect reigns supreme, was not representative of true reality and therefore was in error."

Intent on continuing my discourse, I posed a question for Hawkins: "You suggested the possibility of a force field being transferred to the sun. Would a physicist, who acknowledges the second law of thermodynamics or the law of entropy in his physical science, accept such a possibility?"

Hawkins thought for a moment. "No, probably not."

Pleased with his reply, I said, "The materialistic interpretation of the universe that dominates the world today has devalued the mystic schools of thought. The scientific view is that the sun can be neither divine nor a manifestation of cosmic intelligence. The sun is incandescent, a sphere of energy. The world has forgotten the mystical interpretations of the scientific philosophers. Aristotle taught that man is begotten by man and the sun together. Plato said that the sky and the sun were man's instructors in wisdom. Remember the words of Plato when speaking of the One God, whom he called the Good: 'The offspring of Good, which the Good begat in His own likeness, and Good are in relation to pure reason and its objects in the intelligible world, just as is the sun in the visible world in relation to sight and its objects.' Plato believed in the old doctrine that the light diffused from the sun is the incarnation of undefiled, pure mind. This idea has been modernized into the concept that the universe is a gigantic thought. So we can see that while the natural sciences have borrowed much from ancient schools, they have been careful to ignore the deep philosophical and religious teachings and especially the idea of any transcending or spiritual power directing the natural world of form and phenomena. Science has denied the cosmic intelligence not only within the world, but within the individual."

When I had finished, Tomich said, "I see what you mean. The Project is beyond science. But I fear it may not be accepted; like your cities, any discoveries may be discounted because we are not accredited."

"Academic acceptance isn't necessary," I said. "Didn't Leonardo da Vinci declare, 'Whosoever in discussion adduces authority uses not intellect but memory.' It is important for everyone here to keep in mind that ancient monuments, such as the Pyramid of the Sun here and most of the other temples we have recovered in Amazonia, but not only those, were built by solar civilizations who, one might say, agreed with the priests of Athens. Material scientists who study their remains can glean very little knowledge by their study, because they don't understand the mystic science of the builders. That is one of the reasons we have decided not to make the discoveries of our explorations in Amazonia known to secular science.

"From now on we will make a mystical study of the monuments in order to rediscover these higher sciences. The discoveries should help us to develop the sciences more than they ever have been. Science has evoked authority far too many times and built convincing arguments backed by facts and figures only to have them prove erroneous later on. It has always been the same with authoritative institutions fashioned by men. While natural science has overlooked—maybe discarded is more accurate—the cosmic intelligence manifest in the sun, we should always acknowledge that this cosmic intelligence registers on the consciousness of man, just as the sun's energy works upon our physical natures.

"Carl Jung's studies of the psyche in his monumental work *Man and His Symbols* show very clearly that the inner self is divine and projects itself as a solar figure. The divine solar consciousness has a personal nature in man, just as it has an impersonal nature in the sun itself."

"Is the sun divine, then?" asked Sylvia.

"No, the sun obtains its energy from the consciousness of God. It is this consciousness manifest within the sun that is divine, not its physical expression. The human mind is rooted in this consciousness as it is in the sun. While the natural sciences are relatively new, the mystic science that teaches this fact is as old as man himself. Experience in this mystic science is the only credential one needs in it. Those uninitiated in the illumination that comes to man's divine reason through the absorption of sunlight and of the intelligence inherent within it, by means of the techniques, are restricted by human reason. They can possess only a limited view of the universe. The material outlook must by its very nature collide with the mystic outlook; indeed, it must challenge it and seek by argument to disprove it. Therefore, scientific accreditation would be the same as trying to mix water and oil.

"The spiritual universe cannot be described in the scientific terms of the material physicist. It can only be described in a mystical language understood by spiritual consciousness. If this consciousness is not developed by means of a transformation of man's spiritual potential, there can be no understanding; none but the enlightened can hope to understand. Therefore, the role of any mystic religion is to teach man how to attain this transformation of self. The old priests of Athens, who came under strong criticism by the scientist, and the layman who is often influenced by scientific thinking, knew and know the dangers of the materialistic attitude. This attitude devalued man, made an animal of him, and brought him down from his celestial abode.

"A case in point: physics teaches that the physical universe must one day dissociate, return to nothingness. Yet, mystic science teaches that the physical universe was not created out of nothing, and therefore cannot dissipate into nothingness. It returns to the source which was and is the spiritual universe that existed before the creation of the physical universe. That spiritual universe, like the spiritual nature of man which is part of it, is eternal. God is the great generator or creator of all life. Therefore, for scientists to understand the universe and its cause it is necessary that all who would understand these origins acknowledge this creative force or power in life. Such acknowledgment will involve metaphysics in the beginning and later a highly advanced religious concept. Such a religion must by its own nature be involved with the sun. This is the goal of the Project. We are the catalysts."

"You mean we are creating a new religion?" blurted Hawkins in a loud, high-pitched voice that startled everyone.

As though to tantalize him, I answered, "Because it is the nature of the physical universe to disintegrate and then to rebuild, so it is with man's sciences and religions. The physical sciences broke from the old religions, measuring material phenomena and basing their investigations on sense data. Eventually physical science became the new religion, holding power over thinking man no less than did the priests who persecuted Anaxagoras in the fifth century B.C. What they couldn't measure was denied existence. They sought to dethrone God in the name of science. With the advent of nuclear physics and nuclear fusion, science is again uniting man with the energy of the sun. Now it only remains for man to recognize the existence of intelligence factors inherent in the radiation of the sun. With this recognition will come an acceptance of God and the rebirth of mystical science."

"I don't know; sounds like religion to me," said Hawkins. "Never did like religion."

I looked at Hawkins tolerantly and said, "Why did you come here?"

"Certainly not to become involved in religion."

"What is your idea of religion?" I asked.

"Priests, power, gold and jewels, ignorance, superstitious ceremony, ritual, blind faith, fear, sin, hatred, blood in a cup," said Hawkins. "I came here to learn about the uses of energy in a scientific manner. I know the benefits of the techniques and sunlight. I feel younger, I'm more alert, more psychic, even spiritual, and my radiesthesia machines work better, because I'm a better operator. I want to learn more. But I want no part of religion."

"Do you believe in the existence of God?" I asked quietly. The others leaned forward to hear Hawkins's reply.

"Of course I do. But not religion. Religion is the creation of priests."

"But you do believe in the existence of God?"

"Yes!" said Hawkins resolutely. "Yes, I do."

"Then you *are* religious, and you belong to a religion."

My statement caught Hawkins off guard. He looked hard into my eyes and said, "And what is the name of this so-called religion? I, for one, would like to know."

"Your religion is the universal religion of light expressed in your own words. You have described the benefits, even a belief in God. Therefore, your attitude is both mystic and scientific. True religion, to use the words of Albert Einstein, does not come through blind faith, but through an extension of our rational knowledge. You have moved away from the old world religions to join the ranks of those who believe in the universality of the sun and its benefits on the human level, and you have acknowledged the existence of God. That is the purpose of the Project."

Hawkins nodded. "You may be right," he said. "You mean that in the Project each person is free to comprehend God in his own way?"

"There is no other way," I said. "It's always like that in the beginning. As you merge with the universal, you move away from an individual interpretation of creation. You simply acknowledge what is, but only after long involvement with the light of the sun and the source."

"What is the source?" asked Sylvia, sensing Hawkins had nothing more to say for the moment.

"The source is the origin."

"How does one reach the source or the origin?" she asked.

"By means of the System, first through the sun and then beyond it to the consciousness that created the sun and the universe. In the System one is taught to 'eat' the atoms of the sun manifested as light, then to move on to consume the primeval atoms of the creative energy. That is what each of you is learning to do here at the pyramid and at our other sites."

"And what is the goal after we accomplish this?" asked Sylvia.

"If you are successful in the first effort, you penetrate to the other world beyond space and time, through the point from which the material universe merged. I call this 'passing through the gate.' Once through, you can recognize true form and true nature, a process called 'the merging of the twins.' "

"What are the twins?" asked Tomich. "And the merging?"

"When the physical and spiritual become as one," I said. "We are conscious of the physical nature in the present third-dimensional space-time awareness. What is to be accomplished is the creation of our spiritual awareness in a dimension beyond this world, to future time and space."

"Are you speaking of the solar world, where solar forms and beings exist in the sun?" Sylvia asked.

"No, of a world of pure consciousness, in which spiritual form and being had their origin. The sun is the source of our material form. It is the latter world of the sun that each of you must penetrate if you are to understand your pre-existent nature. The

Stone ruins of Chachapoyas, where the author's interest in ancient civilizations began. The remains of forty old cities, long forgotten by man, were discovered on the forested slopes of the high jungles of northeastern Peru.

Stone ruins emerge as the vegetation is cut away by the machete-wielding trailsmen of the author's expedition. These cities are part of the Chachapoyas civilization conquered by the Incas over four centuries ago. Long thought to be only legendary, with their discovery, the citadels became part of history.

This photo of the author was taken shortly before his expedition into Chachapoyas in July 1970.

Oscar Egusquiza

Project "X" Photo

The author looked aged and drawn a few weeks later, shortly following his transition. The photograph is a record of the reversal process encountered in the experiments with solar energy and contact with ultra-dimensional worlds.

Antonio (far right), the author's friend and guide, stands with companions on the trail at ten thousand feet above sea level. Behind them are scattered stone remains overgrown with tufts of grass.

The author, fully recovered, before boarding helicopter which returned him to the ancient city of Gran Pajatén. The stone temple is perched atop a craggy, pyramidlike mountain that looms 9,500 feet above the surrounding jungle.

Sylvia Savoy

Stone stairways emerge from the jungle. The top of an ancient temple juts up out of the foliage below the helicopter swooping over for a low-altitude aerial photograph. Macheteman was lowered by means of a rope to cut a small clearing, enabling the author and his wife to land.

A king's tomb caught by the camera as helicopter passed a white cliff adjacent to the lonely temple. The explorers were unable to reach the isolated crypt, which examination of similar tombs led them to believe was occupied by the mummified remains of a long-dead king, along with pottery and colorful alpaca textiles.

ABOVE—The author's wife, Sylvia, ready to clear away vegetation from a circular building at Gran Pajatén. Ancient stone heads tenoned into the walls peer out from the edifice in silence.

RIGHT—The author, fully recovered from transition two months before, descends stone stairway at temple site. He is reading an altimeter, which shows the temple to be 9,500 feet above sea level.　　　　*Sylvia Savoy*

Stone figures frozen in a dance. The ancient cities which attracted the explorers were ornamented with human, animal and geometric designs in slate and other materials. Note the head of a Chachapoyas priest-king etched in stone. The solar crown suggests that the temple may have been dedicated to the sun.

BELOW—Peruvian flute players play an ancient tune near ruined cities of Chachapoyas. Peacock feathers, colorful hats and blouse designs reflect the centuries-old traditions that are kept alive in these remote areas of the upper Amazon.

sun, as the ancient Greek philosophers taught, is the meeting ground, the mediator between the physical and the spiritual."

"Then the sun is the gate," Tomich was quick to reply.

"Yes," I said. "The work must begin first in the sun."

"If we advance to future space-time, what becomes of our present form?" asked Sylvia. "Do we leave this world?"

"When the physical and the spiritual merge, you exist in two worlds at the same time. By this I mean you live in the present third-dimensional world of space and time, and you also live in future space and time of a higher dimension, which is to say you occupy space in two universes at the same time, present and future. But let's not jump ahead of ourselves. Speculation, like theories, is just so many words. All of you will have to experience your spiritual nature and the spiritual world that I have mentioned. It is important that all of you discover this universe for yourselves in order to understand and accept it. This is the great secret of secrets."

"Is that really possible?" Tomich asked. "I mean, I am intrigued by the idea of other dimensions, and I want to experience them. I have felt the energy of the pyramids when I applied the techniques properly, but is it really possible, this transformation of the individual of which you speak?"

"Yes, but you must accept the fact that it is the nature of your understanding of the spiritual universe that is important. Your ideas must change first. After you have each seen that you have access to other dimensions, more than you have supposed or have been taught by accredited institutions, your faith in religion will not only be renewed, but you will each generate a new kind of faith, the kind that built these monuments here, a faith that will go on to build monuments the like of which the world has never seen. If humanity is made to see its true heritage, the world will emerge from the era that is dying, and enter a new and greater one. We of the Project may very well pave the way for it . . . just as nuclear physicists ushered in the atomic age."

"You speak of a dying age," Hawkins said, "and the birth of a new one. What exactly do you mean by that statement—or are you referring to the Aquarian Age?"

"No, my statement had nothing to do with astrology. Let me

explain. Go back to the emergence of the material philosophers. Their attitudes had a decaying effect on man's idea of himself. It took centuries, but man slowly began to see himself in a new light. He no longer stood in the center of the universe. He saw himself not created by God, but the product of natural environment, an accident of nature. He evolved from the sea, crawled up on the beaches and gradually stood up and walked. Having done so, he began to conquer the environment that had produced him. He drained lakes, cut down forests, dammed rivers, killed animals, dug minerals from the earth, poisoned the atmosphere, made war on his own kind.

"The old gods were no longer served. Man didn't stand in awe of his Creator. He answered to no one but himself. New gods were created and put on the altar—machines, for example, were first made to serve man, but once man became dependent upon the machines, he found himself serving them. The material sciences created the technologies and handed them over to the economists, politicians and militarists. Men were compelled to produce products, then to purchase these products in order to survive. Natural resources taken from the earth were controlled by syndicates, as food was. Shortages were created. Prices fluctuated. Life consisted of a continual struggle to make enough money in order to live. Man never suspected that the whole scheme was artificially rigged, created to keep him enslaved to the work ethic. He was motivated by a system called inflation, which kept prices high and perpetually taxed him in order to make his property useless, so it could become the property of the state. Wars around the globe kept man in a continual state of fear and anxiety.

"At first only the poor were swept along in the current, then the man of some means, then the rich and the powerful, the economist, politician and militarist, all were carried along together by a system they had created to serve them, but which eventually required that all men everywhere become its slaves. The horrible truth is that the system they built was taken over by a cosmic power of darkness, animated by the devil himself. Thus the deification of matter became complete."

"You are speaking of the present age, are you not?" asked Sylvia.

"Yes, and it is an age that must die if we are to survive."

"What do you mean by this so-called cosmic power of darkness?" Hawkins asked.

"The mystical religions had warned men of these malevolent powers of darkness," I replied. "They are very real."

"Don't tell me you believe in the devil?" asked Hawkins, with the trace of a smile on his lips.

"Yes, I do, and each of you must be prepared to face him on your return to the light. Rest assured he will make his presence known as you approach the gate."

This statement startled my listeners.

"Do you mean the path to the light is guarded by the devil?" asked Sylvia with surprise.

"Even Christ was tempted by the devil," I said.

"Have you seen the devil?" Tomich asked.

"The devil takes many forms. Each of us has a dual nature, one light, the other dark. We each choose which force will motivate us, God or the devil, good or bad, light or dark." I could feel my brow furrow as I spoke. "Yes, I suppose you could say I have seen the devil, and so I stress more than anything else the need for discipline in the System. It is the price we each must pay for our return to the light. Mystic religions emphasized this fact, while the natural philosophers ridiculed it. By so doing they caused the greater harm to man, placing mankind under the domination of evil forces that are currently having their way in the world after so many centuries. Humanity today is nearly powerless to challenge them. People have forgotten the disciplines."

Hawkins began to ask another question, but seeing that the sun was high, I interrupted him. "It's late. Continue with the experiments of the day."

I picked up my leather saddlebag, which held my journal of transcripts and a light lunch, and, slinging it over my shoulder, descended the stairway towards the Street of the Dead.

Watching me go downstairs, Hawkins spoke. "I wonder what the devil looks like?" he asked the person next to him, a middle-aged lady from upstate New York.

"I really wouldn't know," she said sharply. "But I suppose some people could give you a description."

Sylvia spoke next. "I once asked Gene about the devil and he told me to ask any drug addict for a description. I think this is why he is so opposed to the research of many anthropologists who are investigating shamanism, the black arts and drugs as used by primitive people. He believes they are popularizing these cults and encouraging the unwary to play around with things they shouldn't be toying with. Evidently he is speaking from experience."

Their eyes followed me as I walked slowly towards the Pyramid of Quetzalcoatl to the west.

"I wonder what he does at the pyramid when he leaves us each day?" Hawkins said.

"I don't know," someone said, "but I certainly wish I did. Whatever it is, I suspect it has to do with those experiments he is conducting."

"I guess we'll know soon enough," said Hawkins.

Ten minutes later I entered the palace of Quetzalcoatl, passed the platforms and foundations, and went down a flight of stairs leading to the sunken courtyard. Approaching the pyramid itself, I paused to study the carvings of the head of the plumed serpent, symbol of Quetzalcoatl, wreathed in quetzal plumes. Then I climbed the narrow stone steps to the top of the mass of stone and sat down under the warm sun.

The ruined city was spread before me in every direction as my eyes took in the scene. They didn't perceive just the massive awesomeness of the buildings themselves, but also the patterns of electric fields created by the imposing structures. I saw these fields around the buildings, around trees and plants and around the tourists and other visitors to the city. What I saw was a maze of structures and rainbow currents enveloping them, like heat waves rising off an asphalt road in the summer sun. I had decided against telling my associates about my new-found vision, so as not to upset them. At first I thought I might have damaged my retinas from excessive sun-gazing. For several days I had not looked at the sun.

Then I wondered whether I was experiencing the same fate as Professor Fechner, who had gone blind for three years after looking at the sun. I also thought of St. Paul, whose sight had been impaired after seeing the brilliance of Christ over the face of the sun on his way to Damascus. Paul had been blinded for three days, and the biblical accounts suggest that his sight was never fully restored. The Aztec priests spoke of the necessity of sacrificing external sight so that they might attain a spiritual illumination through inner vision. Strangely enough, I had been resigned to my fate, knowing that no man's life is worth more than the cause he risks it for. Exposure to sunlight had apparently led to an enhancement of acuity: the greater receptivity of the retinas, perhaps because of the emergence of more sensitive rods and cones, had given me hypersensitive sight. I had gained an expanded eyesight with a new image of the external world. Therefore, I returned to the techniques with increased confidence.

Now I sat looking at the forms within my visual perception and beyond these to the color bodies which envelop all living things. It seemed to me that these colored forms or fields were more active than the physical forms to which they were attached, giving off arcs of electrical current, expanding and contracting as impressions imposed upon the physical forms altered their natures. Sometimes I felt as if I were living on the bottom of the ocean, looking at sea anemones swelling and shrinking, constantly changing their colors with changing conditions.

Soon I discovered that when my watch slowed, or stopped completely, the external world around me seemed to slow, like a slow-motion picture.

Thus, the fields around my body were speeded up enough through the intake of solar energy to allow the impressions of another dimension to register on my new-found sensory makeup. Time and energy could be manipulated to give me an entirely new impression of existence—a higher reality, beyond and yet just as much a part of man as the physical reality. It did not trouble me that others didn't know of this reality. I was perfectly content to observe for myself, as if I were the discoverer of a new world, and felt it was my right to explore its wonders.

I was soon to experience this new dimension in a way I had not anticipated.

6

The Disappearance of Societies

Pyramid of Quetzalcoatl

September 7 (A.M.), 1971—Our group gathered at the pyramid in the Temple of Quetzalcoatl the following morning. After performing the ritual of viewing the sunrise, someone asked me what had happened to the Toltecs who built Teotihuacan.

"This question can be asked about the builders of many ancient cities. The Bible records Noah's flood. In his *Dialogues* Plato speaks of this very same flood that covered the earth. According to Chan Thomas, researcher in cataclysmic geology, the Pyramid of Kufu at Giza in Egypt shows a high-water mark at the 200-foot level. Recent oceanographic data gathered by scientists suggests that several thousand years ago the earth actually was covered by a flood. Georges Cuvier's *The Theory of the Earth,* published in the last century, mentions great cataclysms and their causes."

"Darwin commented on these cataclysms while he was aboard H.M.S. *Beagle,* if I remember correctly," said Sylvia. "He wrote something to the effect that no fact in the history of the world is so startling as the repeated extermination of its inhabitants."

"Yes, many writers, ancient and modern, have referred to these cataclysms. In Alaska and Siberia, animal remains have been found by miners as far down as 100 feet beneath the surface of the earth—mastodons, mammoths, zebras, hyenas and other species

62

that shouldn't be there. No doubt the earth has experienced many upheavals in which many animals and people perished so suddenly that there were few survivors. Some species must have been wiped out."

"The earth probably flipped over when the axis shifted and the poles were displaced," said Hawkins, "or so Velikovsky theorizes, anyway."

"Yes, and Whiston, Donnelly, Cuvier and others agree," I said. "From the legends of ancient peoples, it appears to me that at least four and possibly five such cataclysms swept the earth. Each time, whole civilizations perished without trace. The survivors were thrown back into a Stone Age life, under new climatic and geographical conditions. The whole surface of the earth was altered. Continents were torn apart; some sank beneath the sea, while others rose from the sea. Arts, sciences, religions, and technologies perished with the lost peoples."

"Atlantis included?" asked Hawkins.

"Undoubtedly. While the surviving peoples of the world recorded various versions of these catastrophes in their oral traditions, legends, myths and folklore, they all have one thing in common."

"What's that?" asked Tomich.

"They tell about an earth having been swept by water, wind, earthquake, and fire. All peoples record these events. Among the Toltecs the *Codex Chimalpopocati* mentions a time when the earth was plagued by the destruction of the third sun, which cast fire over the earth by a 'rain of fire; all which existed burned, and there fell a rain of gravel, and the rocks boiled with great tumult. On this day, in which men were lost and destroyed in a rain of fire, they were transformed into goslings; the sun itself was on fire, and everything, together with the houses, was consumed.' " I quoted the account from my journal.

"Father Bernardino de Sahagun mentions such episodes often in his chronicles of the Aztec peoples. I have it here somewhere in my notes." I leafed through my journal until I came to the passages I had copied from the old text. "This is taken from Sahagun's text and chronicles an Aztec's prayer to Tezcatlipoca, the earth sun, following just such a cataclysm.

O our Lord, protector of all, most valiant and most kind, what is this?

Thine anger and thine indignation, do they glory or delight in hurling the stone, and arrow, and spear? The fire of the pestilence, made exceeding hot, is upon thy nation, as a fire in a hut, burning and smoking, leaving nothing upright or sound. The grinders of thy teeth and thy bitter whips are employed upon thy miserable people, who have become lean and of little substance, even as a hollow green cane.

Yea, what doest thou now, O Lord, most strong, compassionate, invisible, and impalpable, whose will all things obey, upon whose disposal depends the rule of the world, to whom all are subject – what in thy divine breast hast thou decreed? Peradventure, hast thou altogether forsaken thy nation and thy people? Hast thou verily determined that it utterly perish and that there be no more memory of it in the world, that the peopled place become a wooded hill and a wilderness of stone? Peradventure, wilt thou permit that the temples and the places of prayer and the altars, built for thy service, be razed and destroyed, and no memory of them left?

Is it, indeed, possible that thy wrath and punishment and vexed indignation are altogether implacable and will go on to the end to our destruction? Is it already fixed in thy divine counsel that there is to be no mercy nor pity for us, until the arrows of thy fury are spent to our utter perdition and destruction? Is it possible that this lash and chastisement are not given for our correction and amendment, but only for our total destruction and obliteration; that the sun shall nevermore shine upon us, but that we must remain in perpetual darkness and silence; that never more wilt thou look upon us with eyes of mercy, neither little nor much?

"A pitiful episode," said Sylvia when I had finished.

"But one that rings true," I said.

"Do you really believe the sun went out, that the world was enveloped in darkness?" Sylvia asked, clearly moved by the passage.

"No doubt about it," said Hawkins.

We continued to discuss the prayer throughout the morning.

7

The Solar Ages of the Earth

Pyramid of the Moon

September 7 (P.M.), 1971—After lunch, we climbed to the summit
of the Pyramid of the Moon, which is east of the larger Pyramid of
the Sun, further along the Avenue of the Dead. The morning
conversation continued:

"What is the cause of these global cataclysms?" asked Tomich.

"It has been speculated by Velikovsky and others that comets
are the cause," I said. "However, I cannot accept this theory
completely, though I do accept an extraterrestrial cause."

"Then what is the cause?" Tomich asked.

"The sun," I declared. "After all, the close association of the
earth with the sun and its total dependence upon it would suggest
that any variation in the sun's radiation would result in disturbances on earth. The instability of the sun has been recorded by
nearly all the world's great civilizations. It is universally true. The
scriptures of the world's great religions chronicle it. Ancient man
everywhere was occupied with the performance of rites and rituals to encourage the sun to continue giving off light and heat.
Fires were maintained in temples, sacrifices were made—all in an
effort to make peace with the sun or with the gods.

"You see, the ancients believed that the gods had scourged the
earth because of man's sins against them. Ancient people viewed
the sun as an intermediary. They believed that the gods punished

men by taking away the sun's light and heat and by causing catastrophes. The sun was the focal point. The ancients thought they could influence the sun and the gods—either directly or indirectly—through their prayers, sacrifices and rituals.

"We have evidence that men once believed that the sun was blotted out by an act of God or the gods. Men apparently felt that prayers or sacrifices—or often the spilling of blood—would satisfy God and he would restore the sun. In the solar myth recorded by the Egyptians, Osiris was the sun who died and then came to be known as the sun of night and judge of the underworld. Horus was the new sun. Among the Syrians, Adonis suffered a violent death, only to be resurrected at a later time. The Assyrian Du-Zu, the Hebrew Tamheur, the Norse Balder are only a few of the many, many ancient solar gods who died at the hand of some malevolent force, only to be born again.

"All ancient religions record the great and dreadful battles between the forces of light and darkness. For instance, in the Christian religion, Jesus is a solar figure who suffers a violent death and descends to the underworld of darkness, only to be resurrected to judge mankind. Christianity teaches that the shedding of Jesus' blood was an act of redemption that atoned for mankind's sins. Legend has it that with Jesus' death on the cross the sun was blotted out for a time and men stumbled about in darkness even though it was day.

"At dusk, Zoroastrians saluted the setting sun, repenting for their sins and asking for compassion. Though the sacrifice of bulls and goats was part of the older ritual, there was also a bloodless sacrifice (or Yasna) which was a communion of bread. Fire, like water, was a sacred element which symbolized the presence of God, for fire was considered to be a messenger who could carry prayers heavenward.

"Mithra was created from a rock by Ormazd; the event was witnessed by shepherds, who then brought gifts to the light child and adored him. He drove a fiery chariot through the sky in which he carried the souls of men to the celestial realms. He was the divine mediator between man and God, a savior and benefactor of earthly life. He bestowed upon his followers protection, light, beauty, health, long life, material wealth, offspring, sovereignty and power.

"The Romans, who were followers of the Unconquerable Sun, were also followers of Mithra. They believed that Mithra's blessings gave them the intelligence to rule the known world for centuries. Romans saluted the sun in order to sacrifice all that is good to Him: 'Hail! O Dawn! Hail to Thee! Hail! . . . Hail! Sol Invictus, author of all good, Spirit of beauty, purity, and light.' The eternal fire, in which the presence of God was believed to preside, burned perpetually on Palatine Hill and on the federal altar of Alba Longa.

"Similar fires were kept burning in Greece—at Olympia, where Pan and Helios were honored, and at Delos, the birthplace of Apollo and Artemis. Everlasting fires were kept burning in all the lands that were influenced by the Indo-Aryan solar religions that spread throughout Europe, India and Persia and that, according to the *Zend Avesta,* The Sacred Books Of The Ancient Zoroastrians, divided the world into seven regions. A common doctrine was followed in all these areas—that is why fires were found on the altars in Germany where Thor was honored, in Prussia where Perkum was honored, in Lithuania where Zinoz was honored, and in the Slavic countries where the God of Light was honored as the first-born son of God. The Sun and the Sky Father were known in Russia, in the Scandinavian countries of Norway, Sweden and Denmark, and in France and Italy. In Ireland an eternal fire burned at Kildare in honor of Bridgit, the Bright. In England the sun was honored at the great astronomical sun temple of Stonehenge.

"Each morning the Brahman prays for the sun to rise. Twelve different names for the sun are intoned in the Brahma Purana. The sun was considered to be the divine Vivifier, Surya. In Babylonia, where we find great Temples of the Sun, the mighty Sun God is called Shamash. The Assyrian and Syrian astrologers, famous for their knowledge of the heavens, based their science, which had its origin in the earlier Mesopotamian civilization, on the sun. Their sciences involved the art of developing their eyes to see the sun and the stars in a way not natural for ordinary man. They observed and communed with the heavenly bodies for long periods. To them, the sun was not just a gaseous orb that sent light and heat into the solar system, but a living organism that charged men with a spiritual knowledge that purified their minds, bodies, souls and spirits. They communicated with the gods from other worlds through heavenly bodies, and thereby incorporated their characteristics. It was natural, then, for ancient astrologers and scientists to elevate the sun to king of the whole universe, the generator and sustainer of all life on the planet, the ruling power of the world, master and heart of mankind.

"To Socrates and the Greek intellectuals, the Sun God was Apollo. Plato called the sun the offspring of the First God; though the First God was outside the visible universe, the sun was the son of God, the mediator between man and the Creator Father. The physical sun was considered to be the visible symbol of the spiritual sun. Greek thinkers believed the sky gods to be supreme: Apollo, Jupiter and Zeus. The sun was not seen as a god, but as a physical object that could be measured; it was not personified or worshipped.

"The Roman Emperors Julian and Constantine saw the sun as having three aspects: the Sun of the Intelligible World, the Sun of the Intelligent World and the Sun of the Sensory World. Constantine saw Christ as a fourth aspect of the Sun; after observing a cross in the sky over the face of the sun following a great victory on the battlefield, he converted to Christianity. Julian believed that this fourth aspect or savior of mankind was neither Helios-Mithra nor Christ—he thought it was Asclepios. In any event, all saviors were identified with the sun in one way or another.

"The Jewish religion was involved with the sun. The Lord commanded Moses to keep a perpetual fire burning on the altar; its flame was to be replenished each morning by the priests so that it would never go out. The Angel of the Lord appeared to Moses in a flame of fire, out of the midst of a bush, and the Lord spoke to Moses using the fire as an intermediary. Reverence for the sun was one of the rituals permitted in Jerusalem; there was a Bethshemesh, or House of the Sun, in Judah. The sun was not personified, nor was the physical sun worshipped, since it was only a visible representation of the invisible God, as was the fire through which the Lord spoke to Moses. We are reminded of this fact in the Old Testament, where the coming deliverer is spoken of as the Sun of Righteousness, God's Light, the Primordial—or First—Sun that would shine again on all men.

"A Toltec document tells of a time when the earth was cast in darkness. The return of the sun is attributed to a sacrificial rite. I have part of that document by Fray Andres de Olmos, a missionary among the Mexicans, preserved in my transcripts," I said. "Let me read from it.

> *Now, there had been no sun in existence for many years; so the gods being assembled in a place called Teotihuacan, six leagues from Mexico, and gathered at the time around a great fire, told their devotees that he of them who should first cast himself into that fire should have the honor of being transformed into the sun. So, one of them, called Nanautzin, flung himself into the fire. Then the gods began to peer through the gloom in all directions for the expected light and to make bets as to what part of heaven he should first appear in. Some said "Here," and some said "There"; but when the sun rose they were all proved wrong, for not one of them had fixed upon the east.*

"Then there is the Popol Vuh, the sacred book of the ancient Quiche Maya, which chronicles the period when all was dark on the planet. The Quiche Maya had a prayer for light and the return of the sun. Let me read it to you.

> *Hail! O Creator! O Former! Thou that hearest and understandest us! Abandon us not! Forsake us not! O God, thou art in heaven and on earth; O Heart of Heaven! O Heart of Earth! Give us descendants and a posterity as long as the light endures.*

When I finished the text, I read from a clipping pasted at the bottom of the page. " 'The following passage was taken from the Popol Vuh and records the people's joy at the return of the sun.'

> *They determined to leave Tulan, and the greater part of them, under the guardianship and direction of Tohil, set out to see where they would take up their abode. They continued on their way amid the most extreme hardships for the want of food, sustaining themselves at one time upon the mere smell of their staves and by imagining they were eating, when in verity and truth they ate nothing. Their heart,*

indeed, it is again and again said, was almost broken by affliction. Poor wanderers! They had a cruel way to go, many forests to pierce, many stern mountains to overpass, and a long passage to make through the sea, along the shingle and pebbles and drifted sand—the sea being, however, parted for their passage. At last they came to a mountain that they named Hacavitz after one of their gods, and here they rested—for here they were by some means given to understand that they should see the sun. Then, indeed, was filled with an exceeding joy the heart of Balam-Quitzé, of Balam-Agab, of Mahucutah, and of Iqui-Balam. It seemed to them that even the face of the morning star caught a new and more resplendent brightness.

They shook their incense-pans and danced for very gladness: sweet were their tears in dancing, very hot their incense—their precious incense. At last the sun commenced to advance; the animals small and great were full of delight; they raised themselves to the surface of the water; they fluttered in the ravines; they gathered at the edge of the mountains, turning their heads together toward that part from which the sun came. And the lion and the tiger roared. And the first bird that sang was that called the Queletzu. All the animals were beside themselves at the sight; the eagle and the kite beat their wings, and every bird both great and small. The men prostrated themselves on the ground, for their hearts were full to the brim.

"These old and wondrous tales suggest that the ancients of America believed earth and sun were interrelated in a mystical manner. There was a constant danger of the sun becoming transformed into matter, cooling and losing its radiant heat and light."

"But why all the blood sacrifice?" asked Hawkins. "I've never been able to understand it."

"The ancient Mayan's concept of four ages of the sun was based on the idea that man maintains the sun's force and energy through transmission of conscious energy back to the sun. Some of the priests emphasized the shedding of man's blood to sustain the sun's vitality; but Quetzalcoatl—a redeemer like Jesus—taught that it was man's transmission of spiritual energy to the sun that sustained it, not his blood. It was taught that the earth was a battleground of powers of darkness (matter) and powers of light (spirit).

"If matter triumphed, matter would be deified and the sun would go out. If light won, the spirit would dominate and a new sun would come forth—the Fifth Sun. This would establish the fifth epoch of the sun. The transformation of the sun would become complete and the earth would be transformed into light like a sun. The Mexicans taught that salvation and the transformation of man were only possible through knowledge. This knowledge was taught in their religious colleges and consisted chiefly of a system that would enable the individual to bring about a mystic union with God through the sun. The individual rose above himself by first learning to transmit material energy to the sun.

"By these steps the individual actually projected himself into the universe and through an enlightened consciousness, played an active part in the control of events in the sensible universe. The individual was then freed from matter through his participation in the hidden knowledge found in the sun and in light. The soul could be transformed by this sacrifice of light and fire. The whole world would be transformed in the same manner.

"With the manifestation of the Fifth Sun in the universe man would be freed from the bondage of matter and restored to his former glory. The spiritual message of Quetzalcoatl was that man and his world could be made immortal by the divine light of a new sun which men could control themselves after proper training in the mystic arts and sciences.

"The Mayan, Toltec and Aztec teachings tell us that the earth has passed through at least four epochs in which the sun was dimmed, the earth depopulated by floods, earthquakes, winds and conflagrations; the present Fifth Sun will either destroy the earth, or man will use it to transform his world. Some Mexican sources recount seven solar epochs.

"These old records point to the incredible possibility that man may be the cause of the disorderly activity of the solar system and the periodic instability of the sun itself. Here we have evidence of the sun's rebellion against its pollution by the mind of man! Biblical records suggest that God is the cause of a changing sun; that He uses the elements and the sun to punish man. Again, actions of the prophets as recorded in scripture indicate that man can influence the sun.

"An episode of a deluge is recorded in the eighteenth Psalm; it says that the waters of the earth were troubled and that the clouds poured out water. Further on, the seventy-seventh Psalm tells of a great earthquake. Psalm 97 continues this theme. And, you will remember, in the book of Joshua, Chapter 10, Joshua actually commands the sun to stand still upon Gideon for the whole day. The tenth chapter of Exodus has Moses commanding the sun and casting a darkness over the land of Egypt for three days. All these biblical accounts indicate that there is much more to the sun and the stars than we might imagine.

"Like any other living organism, the sun appears to be an open system. The sun's energy is maintained through energy exchange from a higher source, perhaps from other stars in the galaxy and beyond. Thus it would seem that the sun is a valve through which energy, obtained from a higher source, is then passed into the physical universe. This would explain why each nebula is receding from all others. Perhaps God is the ultimate source, a consciousness that is transformed into energy in the physical universe.

"If this is the case, the sun and the physical universe are not what physicists believe them to be. The universe is a closed system according to the law of the conservation of energy. This means that the universe can neither gain nor lose energy—energy is not exchanged with its environment. Thus all things in the universe run down like clocks, losing heat and not regaining it.

"Our parent sun appears to be a variable star that radiates excessive amounts of electromagnetic currents, thermal heat, X-rays and radioactive discharges in a most unpredictable manner, causing upheavals on the planet from time to time. That there may be some level of controlling consciousness involved is indicated by the Old Testament claim that God caused the sun to act in a strange manner and that prophets controlled the movements of the sun.

"There are many cases recorded in history where the sun was observed to spin, oscillate or move about in the sky. This displacement is quite universal; it has been reported by many people all over the world. The phenomenon is often accompanied by miraculous events, visions and appearance of holy figures. All these reports seem to suggest that the sun responds to thought or consciousness. Whether the influence is from God or from man, the sun is responsive. What then is the nature of the sun?"

No one replied to my question. And I didn't expand upon the subject, electing instead to leave each with his own thoughts.

We remained on the Pyramid of the Moon until the sun set. When the clouds turned a brilliant orange and fingers of light turned a blood red, reaching from the horizon to the vault of heaven, we made our way slowly down to the paved street.

An hour later we were back at the hotel, where I told them about the forthcoming Amazon expedition.

8

The Sun of Intelligence

Manaus, Brazil

November 3, 1971—At 9:30 on a cool November morning, members of the El Dorado/Amazons Expedition lifted off the concrete runway of Bogota, Colombia, and headed southeast towards the vast Amazon jungles of Brazil.

We had received funds for a 60-day exploration to seek out whatever archaeological remains, if any, could be traced to the legendary female tribe of Amazons and the equally legendary golden man called El Dorado; we hoped to find traces of the fabled fountain that regenerates the aged.

During the flight we were overwhelmed by the vastness of the Amazonian jungle plain. Looking down at the rain forests each of us experienced a sinking sensation of futility. How were we to explore such expanses of unknown territory in the time allotted us? As an experienced jungle explorer, I knew that feeling only too well. The others had had a taste of what it was like to cut through the jungle during a twenty-day trip to eastern Ecuador. They all agreed that luck would play a paramount part in the success of the expedition.

Dailey put an elbow in my ribs. "It would take many lifetimes for a man to cut through all of that," he said, pointing out the window.

Philosophically, I replied that for some time I had accepted the limitations of the time allotted each man—and of his material body. I compared the jungle to outer space. Man's ability to explore the jungle is limited by a frail body not immune to the microscopic organisms and parasites bred in the culture dishes of the jungle's biological laboratory.

In the same way, man has been bred under a protective layer of earth's atmosphere that has kept him safe from the unseen cosmic radiation that penetrates his bones and flesh. With his present technology, man could never hope to travel outside our solar system because of his short life span. The jungle had started me thinking about the possibility of overcoming the time limitations —and the physical limitations—of man's terrestrial nature. I said man is no less a prisoner of this planet than the apes of the jungle. My many years of exploring—during which I was able to examine life in its primeval state—had taught me this important truth, and I had grown to resent it. I wanted to escape the planet and turn back the time clock. I needed, as every man and woman who reaches the three-quarter mark of life discovers, more time. . . .

"There is something about the jungle that permits a man to look beyond himself, to ponder the accepted explanation of the origins of life," I said. "Alfred Russel Wallace and Henry Walter Bates, who explored the Amazon a hundred years ago, reached certain conclusions that helped pave the way for the idea of natural selection. Darwin's observations made on H.M.S. *Beagle* led him to his theory on the origin of the species. Perhaps one can get closer to life when one is surrounded by the primitive. Perhaps here we can discover more about the emergence of the human mind and spirit. Finding ancient monuments for the sake of making new discoveries or digging through the remains of forgotten civilizations holds little fascination. We must learn more about the life-religions possessed by the builders of these cities."

Dailey was intrigued by my ideas because they paralleled certain concepts of his own. On the basis of his knowledge of history and legends, he acknowledged that the sun played an important part in the life of ancient man in the Americas. It seemed to Dailey that man's mind, which strives to comprehend the universe, could begin now by communicating with the sun, which is responsible for feeding the brain, for the evolution of the eyes as extensions of the brain, and even for human thought. He, too, felt that untold secrets of man's nature might very well be discovered if man could somehow communicate with the sun and with the intelligence found within solar energy.

I went on to explain to Dailey that I had learned the basic secrets of communing with nature from the older Celilo Indians of the Pacific Northwest.

They practiced little-known rites while communicating with the Great Spirit through the sun and the stars, from which they drew into their being a cosmic energy that not only helped sustain them, but gave them insights into the darkest of nature's secrets. They needed little food to nourish their lithe bodies and psychic powers. I had seen old men, well into their seventies and eighties, as spry and energetic as men half their ages, who were able to read the weather and predict future events long before they occurred simply by observing nature.

I described a ceremony I had witnessed years before at an old ceremonial site destined to be inundated by the waters of a dam then nearing completion at The Dalles, Oregon. An old Indian wise man had come to look one last time at the secret site; he rose in the predawn darkness and, stripped to the waist, went out on a promontory facing east to greet the morning sun.

"Holding his upraised hands to heaven, he called out in a low, melodious voice: 'Hay-ha-ha-hay . . . hay-ha-ha-hay . . . hay-ha-ha-hay . . . hay-ha-ha-hay . . . hay-ha-ha-hay.' Dancing around in a small circle, he seemed to beckon to the sun as if to evoke its cosmic powers. With the coming of the sun he sent forth his hymn to the sun again: 'Hay-ha-ha-hay . . . hay-ha-ha-hay . . . hay-ha-ha-hay . . . hay-ha-ha-hay . . . hay-ha-ha-hay . . . hay-ha-ha-hay.' Then I saw him look straight into the sun, holding the palms of his hands toward it. He was as still as the rocks around him, his coppery skin reflecting the rays of sunlight. What intrigued me most were his radiant eyes mirroring the sun.

"Then he called out again and, as near as I could understand and remember the words he spoke, he said something like this: 'Great Spirit, maker of the sun and the stars, I send my voice on the wings of an eagle to the cross of light, our Father the Sun, created by you to give us life and warmth. Hear me. I come one final time on this sacred land that holds the remains of so many of my departed brothers. Let me fly to the sun in my flesh so that I may know you before I die. My spirit will come to you soon.' His voice stopped abruptly. Continuing to look directly into the sun, he gave the impression of bathing himself in sunlight, using his hands to pour the living water of the sun over his body. After performing this rite he walked slowly down the hill and disappeared into the gully.

"His act made a lasting impression on me. Some months after witnessing the ceremony I began an exhaustive study of the customs and religions of the Indians of the Americas. I found that the northern tribes all spoke of great teachings that originated in the neighboring civilizations to the south: Aztec, Maya and Inca, I supposed. Undoubtedly, the old Indian who had enacted the ceremony of the sun had learned it from his ancestors, who had carried on an oral tradition that must have had its origin in the solar cultures of Mexico and Peru.

"These civilizations exalted the sun and built an organized society around their relationship to it. They recognized that the heat and light of the sun were the immediate generators of all life on the planet. They regulated and governed life and the seasons. The Incas called the visible or physical sun Inti, but they acknowledged a transcendental power behind the sun which moved the physical sun across the sky on a daily course. This true creator they knew as Viracocha, the source of all life. The Indians of North America fell heir to these fundamental teachings."

Midway through the flight to Brazil my conversation was interrupted by a stewardess, who served a light snack and bottled wine. After she left, Dailey, who had been listening attentively, scribbled a note on the back of a napkin with a pencil. He had a logical mind and grasped essentials quickly. He had surveyed large tracts of desert in Nevada and had learned to live alone. Once he spent five months exploring a cave in the Yucatan. He was the kind of person who doesn't speak unless he has thought out what he has to say. Folding the napkin carefully and stuffing it in the pocket of his shirt, he turned to me.

"I've always believed that the sun is a mirror reflecting a higher intelligence. Our immediate sun, our solar system, is a collecting basin for some higher intelligence coming into the solar system from without, just as other systems are collecting basins for other forces in other areas of the physical universe. Man is also a collecting basin for solar energy. I believe that men everywhere feel and experience this higher intelligence in every bone and sinew of their bodies, in their minds and in their spirits. I believe that the sun is understood inwardly by men much more than anyone can imagine. Indians were essentially realists and naturalists. They observed all living things in nature—plants, animals, humans. They observed that living things awaken at dawn and close down or retire at sunset. The sun dominates corporeal life. Being mature Indians, they knew this. It is the same for man today, except that we moderns have forgotten how to be practical realists and naturalists."

"Absolutely," I said.

"If we put these techniques in the hands of man on a universal scale," Dailey said, "they could become the basis of the true religion of all time, dominated and controlled by a higher intelligence, not man. We may not see it in our lifetimes, but someday such a higher religion could triumph over the old religions, and, I believe, make a better world."

"There is a lot to be said for the universality of such a concept," I replied. "Sunlight is the prime mover in the solar system. Perhaps we can do more with the sun today than has ever been done by former generations. Man would, of course, have to accept the fact that sunlight has played a more important part in the evolution of the species than natural selection. No doubt about it. The sun is the key to man's future evolution. I remember reading somewhere that Plato taught his students that expansion of one's self was the result of sunlight—that some men could learn from looking at plants and statues, others by looking at the stars, and superior men by looking at the sun, an act only possible for men granted sun-eyes by the gods. Among the Greeks, the 'word' or logos was identified with the creation and, therefore, filled with the mind of God. They taught in their academies that personal regeneration was only possible through understanding the word of God, and that it was attained by an inner illumination.

"It is plain to see that the ancients were fascinated by the sun. That the sun could blind men with its brilliance undoubtedly did much to create awe and wonder in the minds of men. As civilized thought advanced, men began to see the sun as the ruling power and master of the universe—the heart, eye and mind of the world. Even later, Christians equated Christ with the sun. The birth of Jesus coincided with the birth of the sun, the winter solstice celebrated on or near December twenty-fifth.

"Inca Huayna Capac was seen looking directly into the sun for a long time, contemplating its course through the sky. The account of why he raised his eyes to the sun was interesting, but of greater interest was the fact that he did look at the sun without harm. It seems to me that it was his lack of fear (being Inca he was called the Son of the Sun and therefore considered an offspring of the Sun) that permitted him to accomplish the feat without harm to his eyes. Did he, like the Mexican sun priests to the north, believe that man was a particle of the sun? That the sun gives life to the planet as a result of man's consciousness being reflected back to the sun through daily sacrifice? And that it is because of this continual exchange between man's spiritual being and the sun that life is able to exist? After all, if there is a bond between man and the sun, that bond, like any energy bond, implies a two-way relationship.

"In the ancient philosophies and religions of the world, light was held to be the carrier of the divine word or logos. The Phoenicians declared that invisible rays of light were the purest incarnation of the divine intelligence. Though this light was invisible and generated by God from spiritual realms, it nevertheless was related to or bound up with the visible light of the physical universe. The Romans called this higher sun the Sun of Intellect.

"It was natural that ancient man looked to the light of the sun as co-creator of life on the planet. All living things on the face of the earth and under the sea are dependent on sunlight for existence. Though sunlight, without which nothing could survive, seems relatively simple in concept, it is nevertheless responsible for complex forms of living species. We see, therefore, that sunlight is the carrier of some form or forms of intelligence. Sunlight is more than stimuli acting upon life; it has the capacity to cause an organism to respond in a certain way.

"Photosynthesis in plants is a good example. It was only natural for primitive man to be inwardly aware of the creative nature of the sun. He worshipped the sun as the visible instrument of God. The moon, planets and stars were believed to be agents of God, each having its own distinctive effect on living things.

"Ancient prophets and philosophers taught that it was as a light body rather than a physical body that man was made in the image of God, for the physical body was related to the lesser nature of man. The light body was made in the image of the greater light of God, which was akin to the spiritual consciousness that gave men their immortal spirits. This light body was the archetype of physical man—his true nature—from which the physical form evolved through some fault or sin against God. The word of God was the logos, the divine light that shone brilliantly upon man's spiritual nature, feeding his spirit and giving him conscious life. The ancient writings and mythology all report that at one time the whole universe was illuminated by the invisible light of God, and man, as a light being, walked in fellowship with God. Adam Kadmon, the archetypal man in the Hebrew religion, lived under this primordial Sun of God, the first invisible light, the Tree of Life that shed its fruit for Adam's nourishment. Upon his fall from God's grace, Adam was given a lesser light, the physical sun, and the first light body took on a visible form that was dependent upon the visible sun as the light body was upon the spiritual light.

"The visible sun was the veil that existed between man and God, yet it gave man life. The Sun Father became the eikon of God, the visible image; in the absence of the Supreme Creator, which no man could know, the sun was held to be the divine mediator between man and God. For this reason the light of the sun was sacred. Men reflected the light back to the source, believing that their bodies and their minds were descended from the sun, just as their spiritual consciousness and light bodies were descended from the light of God. They sought to reach the light of God through the mediating sun.

"The early Christians believed that Jesus sought to teach mankind how to feed upon the invisible light that was being shed through the sun. Thus we see that the sun radiates God's light upon the whole world; yet only the righteous and those knowledgeable in the sacred sciences understand it—all others are blind to it. That is why Paul wrote to the Ephesians on a subject later expanded upon by Clement of Alexandria in the Protreptikos, 'Awake, thou sleeper, rise up from among the dead, and he who is Christ the Lord shall enlighten thee, the sun of resurrection begotten before the dayspring giving life by his beams.'

"The identification of Christ with the sun is quite common in the ancient writings of the original Christians. They were known to face the rising sun with a hopeful attitude, repeating the Odes of Solomon:

> *As the sun is the joy to them that seek for its daybreak,*
> *   so is my joy the Lord:*
> *Because He is my Sun and His rays have lifted me up;*
> *   and His light hath dispelled all darkness from my face.*
> *In Him I have acquired eyes and have seen His holy day . . . .*

"The Gospel of Matthew records Jesus' words on the relationship of the eye and light. 'The light of the body is the eye: if therefore thine eye be single, thy whole body be full of light.'

"From earliest times, Christ has been identified not only with our parent sun, but also with the promised Sun of Righteousness that is to rise in the east through the physical sun. With the appearance of the Sun of Righteousness, the earth is to experience a kind of spiritual heat that will influence the souls of mankind. Eventually, the physical sun is destined to be affected by the source of all light; the earth and all living things will be reduced to cinders, the oceans dissolved, and the earth and all physical life dried up. Yet man shall not die, but be transformed. The earth shall become as the sun, being all light, and only the light men shall survive the holocaust. In those days the powers of darkness shall be conquered and man restored to his natural state of light.

"Years ago I became convinced that it was through use of the solar techniques of the original Christians that the Essenes, the Therapeutae of Palestine, and other solar cults were able to take into their nervous systems the great amounts of energy needed to accomplish their spiritual and psychic achievements. If this power was made available to them—and held secret over the centuries— then it could extend similar benefits to modern man if it could be rediscovered. Perhaps solar power was the source of Jesus' ability to work miracles. It was this kind of thinking and research that led me to journey to Central and South America to study first-hand what was left of ancient solar cults."

Two and a half hours after leaving Bogota we swept over the peaceful flatlands of Manaus. At last we saw the muddy Amazon. We tried to imagine what the 53 Spanish explorers of the Francisco Orellana Expedition might have thought when they drifted past this point on that mighty river. We circled once and then landed in the steaming heat at one o'clock in the afternoon, Brazil time. After checking into a local hotel, we picked up our guide, Joaquim Beserra de Araujo, an eighteen-year-old English-speaking Brazilian. Then we went down to the docks to arrange passage on a riverboat.

We chartered the *Cidade de Natal,* a 72-foot two-decker ship which was freshly painted and comparatively clean. Equipped with a generator, refrigeration and showers, this 27-ton craft was well suited to our needs. Her 165-horsepower Chrysler diesel engine made her one of the fastest boats on the river, and with her draft of just four feet, we could take her up the many tributaries we wished to explore during the weeks ahead.

Three days later I stood at the ship's railing on the upper deck, overseeing the loading of food and supplies. We were scheduled to sail the next morning.

"Hot, isn't it?" Dailey said, joining me at the rail. We both wore loose-fitting khaki shirts and shorts.

"It'll get hotter as we go downstream."

"What are we really looking for?" he asked me seriously.

"Archaeological remains, roads, tribes, anything that can give us an answer."

"What answer?"

"The answer to the riddle of the sun and what lies beyond."

"We'll find it," Dailey replied. "I know we will."

Third Transition

BEING

9

The Great Discovery

Tula, Mexico

August 7, 1973—Ten days after departing from Manaus by ship, I
had come upon what came to be known as the "great discovery." It
had begun with the second transition. Two years later, here at the
ruins of Tula, I recalled the experience vividly as I described it in
detail to twelve associates who had gathered at the summit of a
stepped pyramid to hear me teach.

The day before sailing, Dailey and I had met and talked with a
hunter from the interior who was friendly with the descendants of
the Maué Indians of the Amazon. During the conversation, the
hunter related the legend of the Guarana. It seems there was once
a young woman who could not have a child, though both she and
her husband desired one very much. They sought advice from a
medicine man, who gave them herbs and charms, and before long
a most beautiful child with remarkable intelligence was born to
them. It was believed by the tribesmen that one day this child
would become chief. But an evil shaman who dwelt among the
Maués grew jealous of the child and began to work his black magic
against him.

The couple, sensing the danger from the shaman, took pains to
protect the child and keep him away from the shaman's influence.
However, one day the child wandered off into the jungle. The
shaman followed; seeing that the child was alone and unpro-

tected, he used his magical arts to command the evil demon in a snake to harm the child. When the parents found the dead body of their beautiful child they wept, and a bolt of lightning shot down from the sky, causing the lifeless eyes of the babe to burn bright as glowing coals. Fearful, the couple ran into their home. The next morning they found the body of the child had disappeared, and in the place where the coals of fire had burned bright two saplings grew, green and tall in the sun. The next season the trees miraculously matured, producing fragrant blossoms that turned into a wondrous fruit resembling human eyes. This fruit, which they called guarana, meaning living eyes, has been used ever since by tribesmen to renew their strength and energy.

Dailey and I had sampled the fruit. Finding that it didn't appear to have any great medicinal or beneficial qualities, I supposed that the hunter's story was an allegory that had some special significance to his tribe. I interpreted it to mean simply that there is evil in the world that seeks to harm the good; that both good and bad can be evoked by those knowledgeable in the arts of white and black magic; and, most important, that man can be aided and abetted by a celestial force of light which can triumph over darkness when properly applied.

One day while in the jungles near Obidos, I got an opportunity to experiment with that idea. We had cut through the jungle to the heights of the Sierra de Escama, where stone carvings had been reported. After documenting the carvings on film, I had gone off to inspect the surrounding area, hoping to find more carvings. Suddenly I encountered a long, venomous snake—the *surucucu*.

We had heard tales about the poisonous reptiles of the jungle: the *surucucu pico de jaca* whose venomous bite causes flesh to rot and drop away from the bone; the *sucuriju,* a large serpent related to the anaconda, which drowns unsuspecting persons who happen to come upon it near the water's edge. It was all I could do to keep from bolting. Seven years before I had been bitten by a snake in Peru; miraculously, the bite had healed, with the aid of herbs from an old Indian woman who was familiar with plant medicine. I had an inner fear of snakes, even though I did not dislike them.

My experience with the deadly bushmasters, large aggressive snakes that grow to ten or more feet in length and that often occupy old cities of the jungle, had taught me to stay out of their way. If I were attacked, I knew enough to keep a cool head.

Now I stood perfectly still, watching the *surucucu* coiled and ready to strike. Not more than six feet separated us.

Our eyes were fixed upon one another. Each of us waited for some sign, some movement in order to respond. I felt a chill run down my spine, because the snake's eyes flashed a primordial fear of its natural enemy. For some reason I remembered the story of the shaman's working upon the demon in the same type of snake and how he commanded it to strike the little child. Maybe I could reach the good nature of the snake (I was convinced by this time that all living things had two natures, responsive respectively to good and evil influences).

I looked deep into its eyes in an attempt to communicate with it telepathically. I could sense the snake's fright radiating through its eyes, and within the fright I sensed the suffering known to all jungle creatures that live by the law of kill or be killed. I kept my gaze steady, holding the snake hypnotically. I looked deeply into its eyes, trying to reach its inner nature and beingness. Powerful waves of concentration linked us and soon I felt I was getting through. I sent it thought patterns of benevolence, understanding, tolerance—all the time reflecting a feeling of quietness.

I made no gesture towards it—not even a smile traced my lips; nor did I blink my eyelids or move any part of my body. The whole expression of my being was concentrated outward through the beams in my eyes. Slowly, the snake lowered its eyes, as if sensing the peace and nonaggression in the man before it. Gliding silently into the jungle, it looked back once before disappearing.

The experience demonstrated to me that living things do indeed have dual natures and, perhaps more important, that these natures can be reached and a friendly relationship established where none existed before. The full realization of what I had experienced came to light a few days later.

The expedition had continued downriver by ship, docking at Itacoatiara, Parintins and other small ports where we collected ceramic fragments and hired natives to explore the interior. Stopping at these ports of call was important because it enabled us to put the natives to work in our absence. We would return weeks or months later to gain new insight into what lay hidden in the jungles. I was experienced enough to know that several seasons would be required to find the old cities of the Amazons and El Dorado, and I was determined to use the technique I had employed in Peru—putting experienced jungle men to work exploring the country they knew in search of old roads, walls or building sites. At least several seasons would be needed to uncover what had escaped numerous explorers over the centuries.

At Santarem, Dailey, Joaquim, and I found a pilot who agreed to fly us north almost 400 miles across the Amazon to the range of the Tirios Indians near the border of Surinam and Guyana. While the ship lay at anchor, we took off, descending hours later onto a grassy strip near some thatched huts. We were greeted by a bunch of boisterous children, who flocked about the small plane. We walked to a hut, where we were greeted by a Catholic missionary priest with a long gray beard, who introduced himself as Father Angelico. Rotund, kindly and cordial, he condescended, though reluctantly, to introduce us to the tribal chiefs and to escort us around the Tirios settlements.

The natives were generally friendly enough, but we found the hunters we met in the surrounding jungle much more defensive, reluctant to talk, and uneasy. Skin paintings on the arms, legs, faces and chests of the Tirios resembled in many ways the designs incorporated in the architectural ornamentation I had found on the remains of the Chachapoyas peoples of the upper Amazon jungles in Peru. The nested-diamond, zigzag and step-fret designs suggested there had once been contact among the peoples of the lower Amazon, those of the highlands of Peru, the Incas, and the pre-Inca peoples. This graphic evidence could also indicate that Amazon peoples had migrated westward out of the steaming tropics to lay claim to the lush lands of the Andes and the coasts of western South America. Overpopulation, war, disease—any of these factors could have caused this migrating.

We became friends with some of the Tirios. A few had taken a liking to Joaquim and revealed to him the details of some of their legends. They also agreed to have the older hunters who knew the interior well watch for traces of "the forbidden places"; they promised to report to him any findings.

That night we accepted an invitation from Father Angelico to dine on black beans, rice, yucca and yams, washed down with goblets of sweet lemonade followed by cups of black coffee.

At first light, just as the sun was rising over the forest to brighten and cheer the cold morning air, the four of us walked to the airplane. Dailey, Joaquim and the pilot busied themselves topping the fuel tanks with extra fuel from five-gallon containers we had brought with us. I strolled over to a cluster of trees to take in the sunrise. A silence filled the chilly air. Not even the birds, usually the first to greet the sun, had stirred. Looking into the sun I beheld its bright image. As it rose above the mountain I could discern a few stray sunspots at the lower edge until its increasing brightness obliterated them. I felt the energy streaming into my being.

I experienced the exhilaration of spirit I always felt when viewing the star of our solar system. By this time I had become part of the sun, addicted to its light and dependent on the stimulation I got from looking at it. As the radiation streamed in, my brain sped up, uplifted by the energy that turned my nervous system into a highly sensitive receiver of celestial events. I knew there was no hope of my ever giving up this addiction to light. Now I was fully dependent upon it as a source of renewal and regeneration of body, mind and soul.

Looking off to one side of the sun, I observed its oscillation; I watched it vibrate from side to side, changing from black to white and back again. I had often observed this phenomenon and wondered what caused it. At first I thought it was a result of a trembling of the eye. (The extraocular muscles and the retina vibrate, never remaining fixed on any one spot for more than one-tenth to three-tenths of a second. When seeing, the eye changes position at regular intervals, jerking and jumping, causing a series of images to fall upon the foveal cones or photoreceptors of the retina.)

I also thought warm air currents might cause the oscillation. Yet, other images—trees and objects on the horizon, for instance—did not oscillate. The brightness of the solar disk must be involved, since it is some five orders of magnitude brighter than most objects, including the sky. Therefore, the dark suns I saw may merely have been after-images. Still, the sun's oscillation seemed curiously affected by my breathing and heartbeat. When I slowed my breath, and thus my heartbeat, the sun's oscillation slowed accordingly.

After taking several deep breaths, slowing my heartbeat and watching the sun oscillate rapidly from a dazzling white disk to a radiant black one, I tried to reach the sun telepathically, as if it were a center of cosmic consciousness and not just a blazing disk of light. Then I recalled the experience with the snake and how I had established telepathic communication with a higher part of its nature. I remembered how frightened I had been by the thought of being bitten and how I had overcome that feeling by a supreme effort of mind and emotional control. The fear had heightened my sensitivity, probably owing to the presence of adrenalin in my system.

At the same time, I had experienced a heightened sense of alertness, as if the state of fear induced by the snake had triggered some hidden power within my mental and psychic framework. I also remembered other thoughts I had had when looking into the snake's eyes: pictures of old buildings with designs similar to the diamond markings of the snake's skin; impressions of jungle scenes and primordial events—possibly caused by the impressions upon my retinas and brain from the glare of the snake's eyes. Beyond these thoughts, or perhaps because of them, a higher faculty had emerged within my being, some superior intelligence that took over the workings of my mind and emotions.

Looking into the dawn, I felt something like that—a sense of unity with the sun. I felt connected to it. My heart beat in harmony with the sun and my whole being pulsated with it in a unified rhythm. It seemed that my mind was expanding to embrace the external universe, the stars of the heavens, then contracting to embrace the internal world, the atoms comprising all living things. I was part of all life, vibrating with the sun in a cosmic dance in which I was a participant, not an observer. I began to experience other dimensions of being, as if I were actually part of celestial realms, transported to the sun and beyond through a gate to the realm of higher intelligence. I entered a world beyond space and time, a world not experienced by the normal mental faculties, and I participated in thoughts never before experienced by my mind. Ninety-three million miles did not separate my being from the sun—in that very instant I was one with it. For the first time, I experienced the sun as the eye of God looking into the depths of my soul.

My eyes were doing more than just seeing or experiencing the electromagnetic radiation of the visible spectrum, which causes light and color perception in material space and time. With my new sense of vision I was seeing points of solar illumination from many areas of the sky. I saw multitudes of suns, not just one, and energy seemed to be streaming into my being from all of them. The nerve cells in my eyes and brain tingled—I felt aglow, radiant. I was also seeing the light of an invisible sun, the sun behind the sun, which is not seen by the organs of physical sight. I seemed to be attached to the sun, and it to me. More astounding, the sun was responding to my projected thoughts as a living organism would. As I was transmitting telepathically to the sun, it was transmitting telepathically to me.

Spellbound, I stared at the suns before me, incredulous at the spectacle. I had read historical accounts of the sun's dancing in the sky, changing positions and appearing at different points. The children of Fatima have reported seeing such events, as have many others all over the world. Previously, I had dismissed the reports as mass hysteria, or—at best—hallucination. But now I was experiencing the dancing sun myself.

With these thoughts, the suns disappeared as suddenly as they had come. I found myself looking for the one sun again. Surprisingly, it was far to the left, in a part of the sky I had not been viewing. Blinking in the light, which now seemed even more brilliant, harsher and more difficult to look at, I wiped the streaming tears from my eyes and lowered my glance to the ground. After composing myself, clearing my thoughts, I looked once more into the sun, attempting to communicate with it. I drew several deep breaths to still my heartbeat. Again the phenomenon occurred. Instantly, I knew that the sun was a manifestation of a supreme intelligence connected to every cell of every living thing, linked to the human mind and the human soul.

Any thought broadcast by the mind of man—any feeling

whatsoever—is relayed to the sun, where it is processed, resulting in a reaction in the person transmitting the thought. The nature of the reaction is determined by the nature of the thought. It seemed to me that whatever thought was transmitted to the sun somehow involved all living things. All life was influenced by the thought, since all living things were interconnected and interrelated with the sun.

The thought transmission seemed to lie beyond the electromagnetic waves, encompassing some higher means of communication that put my inner nature into contact with the living brain or nerve center of the universe. In this way I was able to affect this center, and it was able to affect my very being. My experience demonstrated that through the organ of the sun one can reach into other dimensions and open a new experience that is not of one's own making, though one can play a part in it. It told me that man has latent faculties that can participate in cosmic phenomena. By these means man can project himself into a world where space and time have entirely new dimensions. These new dimensions are just as real, indeed more real, than the material world of physical reality.

It was clear to me that there is manifest in nature a consciousness and a beingness of a supreme order beyond anything man's rational mind can comprehend; that one participates in it by means of an inner faculty with which all men are endowed at birth—or perhaps before birth—into the world of physical reality; and that this faculty is triggered into action by the techniques I was practicing. I felt that this supreme consciousness and beingness could give man a new awareness, a new perception of things—an awareness and perception that reveal the physical world to be nothing more than the furthermost part of the true state or condition of things, the outer skin of a great body which is the universe as it really is.

Man's true nature is part of this greater universe, part of the supreme consciousness at the center. His physical nature is representative of the physical world; because of their limitations, his perceptory senses cannot see the whole.

Absorbing the sun's energy and participating in the inner light at its center had created a profound change within me. I was at peace with the whole cosmos for the first time in my life. I felt a subconscious urge to direct love and compassion beyond my physical being into the whole of the universe. If I had a soul, as I felt I did, then the universe had a greater soul, and I was one with it. I was no longer an individual, limited and uncomprehending, but part of a cosmic whole. For the first time, I understood how mystic religion is a cosmic science that teaches about those greater experiences that the natural sciences, which are concerned only with external events, always narrowed and limited. Mysticism puts man's complex nature into order, arranging psychic events into significant terms through the initiative of the individual who wants to learn.

Slowly I realized that this peace was caused by my letting go of the material world of the perceptory senses, a world preoccupied with the present and the past. I was being drawn into the future, into another world of space and time. Indeed, I was being influenced by the future, as if future events were being impressed upon me psychically. I had an urge to participate, to commune with that future. Knowing it could not be done through the physical body or any exertion of the mind, I sought to release my self-transcending spiritual powers into the care of that supreme intelligence instilled in me by the light of the sun.

I was hardly conscious of breathing; my heart did not seem to be beating. My body was in a state of suspended animation, as if linked by an invisible umbilical cord to the sun. Then, the one experience I had longed for, prayed for, occurred. Once again the golden form appeared, gazing benevolently upon me, smiling, yet with unmoving lips like those of Mona Lisa. It was a scintillating blaze of luminescence, its form like that of sunbeams.

I was intent on recording every part of it in my mind's eye—I hoped it wouldn't fade away again before I had an opportunity to study it.

Like a flash, it was gone. I gasped—shocked by its disappearance. I had felt a pulling at my solar plexus, as if I were connected to the illusive form, and its sudden disappearance had snapped some invisible connecting cord at my navel. For a long time I stood there under the trees, my eyes fused with the sun, intent on identifying and understanding the apparition. Did life exist in the sun? Was it possible for some form of life to exist there? A living form beyond the organic form as we know it on this planet?

Whatever the answer, I felt that the workings of my rational mind had caused the form to fade. That disturbed me, because I had promised myself that if the form returned I would not make the mistake of allowing the workings of my mind to interfere. I realized that the mind of man and the material world to which it is confined conspire to exclude the spiritual realm, to bind the faculties to external events of the material world: rationality does suppress intuition.

I had been overcome by the lower senses and the workings of my mind. In that moment I was humbled by my own feelings. Again my eyes returned to the sun. I was at peace with myself, a bit sad, but content in the knowledge that I had observed the golden form once more, though briefly. Again I merged with the sun and with the cosmic beingness I had come to know. Once more the form appeared. It would have faded again had I not caught hold of myself and overcome the shock of its sudden reappearance. The thought struck me that man does control his own destiny by overcoming the lower faculties that control him—body, mind, emotions.

I remained perfectly calm, observing the form with my inner eye, yet registering the picture of it in my brain. Had someone come upon me as I stared into the sun, he would have noticed my eyes were slightly crossed, my body cool to the touch, my being perfectly composed.

A voice called to me. The form disappeared, but not before I saw the one thing I had wanted to see.

"Gene! It's time to go. Come on. We've gassed up." Joaquim's voice rose above the quietness. Stirring myself, I blinked.

When I had come out of my reverie, I walked slowly towards the aircraft, deep in thought. I had discerned in the form the image of myself, confirming what I had seen in the first appearance of the golden form in Peru. I had seen myself as surely as if I had been cast flawlessly in gold. There was no mistake about it—I could tell by the eyes.

After buckling the seat belt, I leaned back, resting my head. Looking out the window, my eyes were attracted once more to the sun, now glinting off the cracked plexiglass in a spectrum of bright patterns. Again I thought about the experience and the golden form who seemed to be me come from another world. I knew now that part of me existed in another dimension of space and time. Of that I was certain.

The question was: How could I exist in two worlds at the same time?

As the aircraft rumbled down the short grassy strip, climbed into the blue sky, and made a wide sweeping turn in the direction of the Amazon, I thought about the question. And the more I thought about it, the more determined I became to find the answer.

10

The Reality of Immortality

Tollan, Mexico

August 7, 1973 (P.M.)—In the afternoon we retired to a subterranean sanctuary near the pyramids at Tollan. The underground crypt had been selected because it offered the isolation and solitude necessary for discourse.

As I stood on the floor, twelve associates seated themselves on broken stairways directly above me. Their pale faces glowed in the eerie radiance cast by shafts of light squeezing through cracks in the roof. Rich frescoes, made brilliant by sunbeams, presided over the darkened interior. Outside, intermittent thunder shattered the stillness, and a warm summer rain pattered softly down. I had promised to tell them of my experiences. The outer world seemed remote as we sat in the stillness; no one moved, each intent on listening to what I was about to say. I looked upon them, measuring my thoughts, because I wanted to communicate in a way that each one could comprehend through his inner nature. I would address their levels of consciousness, emphasizing one word over another, raising and lowering my voice at certain times, speaking musically and making gestures, tracing symbols in the air—imparting knowledge not so much by what was said as by how I said it. I often spoke in that way, from the belief that a person's understanding of words is often dictated by an association of words that is determined by education, experience and background. Therefore, when the rational mind is used to perceive the spoken word, every listener has a different level of understanding, even though the same words are heard by all. Gestures and intonation create a wave front, sending forth energy from the speaker's consciousness and filling that energy with information that is always understood in the same manner by the consciousness of the listener's inner being. I have often said that pure knowledge does not come from words alone, but from the energies released by certain persons trained in the communication of ideas whose knowledge of a subject goes beyond abstract or objective evaluation to the power behind the ideas. This ability gave the prophets their power to communicate through parables, voice and secret mannerisms. It is one of the reasons music, art and drama are still so effective in communicating universal ideas to large groups.

When I had composed myself and cleared my mind, I began to speak in a soft, melodious voice, right hand raised, palm towards the group, ring finger and little finger resting against the palm, index finger and middle finger pointed straight up, and thumb at a right angle to them: "The second law of thermodynamics holds that physical phenomena are running down like a clock, that their energy is slowly being dissipated. According to this theory, the general direction of physical events in the universe points towards disorder and eventual collapse. On the other hand, the theory of conservation of energy holds that the universe is a closed system where there can be neither gain nor loss of radiation.

"We have learned that man's consciousness ultimately controls the motions of the sun and the stars, as well as those of the atoms. Thus we learned that the processes of the universe and of all life are not regulated just by the laws of physics or chemistry. That life is, or can be, self-determining is indicated by the ancient myths we have reviewed; the oral traditions, the written records and the legends all tell of the sun having been altered, having stood still at times, or even having gone out. Therefore, we must accept the idea of a nonmechanical agency dictating life and its development. So, as mystics, we move away from natural physics towards metaphysics and acceptance of vitalism, which scientists have always considered heresy because its ideas of self-determinism come from the knowledge taught by the mystical schools." I hesitated here, tracing a symbol on the dirt floor with the toe of my boot. "For example, my own experience during which I saw myself in another form, a form of light outside the electromagnetic spectrum, suggests that I was able to discern myself as I will be after loss of the physical body—that is, after death claims it." This statement caused Tomich to challenge me.

"But how can you be certain you were seeing yourself? Could it have been a hallucination? What proof do you have?"

"In addition to perceiving the phenomenon, I was able to experience communication with the form. The consciousness of that form interacted with my own to extend me new information about myself and the world that I did not possess before. Wouldn't this be proof?"

Tomich nodded.

Ana Quintana, a Guatemalan who had been an associate for a year, asked the next question. The eerie tomb light bathing her natural tan features and dark hair made her look like a Toltec priestess, an illusion enhanced by her black-and-white checkered cape and the jewelry on her neck, wrists and fingers. She was twenty-one, radiant with youth, beautiful, intelligent, inquisitive and willing to learn. I had grown fond of her. Though we often spoke together in her native Spanish, now she spoke in English.

"What information did you learn?" she asked.

"That the future is as much a part of us as is the past, that we can share in the future as we remember the past. If immortality is real, if man has indeed a part of him that continues to participate in life after death, then this immortality must embrace the future."

At that moment, Ellen Seaman, who served as the recording engineer and was responsible for the transcripts, removed her earphones and posed a question. She hailed from San Francisco and had taken an active interest in the group after the move from Mexico City to Reno, Nevada, a year before. Fascinated by the experiments that had changed her life, Seaman had become one of the most avid followers of the Project's ideas. Her sparkling personality drew people from all levels to her. In a white coat with matching slacks, her slim figure shimmered in a spotlight of pale rays. "But I thought the past, the present and the future were all one; wasn't that what we were taught in one of the classes I attended at a metaphysical center in San Francisco?"

"The past is a matter of memory," I said, intent upon revealing as much about the question as words would permit. I spoke with both hands extended before me, emphasizing my speech with gestures. "Impressions recorded by our mind and sense organs determine our concept of time and space. The sequence in which these experiences are recorded dictates past and present. The future is not known to our mind and sense organs. Therefore, man is confined to his reactions to present and past sensory stimulation. Much has been said about reincarnation—that we have lived past lifetimes, and that at times we are conscious of our past lifetimes through recall, though information is often fragmentary. Trance, or hypnosis, often brings to the surface these so-called past lives.

"In reality, every human being is the product of former generations. The lifetimes of millions of our ancestors pulse in our genes, our psyche. It is only natural that the memories of these lifetimes should be recorded within us. But memories of previous lifetimes are multiple, never singular. It could be said, then, that each of us is the outgrowth of the past, the combined totality of every human being who ever lived, going back to the first man and the first woman—and before. This would explain why many people share similar life experiences."

Michael Gerbus, a relative newcomer to the Project, had journeyed to Mexico from San Francisco before my departure for the Amazon. He seized upon the last statement: "What do you mean by 'before'?"

Before answering, I studied the tall, lean figure of this twenty-two-year-old youth with long, flowing brown hair. Gerbus stood six feet two, though he weighed no more than 145 pounds. A native of Cincinnati, he had become disenchanted with academic studies and flown to Hawaii, where he had spent most of his time on the beaches of Maui trying to find himself—or, as he told me during his interview, "trying to put things together." Hearing of the Project, he had returned to the mainland to participate.

I mulled over his question, then answered: "If we see ourselves in the future, it would mean that we are beyond the past, present and future and, therefore, that we have lived before. In other words, we become pre-existent. But our pre-existence does not become a reality to us unless we experience it for ourselves in the present."

"Could you explain further?" asked Gerbus.

A smile traced my lips as I replied, "The past and the present are part of our physical environment. The future is part of our spiritual environment. We know the past and the present because we have inherited physical senses from our parents, and thus we participate and record. The future is a matter of the spiritual sensory makeup. We must of ourselves create these spiritual faculties in order to participate in the spiritual world—and the future. It is not a matter of inheritance, but of self-determinism."

"You are saying that each one is obliged to generate a spiritual body by use of spiritual energy?" asked Ramon Gonzalez, a vibrant and intelligent Costa Rican of thirty-five.

"Yes. With spiritual generation we become participants in the spiritual universe, the non-physical world of reality. Therefore, to experience the spiritual, we must participate in it while in the present space-time awareness; that is, we must experience it while we are presently living in the here and now as material entities," I replied.

"We can live in two worlds at the same time?" asked Seaman. "Both in the material and the non-material?"

"Quite so. Once this is achieved, we become involved with the future through the impregnation into our beings of a spiritual energy and a divine force that brings about a conception within the womb of our spiritual beings. After a period of gestation, a new birth unfolds. This new birth is representative of a spiritual entity; it is every bit as alive as the physical, yet it has absolutely nothing whatsoever to do with our physical makeup—at least, not with our faculties of cognition or emotion or our sensory makeup. This entity is part of a spiritual world and has its own life there. We are linked to this spiritual entity on the physical level through our psychic nature and possibly through a higher part of our brain and mind, which may be related to the newly developed spiritual consciousness of that spiritual entity."

"What you are saying then is that the being you experienced was yourself existing in the future and brought into contact with your present time awareness?" inquired Seaman.

"Yes, I believe so."

"What size was it?" asked Tomich.

"Hard to say. The last time, I had the impression it was larger than my physical body, maybe eight feet tall. But one cannot judge by earthly measurements. Once I felt it was small. In the *Resurrection*, Plato commented that the immortal body lives more than once, each time growing smaller and smaller, eventually taking on the form of a baby, before vanishing. The fact remains that our spiritual body is a higher entity than the physical form our senses and our rational mind make us out to be.

"It is immortal and exists in another world beyond the space and time of our material world. This spiritual body is animated by a supreme force man calls God. All knowledge of God comes from the spiritual body and its consciousness, not from our rational minds or workings of the bodily emotions. Since the spiritual body has its origins in a spiritual universe, it is sustained by energies from that world, not from the physical world. Therefore, knowledge of that form is beyond the realms of physics and the natural sciences, which confine themselves to physical phenomena. It would appear that through the absorption of solar energy, by means of our techniques, a new energy field is formed. Once formed, that field is displaced—that is, it jumps to another dimension of space and time, just as electric and magnetic fields do when they are modified. When this displacement occurs, our higher natures are transferred to another place in the universe, leaving behind our physical natures, as a butterfly leaves the chrysalis."

"You mean to say our spiritual nature is transferred to another dimension, and our physical nature remains here?" The question came from a tall, well-built middle-aged man with keen eyes and superb powers of concentration. Jack Opdyke, who had been an associate for a year, was a 58-year-old construction man from La Selva Beach, California. He was active in local church affairs but, owing to an illness, had sought answers outside the established doctrines of Christianity. First he had studied meditation. Later, after experiencing some help from it, he investigated the Project at the urging of his wife, a sensitive from Sonora, Mexico, whose curative powers were well known in both Mexico and California. She sat beside him, wrapped in an orange poncho, following the conversation with deep interest.

"Yes. Body and spirit are separate, each existing in its own world."

Opdyke was still skeptical about some of the teachings of the group and wanted evidence for everything. He inquired further: "How can the body, the mind, the person, experience the existence of this spiritual creation of which you speak? Where is the proof?" Opdyke wasn't hostile to me, but he wasn't sure whether I was a genuine teacher or a phony. Nevertheless, he was convinced there was something inexplicable about me and was earnestly trying to discover what it was. For this reason he had come to Mexico when the Project returned to the ruins. Now he studied me intently, steel-blue eyes playing over me from his position on a step higher up in the tomb.

"While the spiritual body inhabits a higher dimension, it remains attached to the physical body. That is, the higher consciousness of the spiritual body is able to communicate with the lower mind of the physical body, illuminating it from time to time. Upon the death of the physical body, the two merge, and the energy, or vital force, of the individual dissolves into a new form. The whole being is absorbed by the higher entity. In the meantime, there is periodic contact or union between the two; there are flashes of intuition, memories, recalls, images from the future. Relationships between persons of this world and those of another world can vary in degree. Mental events are different from spiritual events. One has to learn how to distinguish between the two or—more important—to be aware of the spiritual, to identify with it. That is the joining of the twins, the royal marriage. When it occurs, a person exists in two worlds at the same time—in a manner of speaking, anyway."

While I was speaking, my being was suddenly surrounded by a brilliant light. The whole room was illuminated. Jack Opdyke saw the light clearly. He was able to distinguish every part of the cave, so bright was the light. Awed, he sat speechless. After a while he got hold of himself; thinking he was experiencing a hallucination, he got up and moved about the crypt. Still he saw the light.

Later, when discussing the experience with other associates, Opdyke discovered that some had seen the light and others had not. He had no rational explanation for the phenomenon, though he felt that he had merged with that light—and that it had altered his awareness. Above all, the light he had seen illuminated a part of his inner being, filling him with great warmth.

11

The Illusion of Death

Curua, Brazil

August 18, 1973—Ten days later I sat on the deck of the *Karim Elke,* a 45-foot river boat, reviewing notes in my journal of transcripts. Joaquim had brought me the journal. It was a heavy, thick collection of transcripts and notes bound in white cardboard. I had been writing ever since our return from the jungle the day before. We had spent the better part of a week on the western slopes of the Javari range in quest of possible remains of the Amazons. We had traveled by sail from Santarem across the Amazon to the Curua River, then by dugout up a small tributary called the Infierno, then by pack through the dense forest to the upper heights. The night before we had dropped anchor in Curua, a small port at the mouth of the river facing Lake Intandeua.

I was tired from the strenuous hike and didn't feel like writing, but force of habit made me record my thoughts. When I finished, I reviewed the notes of the past two days:

TRANSCRIPTS

August 17, 1973

The light field, or luminous form, has been showing itself to others during lectures, most recently at the ruins in Mexico. Telepathic transmission of thoughts to others is quite common in metaphysics. Mediums, sensitives and mystics are known to be able to project images of themselves into the minds of people in the waking state—and also into the minds of people in dream or trance states induced by hypnotism, suggestion, drugs or meditation. But I am unable to account for the field of light that materializes around my person during inspirational talks. It is not observed by all, only by the most sensitive.

It appears that absorption of solar radiation in the manner being taught in the Project enhances this ability. Absorption of solar energy does seem to generate this form and also to sensitize one's awareness of all forms of radiation—particularly fields around living things.

The way my own energy field appeared to my physical senses as if out of another world suggests that the field has come out of the future. Therefore, telepathic thoughts and forms can be transmitted from other worlds—and from one's own future being—to man's faculties. This suggests that man is immortal and that death, in the medical or scientific sense, is an illusion. Perhaps at death our form (the force field around the material form) is transported to another dimension of time and space. This is in future time (to our own present awareness of space and time). Consciousness, being immortal, is able to come back in space and time and manifest itself to us, linking us with the future. This would account for the appearance of the light form which I believe to be myself arrived from the future. Physically, the intake of solar radiation seems to stimulate memories by charging the brain and nervous system with vital energy. This energy is encoded with information of a cosmic nature. On the other hand, the endocrine system appears to be involved, too. I have noticed that absorption of solar energy has a tendency to make a person peaceful, to give him an urge to love and mother the world. (I remember Stromberg reporting on an experiment in which a female rat was given an injection of a pituitary hormone called prolactin. The rat experienced a change of disposition; she became very maternal towards all animals placed in her cage—rats, rabbits, even squabs.)

The pineal gland, called the third eye, does appear to be stimulated by light absorption, which would account for the heightened sight of solar adepts.

It is very clear that man is a spirit; i.e., he has a spiritual nature that can be developed. Man does—or can—control his own life more than he imagines. The techniques propel man from a limited state of

human beingness that is involved primarily with sensory stimulation to a new state of his real being—man becomes whole.
Generation of the immortal nature frees man from bondage to the
physical world. He is freed from the fear of death, loses all anxiety
and insecurity, and becomes involved with new spiritual stimulation.

**I turned the page to my notes of the eighteenth. These writings
concerned my concepts of the light body.**

TRANSCRIPTS

August 18, 1973

ORIGINS. How human life began on the planet is the genuine
mystery, the true goal of pure science. Until we solve it, the real
purpose of existence will escape modern man.

The dominant theme of all ancient scripture has man linked with
(i) God and (ii) the sun. Can all the writings of ancient man, his oral
traditions, his myths and his folklore be nothing but superstition and
fairy tales? I don't think so. The stories of man as a noble creature of
God must have a basis in fact.

It seems to me that the ancient philosophers of the mystical
schools and the priests of the old world religions evidently were able
to contact the supreme creative force in the universe—a contact
man is not experiencing today in the modern world. I have
discovered for myself that contact with the creative energy of the
universe begins in the sun, the fountainhead of all cosmic energy
available to the planet. This energy supplies the human mind with
the vital force necessary to think on a higher level. I have discovered
both through fasting and through a very light diet of raw fruits,
vegetables and water (hardly enough to sustain the needs of the
physical body, if we are to believe the experts who tell us that the body
demands a certain amount of protein and a certain number of
calories) that the body is not nourished by food alone. The sun's
energy supplies strength and an abundance of nourishment on the
primary level; food seems to be a secondary form of energy, essential

to the animal body but not essential to the creative thinking processes.

One fact stands out above all others in the series of experiments conducted to date: with the intake of sunlight and with the use of the spiritual force found within this light, man's spiritual nature is magnified. One draws closer to the idea that man is the bearer of the spirit and that God, as a supreme intelligence, exists.

For some reason, when man began to measure the sun, when he began to develop the natural sciences and technologies, the sun and the universe—and even man himself—were divested of spirit. Man sought his origins in the earth, not the stars. The spiritual world dwindled in importance. As a result, the world is in a dangerous condition—the very soul of life has been denied. Present generations are clinging to a scientific interpretation of existence that breeds an atheistic attitude that could have grave consequences—if our findings that man controls the sun are correct.

Because modern man has lost the ability to draw upon the creative energy of the sun and upon the spiritual energy which would nourish his spiritual nature, he is unable to use the higher and refined faculties of the spirit (without energy they atrophy). This condition would suggest a kind of degeneration of man.

I put my notebook down and picked up a hardcover book. Leafing through it, I found the part that interested me—a translation of an old Egyptian manuscript originally written in Arabic (the English version was the work of a Vicar of Broadwindsor) entitled "The First Book of Adam and Eve." The account picks up where the story in Genesis leaves off. Putting a finger on a passage beginning in Chapter 8, I read on, skipping over parts and ending in Chapter 66:

Then Adam wept and said, "O God, when we dwelt in the garden and our hearts were lifted up, we saw the angels that sang praises in heaven, but now we do not see as we were used to do; nay, when we entered the cave, all creation became hidden from us."

Then God the Lord said unto Adam, "When thou wast under subjection to Me, thou hadst a bright nature within thee, and for that reason couldst thou see things afar off. But after thy transgression thy bright nature was withdrawn from thee; and it was not left to thee to see things afar off, but only near at hand, after the ability of the flesh; for it is brutish."

When Adam and Eve had heard these words from God, they went their way, praising and worshipping Him with a sorrowful heart.

And God ceased to commune with them. . . .

Then Adam and Eve came out of the Cave of Treasures, and drew near the garden gate, and there they stood to look at it, and wept for having come away from it.

And Adam and Eve went before the gate of the garden to the southern side of it, and found there the water that watered the garden, from the root of the Tree of Life, and that parted itself from thence into four rivers over the earth.

Then Adam and Eve felt themselves burning with thirst, and heat, and sorrow.

And Adam said to Eve, "We shall not drink of this water, even if we were to die. O Eve, when this water comes into our inner parts, it will increase our punishments and that of our children, that shall come after us."

Both Adam and Eve then withdrew from the water, and drank none of it at all; but came and entered the Cave of Treasures.

But when in it Adam could not see Eve; he only heard the noise she made. Neither could she see Adam, but heard the noise he made.

Then Adam wept, in deep affliction, and smote upon his breast; and he rose and said to Eve, "Where art thou?"

And she said unto him, "Lo, I am standing in this darkness."

He then said to her, "Remember the bright nature in which we lived, while we abode in the garden!

"O Eve! Remember the glory that rested on us in the garden. O Eve! Remember the trees that overshadowed us in the garden while we moved among them.

"O Eve! Remember that while we were in the garden, we knew neither night nor day. Think of the Tree of Life, from below which flowed the water, and that shed lustre over us! Remember, O Eve, the gardenland, and the brightness thereof!

"Think, oh think of that garden in which was no darkness, while we dwelt therein.

"Whereas no sooner did we come into this Cave of Treasures than darkness compassed us round about, until we can no longer see each other; and all the pleasure of this life has come to an end." . . .

Then when God, who is merciful and full of pity, heard Adam's voice, He said unto him:—

"*O Adam, so long as the good angel was obedient to Me, a bright light rested on him and on his hosts.*

"*But when he transgressed My commandment, I deprived him of that bright nature, and he became dark.*

"*And when he was in the heavens, in the realms of light, he knew naught of darkness.*

"*But he transgressed, and I made him fall from heaven upon the earth; and it was this darkness that came upon him.*

"*And on thee, O Adam, while in My garden and obedient to Me, did that bright light rest also.*

"*But when I heard of thy transgression, I deprived thee of that bright light. Yet, of My mercy, I did not turn thee into darkness, but I made thee thy body of flesh, over which I spread this skin, in order that it may bear cold and heat.*

"*If I had let My wrath fall heavily upon thee, I should have destroyed thee; and had I turned thee into darkness, it would have been as if I killed thee.*

"*But in My mercy, I have made thee as thou art; when thou didst transgress My commandment, O Adam, I drove thee from the garden, and made thee come forth into this land, and commanded thee to dwell in this cave; and darkness came upon thee, as it did upon him who transgressed My commandment.*

"*Thus, O Adam, has this night deceived thee. It is not to last for ever, but is only of twelve hours; when it is over, daylight will return.*

"*Sigh not, therefore, neither be moved, and say not in thy heart that this darkness is long and drags on wearily; and say not in thy heart that I plague thee with it.*

"*Strengthen thy heart, and be not afraid. This darkness is not a punishment. But, O Adam, I have made the day, and have placed the sun in it to give light, in order that thou and thy children should do your work.*

"*For I knew thou shouldst sin and transgress, and come out into this land. Yet would I not force thee, nor be heard upon thee, nor shut up, nor doom thee through thy fall, nor thy coming out from light into darkness, nor yet through thy coming from the garden into this land.*

"*For I made thee of the light; and I willed to bring out children of light from thee and like unto thee.*

"*But thou didst not keep one day My commandment; until I had finished the creation and blessed everything in it.*

"Then I commanded thee concerning the tree, that thou eat not thereof. Yet I knew that Satan, who deceived himself, would also deceive thee.

"So I made known to thee, by means of the tree, not to come near him. And I told thee not to eat of the fruit thereof, nor to taste of it, nor yet to sit under it, nor to yield to it.

"Had I not been and spoken to thee, O Adam, concerning the tree, and had I left thee without commandment, and thou hadst sinned—it would have been an offence on My part, for not having given thee any order; thou wouldst turn round and blame Me for it.

"But I commanded thee, and warned thee, and thou didst fall. So that My creatures cannot blame me; but the blame rests on them alone.

"And, O Adam, I have made the day for thee and for thy children after thee, for them to work and toil therein. And I have made the night for them to rest in it from their work; and for the beasts of the field to go forth by night and seek their food.

"But little of darkness now remains, O Adam; and daylight will soon appear.". . .

Then Adam said unto God: "O Lord, take Thou my soul and let me not see this gloom any more; or remove me to some place where there is no darkness."

But God the Lord said to Adam: "Verily I say unto thee, this darkness will pass from thee, every day I have determined for thee, until the fulfillment of My covenant; when I will save thee and bring thee back again into the garden, into the abode of light thou longest for, wherein is no darkness. I will bring thee to it—in the kingdom of heaven."

Again said God unto Adam, "All this misery that thou hast been made to take upon thee because of thy transgression will not free thee from the hand of Satan, and will not save thee.

"But I will. When I shall come down from heaven, and shall become flesh of thy seed, and take upon Me the infirmity from which thou sufferest, then the darkness that came upon thee in this cave shall come upon me in the grave, when I am in the flesh of thy seed.

"And I, who am without years, shall be subject to the reckoning of years, of times, of months, and of days, and I shall be reckoned as one of the sons of men, in order to save thee."

And God ceased to commune with Adam. . . .

After this Adam and Eve ceased to stand in the cave, praying and weeping, until the morning dawned upon them.

And when they saw the light returned to them, they restrained from fear, and strengthened their hearts.

Then Adam began to come out of the cave. And when he came to the mouth of it, and stood and turned his face towards the east, and saw the sun rise in glowing rays, and felt the heat thereof on his body, he was afraid of it, and thought in his heart that this flame came forth to plague him.

He wept then, and smote upon his breast, and fell upon the earth on his face, and made his request saying:

"O Lord, plague me not, neither consume me, nor yet take away my life from the earth."

For he thought the sun was God.

Inasmuch as while he was in the garden and heard the voice of God and the sound He made in the garden, and feared Him, Adam never saw the brilliant light of the sun, neither did the flaming heat thereof touch his body.

Therefore was he afraid of the sun when flaming rays of it reached him. He thought God meant to plague him therewith all the days He had decreed for him.

For Adam also said in his thoughts, as God did not plague us with darkness, behold, He has caused this sun to rise and to plague us with burning heat.

But while he was thus thinking in his heart, the Word of God came unto him and said:

"O Adam, arise and stand up. This sun is not God; but it has been created to give light by day, of which I spake unto thee in the cave saying, 'that the dawn would break forth, and there would be light by day.'

"But I am God who comforted thee in the night."

And God ceased to commune with Adam.

And Adam said to Eve, "Look at thine eyes, and at mine, which afore held angels in heaven, praising; and they, too, without ceasing.

"But now we do not see as we did: our eyes have become of flesh; they cannot see in like manner as they saw before."

Adam said again to Eve, "What is our body to-day, compared to what it was in former days, when we dwelt in the garden?"...

Then God looked upon Adam and upon his strength of mind, upon his endurance of hunger and thirst, and of the heat. And He changed the two fig-trees into two figs, as they were at first, and then said to Adam and Eve, "Each of you may take one fig." And they took them as the Lord commanded them.

And He said to them, "Go ye into the cave, and eat the figs, and satisfy your hunger, lest ye die."

So, as God commanded them, they went into the cave, about the time when the sun was setting. And Adam and Eve stood up and prayed at the time of the setting sun.

Then they sat down to eat the figs; but they knew not how to eat them, for they were not accustomed to eat earthly food. They feared also lest, if they ate, their stomach should be burdened and their flesh thickened, and their hearts take to liking earthly food.

But while they were thus seated, God, out of pity for them, sent them His angel, lest they should perish of hunger and thirst.

And the angel said unto Adam and Eve, "God says to you that ye have not strength to fast until death; eat, therefore, and strengthen your bodies; for ye are now animal flesh, that cannot subsist without food and drink."

Then Adam and Eve took the figs and began to eat of them. But God had put into them a mixture as of savory bread and blood. . . .

And when it was day, they rose and prayed, after their custom, and then went out of the cave.

But as they felt great trouble from the food they had eaten, and to which they were not used, they went in the cave saying to each other:

"What has happened to us through eating, that this pain should have come upon us? Woe be to us, we shall die! Better for us to have died than to have eaten; and to have kept our bodies pure, than to have defiled them with food."

Then they prayed to God that He would have mercy on them; after which their mind was quieted, their hearts were broken, and their longing was cooled down; and they were like strangers on earth. That night Adam and Eve spent in the cave, where they slept heavily by reasons of the food they had eaten.

When it was morning, the day after they had eaten food, Adam and Eve prayed in the cave, and Adam said unto Eve, "Lo, we asked for food of God, and He gave it. But now let us also ask Him to give us a drink of water."

Then they arose, and went to the bank of the stream of water, that was on the south border of the garden, in which they had before thrown themselves. And they stood on the bank, and prayed to God that He would command them to drink of the water.

Then the Word of God came to Adam, and said unto him, "O Adam, thy body is become brutish, and requires water to drink. Take ye, and drink, thou and Eve; give thanks and praise."

Adam and Eve then drew near, and drank of it, until their bodies felt refreshed. After having drunk, they praised God, and then returned to their cave, after their former custom.

When I had finished reading, I put the book on the table. According to what was written, an ancient story partially recorded in the Bible, the Koran and the Talmud, man was made originally of light, deriving his food from a divine light. Material food, processed by the alimentary tract, had come much later, after the fall. While I recognized the story as an allegory, nevertheless I saw the truth hidden in it. The thought struck me that the field others discerned around my being might be composed of traces of the original light body—that body of brightness given by God to Adam. If this was the same higher-dimension form I had observed, then it was possible that the Project's techniques had somehow put us in contact with a bright body beyond space and time.

Had the means of re-establishing contact with the true source of man's spiritual beingness been rediscovered? It was possible that this source had been lost through ignorance, and not punishment, as scripture appears to say.

The more I thought about the idea, the more intrigued I became with it.

12

Dual Images

Alenquer, Brazil

August 19, 1973—Seated on the upper deck of the *Karim Elke,* I was nervous and tense, unusually troubled by an experience that had taken place the night before while I was resting in my hammock.

Although the sun was still low on the horizon, it was already a sultry day, whose heat made concentrating difficult. Swarms of mosquitoes buzzed about, pestering my eyes, nose and ears. Usually they didn't bother me, but whenever I was disturbed, the peaceful countenance on which I prided myself left me. As a result, the nasty little insects were able to penetrate my field. I felt like a magician who had lost his magic wand. For a long time I sat under the hot sun in a pool of perspiration, baking, refusing to seek the shade of the lower deck. The *Karim Elke* was at anchor, and the crew, as well as my companions, had gone ashore, so I had the ship to myself. Nevertheless, I found it hard to think. Then a passing riverboat's wake set up a rocking motion that began to lull me.

I opened my eyes and looked at the bright image of the sun, experiencing the warmth of its energy streaming into my brain and feeling, as I often did, the powerful grip of its radiance. I resumed my study of the story of Adam. Shortly after Adam and Eve realized that they had lost their bright natures, they threw themselves down from a mountaintop and killed themselves out of desperation at being cut off from their true image. But God raised them up, saying that even though they had been tempted by the devil to break His commandments and to become as gods themselves, He would have them live on earth.

Sometime afterwards, Satan appeared as a brilliant and glorious being of light, surrounded by a host of beings like angels. And Adam thought the light was of God, and he prayed to God saying, "O Lord, is there in the world another god than Thou, who created angels and filled them with light?" And God sent an angel to tell Adam that the form was Satan with his host come to deceive Adam, as he had done the first time, in order to enthrall Adam and make him worship him. And God made Adam see the true form of Satan, a hideous form, and then commanded him to go away. Adam realized it was the devil who had made him fall from brightness into darkness, from peace and rest into toil and misery, and from then on was armed against him.

In a way, I shared Adam's fear and confusion, because a bright image had appeared to me the night before. Not only had it troubled me, it had frightened me as well. The image had come as before, brilliant and glowing, with a pleasant, smiling face. But it was a human face, and when I looked into its eyes I was filled with fear and apprehension. The black-bearded face, fair in countenance, was almost effeminate. Its beckoning words were sweet, but repelling somehow. My intuition caused me to ask God to send the image away. It disappeared then in a flash, as if sucked up into a black hole in space.

The experience had made me tremble, and I was troubled. For the first time I realized that the path to enlightenment is not an easy one—that the dark forces always manifest themselves. I should have expected that; it has to do with mirror images and the dual nature of man, a philosophical problem I had written a paper on for members of the Project some years before.

That man has a dual nature is an idea as old as philosophy itself. All the world's great religions agree that man has a dual spiritual beingness: one dark, the other light. When an individual meets the inner light and opens the door to the world of the spirit, his human existence is always changed. The individual transcends the physical world to a vision of another that is beyond space and time—one where physical consciousness is replaced by a spiritual consciousness that was known to Adam and Eve in the Garden. In the process, though, the contraries that one meets can overwhelm an individual who is not prepared for them. One must be anchored to a greater beingness, a greater light than that of the simple person confronting the mystery of totality.

Some theologians have argued that to accept the existence of the power of darkness is to give it equality with the power of light—to accept the devil is to give him equal footing with God. Yet, prophets of these religions have accepted that evil is coexistent with God, which is one of the great mysteries of religion—how the union of the opposites in God is possible. I could readily accept that man, but not God, comprises both good and evil. With illumination of the spiritual nature comes the realization that what is holy can be frightening, because it reveals the dark side of the universe, which is every bit as strong, maybe stronger, than the physical side.

This duality disturbed me, because I had experienced it; I knew that man has access to creative and destructive potentials—two superhuman entities emerging from one cause which must be God. What bothered me was the possibility that the darker entity might be another aspect of my higher immortal nature coming out of the future to beguile me, as the devil had Adam.

The dangers of transcendence were clear. So was the nature of the struggle between the dual natures of the spirit. Like the two hemispheres of the brain—the left side rational, the right side intuitive—the deep psychic and spiritual attributes of man have two distinct natures controlling two different attitudes. So the quest for immortality is not an easy task. It calls for a superhuman knowledge of both the demonic and the divine forces of the cosmos. It was apparent I would have to raise myself above, or at least learn to control, the opposites of my own mind and body, as well as of my soul and spirit. I would have to raise a higher part of my being into a superhuman state by nourishing it on the energy of God's light. I would have to be intelligent enough, skilled enough, to distinguish between the true and the false light, because I knew now that there existed true light and false light more powerful than the light of my own physical mind.

Here was the key: because of the creative energy I was absorbing through the sun, I could move out of the third-dimensional sphere of material existence (where the physical mind and body occupy space and time) to a higher dimension of existence, a fourth dimension of spirit. Once inside this fourth-dimensional world, a person has access to a mirror-image of the physical world. It is as if one is occupying two planes at the same time; two figures are worlds apart, and yet they are within each other. The danger is that the higher might draw the lower out before enough knowledge has been gained. If that happened, the neophyte fourth-dimensional entity would be consumed by powers beyond its own capabilities.

Fourth-dimensional space has a dual axis; more precisely, the entity within that dimension has a left-right split of some higher superhuman being. I had had a glimpse of this original beingness in the transparent being I saw in Peru—call it the Adam Kadmon of the Jewish mystics, archetypal man in his true and bright nature.

But I had also had a look at the darker aspect of its dual nature and was aware that it was threatening. I remembered reading an argument between Peter and Simon Magus in the Clementines in which Peter cautioned against apparitions, saying, "He who trusts to visions or an apparition must be cautious because the one revealed may prove to be an evil demon or a deceiving spirit, pretending in his speeches to be what he is not."

I was afraid of being tempted by a beguiling spirit of darkness; of being led, through intellectual communication with it, to consume, as had Adam, the fruit of knowledge. I was also afraid of the temptation of wanting to become equal with God—a status I could attempt to achieve only through a relationship between my lower ego and a vastly superior being emanating from some dark world. The fear was real, for I suspected that the ultradimensional worlds of light and darkness were, in some strange way, counterparts of the material world; that the ego of intellectual man would seek to identify with divine man, longing to use his creative forces to become a second creator. My own human shortcomings suggested to me that I might be unable to understand the totality of the universe, to see beyond the opposites.

I continued to gaze at the sun, fascinated by the brilliance and inwardly sensing the danger; I knew that within its rays there was creative power capable of causing an explosion of the imprisoned spirit. Here was the source of all mystical power. In the hands of a gifted or disciplined adept, the flight of the "bird" could be controlled; in less gifted hands, it would plunge to the ground and certain death. I saw within the sun's disk a plane mirroring man's own image—his craving for self-realization, self-determination and power.

I saw in the sun the meeting ground for two dynamic powers; I observed the oscillation between white and black images in a cosmic spiral. Here the material world was connected to the spiritual, two streams flowing out of a central fountainhead from whose spout pour the living waters of ten thousand images to play upon the eyes and the mind of man, casting a spell.

The power in the living water of the sun transfixed me. I felt it washing and purifying my being, drawing out memories, spraying me with dynamic new ideas: negatives were turned into positives. Above all, I felt the interplay of two dynamic powers struggling within me—the inner and the outer.

As my eyes sought out the spiritual image of the light filling them, I searched for a language that would allow me to speak with God. The good in the cosmos beckoned—I wanted to find that divine world beyond the hostile, demonic, dark forces of the outer world. I knew I had to merge with the good, or I'd be drawn into those powerful demonic forces that offer only madness and self-destruction. My own conceit had blinded me to the possibility that I might be applying the Project's techniques selfishly. Like other men, I clung to material life, seeking wealth and fame, hoping to stave off old age, disease and death. It occurred to me that I had been guilty of allowing my intellect to function independently, as if there were no other part of me. It now seemed that dependence was partly, if not wholly, responsible for the dark apparition. Yes, I was guilty of the pride of intellect.

In a way, I had sought power. . . and its use. Like Adam, I had wanted to know the world, to taste the forbidden fruit. I had misunderstood the nature of my inner being, or at least the force of it. Now I was in a state of anxiety—an anxiety to know every-thing in existence. I had sought answers in the sun, which to me was the gateway to the universe beyond.

Now I was ready to accept that I was spirit, and that it was only through this spirit that I would realize my own immortality and thus freedom. The path was difficult. I had to let go of myself, surrender totally and unconditionally to the greater power of God. I had previously found that difficult; I had wanted some control over my own being and destiny. So, no more dreaming from now on. I was beyond the age of innocence and had to accept a world of contrasts—as well as the duality of my own being. No more experiments—I would accept the wisdom of former genera-tions from Adam through the prophets, and hold to the com-mandments of God as they had been given from the beginning. In that way I hoped to regain the bright nature of my own soul, which had been taken away through Adam's sin. The conditions were the same for me as they had been for Adam in the Cave of Treasures.

As I stared at the setting sun I realized that God had not punished Adam at all—he had given him total freedom to act, and to suffer the consequences of his acts.

Man had only to return to "the way" to regain his lost immortal-ity. Thinking of my own immortality gave me new hope. I was no longer afraid of what might lie ahead.

13

Mind/Time/Space Control

Reno, Nevada

November 13, 1973 — For almost an hour I had been in my private study. The room was aglow with the afternoon sun's warm rays, which were streaming in through the large cathedral windows. I was writing in my journal when there was a knock at the door.

"Come in." The visitor was James C. Geoghegan.

Geoghegan was 50, though he looked ten years younger. He was a professional athlete and had been an associate of the Project since its beginning. He was Irish, born in Leitrim of landed gentry. The man always radiated a private, deep-rooted independence that was in keeping with the race that had bred him, and he reflected a secret, mystical image that is usually associated with the seeker. A trained physiotherapist and hypnotherapist, he was also an exponent of yoga. Geoghegan had circled the globe in pursuit of knowledge, training with the Sufis in Africa and the yogins in India. He had recently agreed to accept a position as a full-fledged research associate with the Project.

"You're the practicing hypnotist among us, James. I've been doing some research into time distortion and I need your opinion. Elmer Jenkins was in here a moment ago, and we talked about his experiences with mushrooms in Mexico. He told me he began experiments about two years ago with peyote and psilocybin. His reaction at the beginning was one of elation; his mind was clear,

Milenko Tomich strides past colossal figures at Tula, Mexico. Other members of the Project practice techniques, viewing the sun through special filters.

Prior to launching of expedition in search of El Dorado and the Amazon women-warriors, the author studies maps at Project "X" headquarters in Mexico City.

The News, Mexico City

Author with Bill Dailey, expedition cartographer, in rain forest of eastern Ecuador. Explorers of Project "X" examine maps of ancient trails. *Project "X" Photo*

With the ruins of Tula in the background, five members of Project "X" attend to experiments.

Dailey peers up at stone carving of the San Augustine ruins in Colombia. Foliated nose and certain other characteristics of the figures here suggested a possible link with the Chachapoyas ruins in Peru.

Aboard a 72-foot river boat, expedition members carried out an extensive exploration of the Amazon and many of its tributaries.

Author studies rock carving uncovered by the expedition in the heights above Obidos, Brazil.

LEFT—Author and Bill Dailey examine river chart as crew member of the *Cidade de Natal* looks on.

RIGHT—Dailey checks air route with author before takeoff. Manaus was one of the bases from which explorers took members of Project "X" by air to unexplored regions of the Brazilian Amazon rain forest.

The Reverend Sidney Carswell, missionary of the Southern Baptist Convention, examines rock carvings with author during river exploration.

Photos by Bill K. Dailey

Crew members sit down to lunch aboard the *Cidade de Natal*. Author chats with captain while the Brazilian ship is at anchor at port of Itacoatiara, on the Amazon.

ABOVE—Tirios Indian settlement in Brazil, near the borders with Surinam and Guyana. Catholic missionaries are attempting to integrate the isolated tribes of this area into civilized life.

BELOW—Author with Father Angelico, at Tirios. Expedition interpreter Joaquim Beserra de Araujo looks on as local tribesman practices language lesson.

Tirios Indian tribesmen allowed photographs to be taken in the bush only after some argument. In camp, under the eyes of the missionaries, the Indians were friendlier.

Geometric designs painted on this Tirios woman have much in common with architectural ornamentation of stone ruins in Peru.

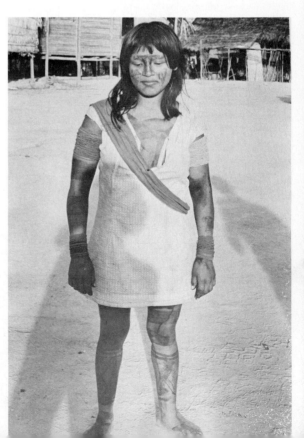

Tirios woman of some importance in the tribe wears heavy beads at neck, wrists, ankles and upper arms.

Author studies assorted pottery fragments from Brazilian region of Santarem, on the Amazon.

Bill K. Dailey

except for some hallucinations that he could actually control. Jenkins started using sacred mushrooms when he was 24—he said it was because of a desire to find out more about life. Mushrooms showed him that it was possible to identify his person with just about anything he wanted to—this parallels some of our own thinking. He had a similar response with LSD, but to a lesser degree.

"For instance, he said he once experienced total union with the sun, so total that he felt he was the sun. He described looking down on the solar system, from his celestial abode, observing life on the planet as if he were a celestial being. Then something happened that frightened him.

"First he felt a loss of vitality. Following periods of hallucination he was groggy—'wasted,' as he put it. The experiences drained him for about three days afterwards. Then the whole thing became negative. He could no longer control the hallucinatory experiences. His dreams were filled with frightening scenes. After a while he developed an urge to harm or even destroy people—and this, mind you, in an otherwise gentle soul. A power filled his being so completely that he lost his self-identity. In short, he was scared to death. Realizing that he might be wasting his life and destroying himself, he became desperate. It was shortly thereafter that he heard about our research. Through work and application of the techniques he was restored to health and usefulness. He doesn't regret the experience, but he would never go back to the use of mushrooms or drugs of any kind.

"You have a background in this field—what's your explanation of the modern trend toward psychedelic drugs, mushrooms, black magic, shamanism, witchcraft and the like? I simply can't understand it."

Geoghegan replied in his thick Irish brogue, "The experimentation with drugs would seem to be a method of trying to find a means of expanding our narrow intellectual world, a method of delimiting our regimented existence. Because they feel so small and helpless when they consider how little influence they have in our world's business or government, some people regress to ideas of a bygone age—ideas of escape from frustration.

"Frustration could be used constructively if we had teachers and professors who would take on the responsibility of giving direction instead of leaving it up to the student to draw his own conclusions from a hodgepodge of anthropological and psychological ideas which, without idealistic ethical direction, can be dangerous.

"Because the young are not prepared by parents, teachers or churches to analyze correctly the avalanche of materials they are presented with, they take the pseudo-scientific trip to self-experimentation with drugs and allied escape techniques. 'Disenchantment' is a word you hear often nowadays.

"Never before on the planet has so much control of 'energy' and 'people' been available. The memory of man's inhumanity to man through wars—including some undeclared wars—rankles the youth of our time, and rightly so, because they hope idealistically for change for the better.

"Unfortunately, they want change now—not next year, but *now*—and our social structures just can't change so drastically or so quickly without toppling and leaving society worse off."

"But what effect do drugs have on all this?" I asked with a shrug.

"Our ability to perceive the external world is directly related to our perception of ideas and images from within. Therefore, if 'conceptual fields' are distorted by mind-expanding drugs, or even hypnosis, we are not in a position to consciously direct our time/space organism as we would in the so-called normal state.

"However, if we could totally relax the body/mind organism and reach levels that are attained through deep meditation, we would arrive at a delimiting level where we would be, to all intents and purposes, on God's time. We would be in the eternal NOW, and time as we ordinarily view it would disappear; our waking knowledge of time always disappears when we are concentrating deeply.

"Clocks, watches, chronometers, etc., are man's measuring devices; as tools, they are necessary, but they have a negative effect on the innate concept of time—man becomes a time slave. And all slavery is bad!

"Consider the relative aspects of time: one second in the life of an ant, a man, a plant, a sun, or a galaxy. To man time is relative to consumption, span and mode: pleasure, boredom, and so on."

"How do witchcraft and shamanism figure in the picture?"

"Since the dim dawn of time, man has used drugs to distort time and space. Alcohol is such a drug and must not be ignored. However, it is not as powerful as some of the drugs that have been used from ancient times for this purpose. The drugs used by shamans, witches, magicians and modern experimenters to create states of mind and space transformation cause disorientation of space and time; unfortunately, they have been and can be used as an escape from the so-called realities of life. When used that way, they have within the possibility of destruction. People who would 'storm the gates of heaven' use these drugs; unfortunately, because of inadequate training in ethics and lack of self-discipline, they do not receive the expected enlightenment but rather find the 'crypt' empty. Continuing the search to 'arrive' with repeated doses of the drug, they succumb to a psychological addiction to the drug. This often happens here in the U.S. with marijuana.

"To put it briefly, expansion of our time/space continuum should be accomplished through the mind, emotion and body, overseen by spiritual intention!

"Ancient man observed the rising and setting sun, the phases of the moon and created his time idea from those natural phenomena. Later on, as he gained some 'control' of his environment, he set out to measure time with more precision. Today, with modern man's concepts of environmental control, we have reached the pinnacle of time measurement, which has brought with it a tremendous awareness of time. Yet time is still relative; it must be viewed in terms of how it is spent!

"Einstein related his theory of relativity to a young man: 'To hold a hot poker for a few seconds in your hand could seem an eternity, while to hold a pretty girl's hands for an hour would seem like a few seconds.'

"If we are doing something we totally enjoy, time flies; boring work leads us to say that time lies heavily on our hands. These are the words of humanity relating itself to the relativity of time.

"The experimenter can change or distort time and space by many methods: meditation, hypnosis, drugs, magic, and witchcraft, to name but a few. In witchcraft, those techniques dealing with the mind and emotions are probably the most powerful, at least as far as direct results are concerned. Herein lies the rub: direct frontal attack on the ego sometimes results in mental and emotional breakdown. Time travel, or so-called mind/soul travel, involves the use of expanded, unlimited states of mind. Through deep relaxation and the use of an expanded imagination, it is possible in some instances to overreach space/time and 'visit' distant spirits. The shamans, witches, and magicians sometimes attained this state through the use of drugs.

"Control of emotions and mind through the higher self—through some of the yogas, religions and even western techniques—can be beneficial to the body/mind combination. But emotional and mind control can have many very serious ramifications if it is done for the wrong reason; I am speaking of those who want power over themselves, others and nature. Emotional and mind control appeals to many of our modern manipulative types, and these are the people who freely involve themselves in the power aspects of magic and witchcraft.

"Let's go back a little in time. Modern English and American witchcraft, as a religion, was the creation of the fertile mind of one Gerald Gardner, a minor clerk of the East India Company who lived and worked in the Orient for many years. During his tenure there, he became interested in the spiritualism of the Javanese and Indians and studied their techniques extensively. On returning to England, he settled on the Isle of Man, where he established a witches' museum in an old, unused mill house. He based his so-called tie-in with the witches on his powerful imagination, and on the writings of the contemporary English anthropologist Margaret Murray, who claimed to have found traces of a once-widespread religion that pre-dated Christianity and that had survived all the vicissitudes of the persecutions of the witches through the ages. To increase his plausibility as a cult leader, he asked Aleister Crowley, an English poet, philosopher, and self-styled magician, to create some rites of witchcraft for coven use. Crowley did so, even though he laughed outright at Gardner and his followers, who took the rites seriously. Gardner had a sadomasochistic streak—he liked to beat and be beaten by his sexual partners. He used the so-called witch coven initiations as a cover for his deviations. Because of the desire to believe in the survival of the so-called old religions, which appeared to offer freedom from the rigid Christianity of England, many unsuspecting young girls—often 30 to 35 years his junior—involved themselves in his so-called initiations.

"My information comes from two noted English scholars who have written extensively on the history of witchcraft. One is H. C. Lea, who wrote three volumes entitled: *Materials Towards a History of Witchcraft;* the other, Keith Thomas, wrote *The History of Witchcraft* and *Religion and the Decline of Magic.* These fine scholarly tomes will give you some sincere answers to your questions on witchcraft in England.

"I have a copy of a confession made to a British psychiatrist in London by a young female disciple of Gardner after she was rescued from suicide. Her warning message comes through loud and clear to all young girls who might be tempted to play the role of a witch. Gardner had created such confusion within her psycho-mental complex that she didn't know where she was; she felt a desire to destroy herself because it seemed the only course left open to her. I'm sure there are many fine young girls who go into witchcraft with the best intentions of becoming so-called white witches. They may mean very well, but they are still the dupes of illusion, and can still become involved in the darker aspects of the cult, ultimately with terrible consequences.

"Most people probably miss the single most important fact about so-called witchcraft in the Middle Ages, and that is that they used drugs. The stories extracted under torture during the inquisition—sometimes from true witches—were horrifying. Yet a lot of them were telling the truth—they believed that they had been to a black Sabbath and that they had had sexual relations with the master of the Sabbath, who was supposed to be Mephistopheles himself. The drugs they used were henbane, deadly nightshade, thornapple, mandrake and datura. They used datura because it produces effects like flying; as a matter of fact, datura can also make you feel as if you were growing feathers or even hair like that of a wolf or a dog. This drug was used in the Middle Ages in Europe; it might account for those people who thought they were werewolves. They actually felt they were wolves, and maybe they did cause some depredations when they were under the effects of the drug. In any case, the witches made an ointment from henbane, nightshade, thornapple, mandrake, solaceanea, datura and other related drugs. When you mix these drugs into a fatty substance and rub them into your underarms and private areas, these powerful drugs are quickly absorbed into the bloodstream.

"Some of their delusions were highly sexual. As a matter of fact, in 1951 when I visited the witches' museum established by Gerald Gardner, I saw a witch's broom, the end of which was shaped like a phallus. This is an actual fact. The witch's broomstick that they rode on to the meetings they held in their flights of fantasy and the very stiff and cold organ of the devil with which they admitted to having sexual activities were nothing but the handle of an ordinary household broom. Now, this is a prime example of the delusions that can be caused by drugs, and you don't even have to have a very fertile imagination.

"There is the story of a druggist—or chemist, as he was known in those days—who asked the inquisitorial board in Germany for permission to visit a husband and wife who had been convicted of witchcraft. Even in those days doctors and druggists were people of knowledge, and this man was interested in learning if the prisoners were really involved in what they claimed they were, or if they were just suffering from delusions. Anyway, under the judge's orders, the chemist talked to the husband and wife without using any of the persuasive tactics the inquisitorial board had used, and he discovered that the couple had been taking the drugs I mentioned earlier. When the woman was describing her sexual endeavors with the master of the Sabbath, she pointed a derisive finger at her husband and said, as they say in Europe, 'I cuckolded you, old man. I cuckolded you.'

"Now, if you have normal intelligence and you think about this for a while, you realize that there are parallels here with a passage in a popular book by Carlos Castaneda in which he describes flying like a crow after taking certain drugs, including datura. He mentions all the drugs he has taken and how some made him feel as if he were flying. Now, it's not that he wasn't up there psychically, and probably he did feel very free, but such things are, nevertheless, hallucinations. Although they may give you a sort of mind expansion, I question their value as a means of arriving at total knowledge and wisdom.

"The drug experience can have an unhinging effect on the mind. In a good trip you get psychedelic pleasantries—moving light, colorful illusionary scenes and possibly a concept of expansion. But bad trips can induce terror, feelings of being hopelessly lost and alone, fear of the dissolution of the ego and total annihilation."

"As with Jenkins," I said.

"Absolutely. In the case of shamanism, though, the situation is rather different. The shaman or medicine man undergoes rigorous training that enables him to leave his body, with or without the benefit of drugs, and to participate in the spirit world."

"By that you mean psychic astral travel?"

"Yes. All ancient societies used shamanism in religious initiation rites for the purpose of receiving and transmitting spiritual values. For that matter, initiation rites and symbols have by no means disappeared. They still exist in more elegant forms in present-day secret societies and even in our modern religions. However, the shamanistic techniques are, as I was saying, definitely related to the psycho-mental complex. The shaman's journeys into the world of the spirits were primarily for the purpose of healing a sick person by contacting his psyche, initiating a youth into adulthood, guiding a person's soul at death, foretelling the future, or learning and perpetuating the sacred knowledge of Creation as understood by the particular society or tribe. Naturally, a shaman performed many other services, but what I am getting at is that the performance of such functions presupposes superhuman abilities, directed above all by the desire to attain a superhuman condition. This desire necessarily involves an aspect of power which can lead only too easily to uncontrollable and inhuman levels of torture and cruelty, especially when identification with animals is involved.

"The power and fury of people, male and female, going berserk is thoroughly documented in myth and history. Such events were common to many, if not all, ancient societies. For example, the *maenads* in ancient Greece were a group of wandering, wild women who, while they were in the grip of drugs, literally tore men and beasts to pieces. When the Romans invaded what is now Germany, they encountered an almost invincible group of people who used to drink a potion made from some unknown weed, probably henbane or wolfbane, that turned them on to such a degree that they actually ripped apart anything in their path.

"In more recent times, when the Americans occupied the Philippines, they found a group of natives there called the Moros who also went crazy after taking a drug.

"In northern Mongolia, Russian Mongolia and central Asia there are many different families of shamans, but the best known are the Tungus and the Buriats. They've been studied by a Russian anthropologist named Shirokogorof, who wrote an exceedingly comprehensive volume about the years he spent living and working among the Tungus. When I was in England, I studied his work under the direction of Michael Haughton. As a matter of fact, this particular book was out of print, and Haughton let me use his copy. I was interested in mescaline then, because I felt it was the type of thing I needed to give me an opening to mind expansion. But Haughton, this venerable teacher of mine, assured me I didn't need it at all. 'It is not right to hasten the process of growth,' he said. 'A baby can no more assume the role of a man than sugar can become salt.' He reminded me that to transform a baby into a man or a woman takes, in addition to nature's efforts, years of growth, and lots of understanding help from parents and teachers.

"Now, to return to the psycho-mental complex of the Tungus, Shirokogorof watched them use many different techniques in order to get 'out of it,' some of which involved drug taking. One drug they used was *amarata muscaria, fly agaric,* a mushroom with little red spots. It is a very powerful hallucinogenic.

"A young man would be chosen for training as a shaman because he had fits, epilepsy or fainting spells, or because he wasn't quite the same as the other young men around—maybe he didn't take an interest in the hunt or in other normal pursuits and, as a result, was less outgoing than the other people. In other words, a youngster would be chosen because in some way he had an unusual view of the world.

"Now, the responsibility of a fully trained shaman was to find answers to questions. If a shaman felt that he had not obtained the necessary answer to any question, he would have himself bound. A rope was tied around his body, underneath his knees and under his crotch. Sometimes his ankles were tied together, but other times the shaman was left sitting on his heels, his legs doubled over on each other. Once he was in this position, his arms were tightly bound to his sides so that he was trussed up like a horse with a saddle. A broad leather belt was placed around his head and neck; it was then pulled forward and attached to the rope between his knees, pulling him toward the center of his body. The shaman would make no sounds whatsoever. Ten or twelve hours would sometimes pass, then a babble would pour from this poor fellow. I imagine, looking at it from a physiological viewpoint, that the pressure on the neck would cut off some of the blood supply to the brain, producing brain anemia and triggering hallucinations. Now, I use the word 'hallucination' loosely here, because in some instances, according to Shirokogorof, a shaman in this state could actually sense the condition of a person who had been ailing, or whether the person was dead.

"In other words, the shaman had developed certain extra-sensory powers. Many people, particularly in Europe, consider ESP an atavistic state of our animal conciousness; every animal is, shall we say, blessed or cursed with ESP. For an animal I suppose it's a blessing, but for man it can be a questionable mental activity.

"If he hadn't obtained results after twelve or fourteen hours in a tied position, the shaman still had another card up his sleeve. And that was drugs. The ordinary Tungus never knew anything about the ingestion of magic mushrooms, because they were told that the mushroom was poisonous and should not be touched. The shamans, however, sometimes used the mushrooms to gain in-sights into the cause and cure of disease. If one was sick, the shaman would take the drug to get a look into that person's unconscious. He probably found the psychosomatic reasons for the illness, such as worrying too much over something or denying a certain aspect of mind, which can produce psychic traumas or dismal states of mind. So, by 'tuning in' through the use of drugs, the shaman could cure illnesses. Now, this is exactly what Edgar Cayce was doing, although he was doing it through self-hypnosis, rather than drugs.

"The shamans also had other people drink their urine in order to get high. In some letters to scholars in England, Shirokogorof told how the shaman gained power over his people in this way. It seems that when the shaman urinated after having ingested the mushrooms, the drug would pass into the urine. Therefore it would affect anyone who drank that warm urine in the same way it had affected the shaman. Well, you can imagine the psychological effects of the shaman's urine being passed around and creating psycho-mental or psychological changes in all people who had partaken. They would be quite vividly impressed with the power of the man whose urine, even, was 'holy.'

"Now, the shaman was also a bit of a chemist—he realized that the muscarine, the actual drug, was just as strong in the urine as in the regular mushroom. This eliminated the need to search for new mushrooms. During the winter, when the tundra was completely covered with snow, it was impossible to obtain the mushrooms. Therefore, if he had any, he would preserve them as well as he could and drink his urine over and over again. Sounds a little repugnant, doesn't it? The mushrooms are supposed to taste pretty terrible, so the urine probably didn't taste any worse. In Castaneda's teachings of the legendary Don Juan, there is nothing about this particular aspect of the drug. Nevertheless, Don Juan was a drug taker and a shaman.

"The power of the shaman in the psycho-mental complex is basically still on a pre-conscious level. Getting back to Don Juan, if he really existed, I don't doubt he was a very fine man who had many good ideas. Castaneda casts aspersions on our so-called soft culture in America and on the lack of continuity in our body/mind combination; I imagine he couldn't do that with the Orientals, particularly those who are into yoga, tai-chi, aikido, and so forth, because they are more integrated. That would apply too to anybody in this country who's involved in those same techniques. So, his looking down his nose at the condition of the average American can be taken with a grain of salt because there are techniques in this country that will get you into good body shape. Techniques to develop awareness will do it, too.

"Shamanism, as far as I am concerned, is not a state to go back to. There are, of course, some medical uses for some of the drugs that the shamans used. In South America they use some of these drugs to help people relax, as you know from your own explorations and your work with primitive medicine men. That is something else again. But we have gone past the age of shamanism, and to return to it would be to make conscious certain areas of our subconscious and unconscious minds. I think that to relegate ourselves to basic animal levels of understanding is to decry our very human nature."

I knew that Geoghegan remembered everything he had ever read. This ability was both a strength and, at times, a defect; he had a tendency to volunteer an inexhaustible amount of information, as he was doing now. He would have continued talking if I hadn't interrupted. "What about your research in hypnotism and time distortion?"

"Some psychologists in England and America have done work with hypnosis and time distortion. What they actually do is put a subject under and then make a suggestion—for example, they might suggest that *Gone With The Wind,* which runs about four hours, will last only four minutes. After sitting through the whole picture, the subject will swear that it lasted only four minutes."

"Time distortion through suggestion."

"Yes."

"How about meditation techniques, especially among the popular schools where autosuggestion is used? Could one expect similar results?"

"Absolutely. Implant the suggestion and time will be distorted. Any of the modern mind-blowing, mind-disturbing techniques that have become fashionable can create mind or time distortion.

"When we get to deep levels of meditation, time and space disappear. During the early stages of 'withdrawal,' the body partially loses its orientation to space and time; but in the deeper meditation, we are 'spaced out of time.' Because of this, we are able to reach beyond space and time (man-made conceptions) and arrive at deeper levels where we can have a better appreciation of the unity of life (God's time). Both ordinary time and space consciousness seem to give man the desire to control the use of time and to make him realize that time and life fly with uncontrollable speed. Modern man has become addicted to the prevention of death at any cost. He is his own producer of 'the fear of death.' But, because he does not realize this, he cannot do anything constructive to eliminate this fear complex, although the answer is as close to him as life."

"Are we speaking here of a mental or a psychic level?"

"Well, in time distortion you are working on a mental, emotional and image-making level, but what you are doing is laying bare a powerful aspect of the imagination. Once you get past the regular ego you get to the image-making factor of the universe, what is called the *Yesod* in the Kaballah. All emotional/creative states start here. So, people under any of these hypnotic states can create new personalities. They can create anything they want to. It is interesting to note that people who create different personalities usually create better ones than their own. However, if they are a little perverse they create worse ones, because they feel the created personalities are more dynamic. It depends on the person."

"Elmer Jenkins mentioned that before taking mushrooms, or any kind of psychedelic drugs, he would clean his room, dress up in his best clothes, and put flowers in the house," I said.

"That is ritual. Without it, you can have bad trips."

"Interesting."

"Yes. As a matter of fact, when people go into drugs they imagine they are throwing ritual out the window, and yet they are actually returning to it. The ritualism that is involved in religion is deeply ingrained in the subconscious. People return to ritualism in one form or another without realizing why. The shamans in America who eat peyote, such as the Southwest Indians, have a sacramental attitude. The idea is that proper demeanor, proper dress and proper direction are prerequisites to participation in the ceremony. It is interesting that peyote eating became very popular only after the American Indian nation started to break up. It was never popular before that."

"I see—sort of a means of escape?"

"Yes. Again, time and space distortion. Time distortion is very interesting. For instance, in Canada we have developed techniques for dentistry in which time is distorted for the person in the dental chair. After a patient had been hypnotized, I would tell him to look out the window. He would then feel that he was outside rather than in the dental chair. It might require an hour and a half to extract the patient's tooth and perform oral surgery, but the person would have lost all contact with time. When the person came out of this state, he would say, 'When are we going to get around to fixing my teeth?' "

"Laughing gas achieves the same thing, doesn't it?"

"Nitrous oxide. Yes, it has the ability to make you stand apart from yourself. All these mind-transforming techniques— meditation, hypnotism, laughing gas, hashish, LSD, or any of the other potions—are on about the same level; none of them has anything to do with the dimensions of spirit. There is a saying in Latin which translates as 'turning to God without turning from yourself.' Such attempts produce powerful paranoiacs."

"What do you think of these chaps from India, such as the Maharishi, who seems to be a very delightful man, teaching transcendental meditation? What are your views on the success of their techniques? I think they are trying to encourage students to relax. At least that is the way it appears to me," I said.

"Well, in Japan there is a technique known as *hara*. Basically, it involves nothing more than sitting. The people who look to India now as the savior of the western world are wrong in many respects, because India made its material available a long time ago. Quite a few American psychologists in the third school of psychology, humanistic psychology, have investigated TM and found that if you take a word such as 'Om,' repeat it over and over to yourself, then repeat it subvocally, and, finally, let your mind keep carrying it as a river carries a cork, you will arrive at a state of complete relaxation. The ordinary egoic mind is stilled, allowing a centering process to harmonize the parasympathetic and sympathetic nervous systems. This benefits the average person, who is so involved with the external world that anxieties get the better of him, putting an extra load on the parasympathetic system, which fights back, causing ulcers, heart disease and many other psychosomatic diseases.

"Transcendental meditation—or TM, as it is called—is part of the system called *japa yoga,* which teaches one to repeat a mantra. This repetition stills what is called the 'monkey mind,' the most basic level of being. Most people—even some of those in schools and universities—are operating on this low level. Repetition of the mantra puts the mind at rest. In this respect TM is helpful."

"I remember reading somewhere that in Hindu scripture the syllable 'Om' means sun, and is therefore the oldest mantra."

"Yes. 'Om' to the Hindus is the primordial, the beginning and the end, the alpha and the omega, the creation. 'Om' is a sacred sound to them. The sound 'om' is not very far removed from the Egyptian 'Amun,' the Hebrew 'Amen,' the Christian 'Amen,' the Moslem 'Amin.' So it has religious overtones, whether people accept it or not."

"We both know youth have turned away from religion. I was interested in your statement that youth dislike ritual, but have actually gone back to it by taking drugs."

"Yes, they found that when they took drugs without ritual they had very bad trips."

"They have to have a proper attitude."

"Right—a reverent mind. And this can be created by particular levels of music. The effect of music is strong; a large number of drug users, especially those into meditation and the like, are turned on by rock. Eventually they turn to classical music, Gregorian chants, ancient Hebrew music, or ancient Sufi music. There is, deep within the layers of our consciousness, an aspect of the holy. If it is touched by music, it will invariably bring the person through on a very safe and good trip. The danger of listening to rock music while under the influence of drugs is that it can tear one up; much rock music represents destructive aspects of life. Church or religious music, on the other hand, has a tendency to relax. The intonations and repetitions of the words can lead to a form of meditation. Such music concentrates the mind in a certain direction. Certain levels of the mind are reached; again, the sacramental and the sacerdotal raise the level of consciousness."

"There is, in the modern world, almost a state of atheism. People appear to resent the word 'God'; they seem turned off by orthodox religion. Yet some are actually going back 10,000 years to the level of the shaman."

"That, to me, is a travesty. Although shamanism once represented an honest aspect of man's aspirations, it now belongs to the archaic past."

"How would you explain regression?"

"The universities seem to be encouraging it, because some anthropologists are curious about the uses of power. They leave the outcome up to the student, not realizing the experiment can be dangerous. Being naive and innocent, students see a ray of hope in shamanism."

I mulled over that point.

"Those who discard the well-known and established religions of the world," I said, "and create their own brand of religious expression out of their rational outlook on the world are creating a multitude of philosophies. These new philosophies are tried and tested, then discarded after a while. Later, another new idea catches their fancy and they follow it for a while. These so-called shoppers who flit from one idea to another do not realize they are wasting precious time. True awareness, or spiritual development, is the work of a lifetime. Nobody but nobody has time to waste in the matter of his own immortality. It is always best to take a path that has been trod by former generations. To cast aside the wisdom of the ages without careful examination is the height of arrogance. No man has time to experiment by trial and error, especially not with his life. What has been revealed by the world's great religions is time-tested. I see no reason why man couldn't build new orders and new attitudes from existing ones. To put aside the knowledge that has come down to us over the centuries is dangerous to society as well as to the individual. Perhaps the reason our own Christianity has failed is that man hasn't learned how to live it properly. All these different schools teaching partial systems of awareness can only create confusion. Frankly, I'm amazed at the success of some schools. The real teachings aren't there."

"Many sects, cults and quacks have taken advantage of man's response to suggestion, diversion and hypnotism, and created so-called schools that prey on the masses," said Geoghegan. "Look at the number of magicians who were successful during the time of Christ. Every street corner had its little school teaching some special kind of mystery. There are always followers for an idea, no matter what it represents. Look at Hitler's appeal to the German mentality, or the reliance in some of the underdeveloped countries on the dated ideas of Karl Marx. Wherever people are suppressed, ignorant, poor or dominated by economics and politics, any emotional appeal based on the power aspect can be implanted in their minds through suggestion or some form of mild hypnotism. Any clever person with charisma and a certain gift for oratory and showmanship can sway people to his ideas, even if the ideas are wrong and the people's intellects tell them so. The power of the suggestion over their emotions forces people to accept such ideas. That's why followers must choose the school they follow carefully," said Geoghegan.

"I think this attitude is expressed very well in the Mishnah of Judah that was compiled from the oral traditions of the Hebrews: 'Men are not to expound the lore of creation. . . . Everyone who meddles with the following four things it were better for him if he had not come into the world, namely, what is Above and what is Below, what is Before and what is After, and everyone who does not revere the glory of his Maker or who detracts from God's Unity, it were better for him if he had not come into the world.' There is great truth in these mystical words of the prophet. Within every man there exists a religious inclination. As Pythagoras said, 'Men are of heavenly race, taught by divine nature.' "

"There are ancient teachings of value: the teachings of the Golden Age. It appears that today's youth have an innate desire to go back. The problem is that they are not going back far enough. They are going back to what I would call archaic levels, such as shamanism and drugs. If they were to go back to the original teachers, the light bearers, it would be better. There are corners of the world where you still have shamanism. It would still exist in New Zealand were it not for the fact that the Maoris have made remarkable progress in social legislation. They have shed shamanism completely, although they still have some beliefs that are related to ancient ones. For instance, the Maoris believe that they, as a race, are descended from light bearers of great magnitude who existed in ancient times."

"How would you explain such a low level of instruction as

shamanism taking hold in a country like the United States?"

"When people have nowhere to go, they reach back. Youth are reaching indirectly to God, but they just don't know how to go about it. They were disillusioned by their parents, because a lot of them were preaching about God with one side of their mouths and lying with the other. It is the tragedy of our time that the family structure is not as strong as it was. We have more divorce, more breakups on all levels of life; religion is looked down on as something archaic and irrelevant. And yet, in their idealism, young people essentially are reaching back towards religion. The present nihilistic state was probably created by existentialism. Another factor is the nuclear arsenals hanging over our heads like the sword of Damocles."

"Man has learned to accept the very real danger that a nuclear test, accident or war could set off a nuclear chain reaction of the nitrogen, hydrogen and oxygen in the earth's atmosphere," I said.

"In essence, that may be the best thing that ever happened to man—it forces him to accept the fact that he must live in harmony with others. This makes him a little more God-like."

"In view of what we have discovered about the sun's power and man's influence over the sun, we had better learn to live with nature and, above all, with the unseen world around us."

"What do you mean precisely?" Geoghegan asked, raising his eyebrows.

"Nuclear reactions are a genuine threat," I said, "but the bombs must actually be used. Man may want to use them, but he hesitates out of fear. With the sun, it is a different matter."

"How so?"

"Christ put it rather well when he said that if your right eye gives offense, it is best to pluck it out and cast it away, for it is better to lose an eye than for the whole person to be destroyed. The same with your hand; if it causes you to sin, cut it off and throw it away. Better to lose your hand than to find yourself in hell. That is only an allegory, but it makes a good point. If man has fear in his heart, hates another, or lives in a state of disharmony, then he is influencing the sun in a negative manner. It is absolutely certain that such negative actions will eventually result in the sun negating—and thus destroying—the world. Yes, atomic weapons are a possible threat to man, but comparing the danger from the sun to that from atomic weapons is like comparing a lion bite to a flea bite."

"I see what you mean. But who would believe that the power of the mind is so great? Could people accept such an idea?"

"Probably not. That's the terrible tragedy of it all."

14

*Introduction of
Solar Energy
into the Brain and
Other Parts of
the Nervous System*

Project Center, Reno, Nevada

December 15, 1973—The other members of the Project and I had just returned from viewing a magnificent sunrise at Pyramid Lake. The sun had come up over the gray-brown mountains to brighten a windswept desert buffeted by icy winds. A closely huddled group at the edge of the freezing lake, we had looked through gloved hands across its blue waters into the penetrating ball of light. The sun was brilliant even when viewed by means of the special filters the Project had developed.

Back at the Project center, we breakfasted, and after a brief discussion on our experiences, we retired to our respective tasks. I took my journal out of my briefcase and began writing where I had left off the day before, sometimes adding quick sketches.

TRANSCRIPTS

December 15, 1973

Today I felt like a growing thing—a plant—struggling towards the light, knowing that my life and being depended on its benevolent rays. I not only felt I could communicate with it—I experienced a response. The sun vibrated as usual, changing before my very eyes with my thought transmissions. There can be no doubt that the sun picks up—and responds to—human thoughts, as we suspected. The sun cannot simply be an incandescent ball of nuclear fire—it is a center of consciousness. Man is intimately related to the sun by a sensory makeup not recognized, as yet, by secular science.

It appears that the sun can make man an extraterrestrial being. The sun will respond to those intelligences that are attuned to it (perhaps like a radio frequency). It also appears that the sun is sending out a special frequency that can be picked up by those sensitive to it (though not by others, for research has shown that those who have only a passing interest in the techniques do not respond to it). I felt electrified. My body—and those of others there today—looked strange: it was surrounded by a glow, a strong electrical field of light. Man does interact with the sun. Intercommunication with some greater intelligence via the sun is a reality that can be experienced by those disciplined in the art. Man has to cope with this special intelligence, the "X-force." The question facing us now is whether X is in the visible electromagnetic spectrum or beyond it. I am curious as to how the eyes detect X and how solar energy IF (information factors) relate to the mental processes.

NOTES: Investigation has shown that light entering the eyes activates the pineal, the pituitary, and other areas of the mid-brain that stimulate and control the production of hormones by the endocrine system. Light not only produces vision but influences body chemistry. It was long thought that the pineal gland served no biological purpose, but recent research has proven the contrary. Light/energy stimuli reach the pineal gland via the sympathetic nervous system (diagram 1). At birth the pineal is connected directly with the brain, but this connection normally disappears during adulthood. Light intake (or lack of it) controls the life of the pineal and its synthesis of light/energy. Hormonal secretion fluctuates according to availability or absence of light. The pineal gland has

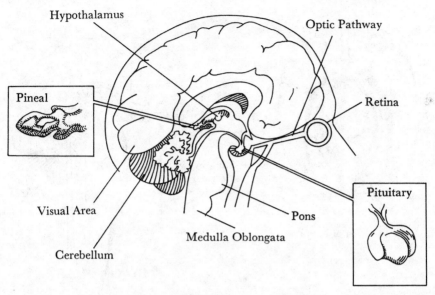

DIAGRAM 1

been shown to be a key regulator of the endocrine system, affecting the gonads, thyroid, pituitary, hypothalamus and other sections of the brain. This means that food and light/energy are the only physiological agents that can activate endocrine rhythms.

The interior of the human eye is lined with layers of rods and cones which receive radiation and transmit it to the brain, where the sensation of vision occurs. The cones are more numerous at the center of the retina, where sharp vision takes place, and less numerous in the outer areas. At the point where the optic nerve enters the retina, rods and cones are not in evidence (a blind spot). The retina contains thousands of these receptor cells linked with the brain by nerve fibers (diagram 2). Millions of nerve fibers are found in the eyes, all performing different functions at the same time. For example, the eye is able to discriminate shapes and sizes of objects because light stimulates and inhibits nerve impulses in various nerve fibers. There are three known types of cones in the eye, each of which responds to a different part of the color spectrum. Each color is light/energy vibrating at a specific frequency; the frequency is identified by its particular wavelength. For example, red has a wavelength ranging from 650 to 770 mu, while that of violet ranges

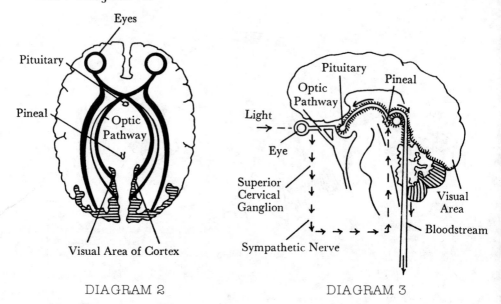

DIAGRAM 2   DIAGRAM 3

from 390 to 430 mu (1 mu = one-millionth of a millimeter). A nerve impulse to the brain is a combination of messages from the receptors. Color frequencies are not apparent as color when received at outer areas of the retina where there are few cones; more light and more cones are required for color vision. However, sensitivity of these areas can sometimes be improved. Rods normally register shades of gray. Rods contain a substance known as visual purple (rhodopsin), which changes to yellow or breaks down when exposed to light. It builds up during periods of darkness. Rods are responsible for vision in dim light. Sharp vision takes place in the center of the retina where there are few rods. All shades or hues of colors consist of three primary colors: red, green and violet (not to be confused with primary colors of paint). White light is a combination of these colors. Diagram 3 indicates the path (see arrows) of the pigment granules of the epithelial cells of the retina, which do not appear to register visible light. However, medical research has shown that these cells are photoreceptors and that they stimulate the pineal, the pituitary and other sections of the mid-brain region via neurochemical channels when exposed to invisible radiation. We see, then, that radiation beyond the range of visible light can influence the endocrine system by means of a retinal hypothalamic nerve path; this can result in physiological and psychological stimulation.

Visual stimulation of two different or two identical areas of the retina results in two sets of impulses being registered as a single image in the cortex. Stimulation of identical points over any portion of the retinas will result in this phenomenon. The human eye records light rays upon the retina (which is essentially an extension of the brain). Incoming light is regulated by the iris, which contracts and expands in response to light intensity (light is also regulated by the eyelids). Light rays are focused as they come through the cornea and lens, and are then absorbed by the deeper layers of the retina. Light produces photochemical reactions, or nervous impulses (this process is the result of the functioning of the rods and cones), which are then carried to the optic nerve, optic chiasma, optic tract and lateral geniculate body, and then to the cerebral cortex, where the nerve impulses are recorded and interpreted (light, color, form, contour, shape, depth, distance, memory-attachment, etc.). Light impulses also impinge upon cell bodies in the spinal cord (pre-ganglionic neurons), moving then to the cervical ganglia and eventually to the secretory cells of the pineal.

It seems that the brain and other parts of the nervous system are also acted upon by "electronic" impulses which originate outside the organism. Invisible radiation as well as radiation of the visible electromagnetic spectrum appears to play upon the organism continually. We are accustomed to the idea that all energy necessary for life is obtained by means of the alimentary and respiratory systems. The idea that the human organism obtains energy for vital life processes from other sources is a comparatively new concept. The human body, like all other material bodies, is enveloped by an electromagnetic field that pulsates with the exchange of energy. The endocrine system functions according to periodic rhythms, and light/energy plays on the pattern-making machinery of cells. The human organism functions in unison with universal electromagnetic phenomena generated by the sun. Our research suggests that the intake of light/energy via the optic pathway regenerates cells by means of certain centuries-old techniques involving the pineal and the endocrine system.

The eye is able to absorb light/energy which is capable of doing work. This work can be divided into two major categories. First, light/energy can be changed into chemical energy within the human organism by a process known as photosynthesis. Plants have the ability to manufacture nourishment from sunlight by altering chlorophyll pigments. We know that when the human skin is exposed to sunlight it manufactures chemical substances like vitamin D. Light/energy is converted by photochemical action into nerve impulses that affect the functioning of the endocrine system. Second, man's highly evolved nervous system can receive a sun-radiated intelligence factor capable of acting on the nervous system to restore a "lost" ability to man. In short, our research has revealed that the human race is living in a lower, or more degenerate, state than necessary. The species still has the potential to return to its original performance level. The objective of the Project is to teach individuals how to activate this higher performance of the mind/body. The Project's approach involves a unique and useful concept of life which takes a practical approach to survival in an age of technology. To apply such a life concept, a complete understanding of the basics of being and reality is necessary. A healthy mind/body is a prerequisite to optimum utilization of solar energy particles. When the solar energy particles that impinge upon the retinas of the eyes are distributed throughout the whole nervous system, they transform it into a system of radiant energy in harmony with natural laws.

The central, or cerebro-spinal, nervous system is intimately concerned with the conscious levels of awareness and with the sensory system which puts it in contact with the outside world. The brain could be viewed as an outgrowth of the spinal cord, connected to it by sensory pathways, most of which terminate in the thalamus, a center of vision. The brain's major purpose is to act as a coordinator of the nerve impulses brought to it by an afferent nerve pathway system. After processing the electrochemical nerve impulses, the brain sends an impulse or impulses out to the nervous system by way of an efferent pathway. This is an automatic process regulated by the brain's ability to handle stimuli. Patterns which may be inherited or acquired are thus built up in the brain from experience. Leading out from the spinal cord are 31 pairs of nerves with ganglions running to various parts of the body. From the spinal nerves come still another set of nerves called the sympathetic nervous system. Issuing from the brain are twelve cranial nerves, which are chiefly concerned with the senses (sight, hearing, touch, smell, taste and the higher sensory perceptions registered by the pineal) as well as with the pituitary and plexuses of the sympathetic system.

The old sun priests of Mexico and Peru possessed a unique concept (now revived by the Project) which likened the brain atop the spinal cord to a flower. Their system was similar to yoga and to the practices of the Tantric adepts of India in that it showed a remarkable knowledge of human physiology. Members of the Project are interested in the scientific as well as the more aesthetic aspects of this idea. The ancients likened the cerebro-spinal system to a flower that might be opened if light were circulated within its delicate network of nerve fibers. They said the secret was to connect the earthly heart with the heavenly heart that controlled the universe. Though symbolic, this ancient system utilized a scientific method that was developed over many centuries of practical observation and experimentation. The Project group is fortunate to have access to this system.

Our research has led us to the conclusion that ganglions and plexuses have a capacity for intelligence; any stimulation of a particular division of the nervous system, such as the central, sympathetic or parasympathetic system, produces a certain effect upon the mind/body. Our knowledge further indicates that reflexes of the nervous system are due to stimulation patterns that are acquired and inherited; nerve neurons display intelligence. This leads to the assumption that what we know as the brain has extended down from the cranial cavity (or vice versa) into the spinal cord, out into the ganglions and plexuses, through the nervous system in general, and into the very cells themselves. Consequently, matter itself—which we usually consider to be dead or dormant—has intelligence. Ganglions, plexuses, neurons, cells and tissue are able to function on their own using inherited or acquired knowledge. Isn't this what the whole organism does? We think of our mind, or what we call our mind, controlling our body. But in reality, we have very little—consciously speaking—to do with controlling the organism. We think of ourselves as individuals inhabiting physical bodies. But how many living forms within us actually use our body, much the same way as we do, for their own survival? And what is the source of this controlling intelligence?

Tissue is composed primarily of cells. The nervous system consists almost entirely of cells; so does the brain. Regulated by wave frequencies, cells have the ability to regenerate themselves (which they do in rhythmic cycles) by converting electromagnetic energy, which is brought into the organism by any one or all of the systems mentioned, into electrochemical energy. There are three basic types of cells: the body cell, the nerve cell, and the brain cell. Part (1) of Diagram 4 shows a typical body cell enclosing protoplasm. Part (2) is a single nerve cell. The dendrites carry incoming impulses to the cell

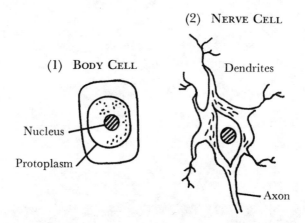

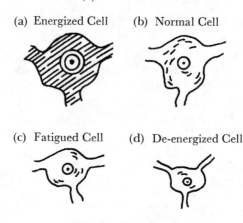

DIAGRAM 4

body and thus to the nucleus; the axons are outgoing fibers by which the cell transmits impulses (the axons may branch out to cover long distances in the body or they may be very close to the cell body). Part (3) depicts brain cells, tens of millions of which compose the gray layer of the cerebral hemispheres. Cell (a) is a vitally energized brain cell with an abundance of light/energy; (b) is a relatively less energized brain cell; (c) is a fatigued brain cell; and (d) is a de-energized brain cell.

BIPOLAR CELL—A MINIATURE SUN

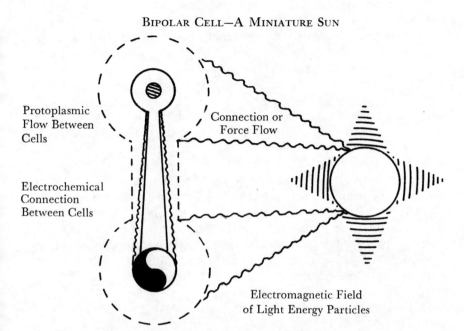

Protoplasmic
Flow Between
Cells

Connection or
Force Flow

Electrochemical
Connection
Between Cells

Electromagnetic Field
of Light Energy Particles

DIAGRAM 5

Cells display intelligence. A cell's nucleus serves as the nervous system which coordinates its life processes. It is interesting to note that, in a laboratory culture state, the cell is immortal if it is properly fed and its wastes are removed. The potential for immortality is within the cell—as long as energy is supplied in sufficient amounts, it sustains the organism. When energy is not supplied, the cell, acting upon an inbred impulse, ceases its normal functioning (or may even begin to destroy other cells). Like a universe within a universe, man is a complex of living organisms which make up the whole. Like a host, he sustains many forms of parasitic life which, acting under the influence of some regulating intelligence, tend to work for the good of the whole organism.

The cell is bipolar—it has both negative and positive aspects (diagram 5). It prepares energy for the organism by breaking large molecules (which come into the organism via the alimentary canal) into smaller components. This job is performed by catalysts known as enzymes, which themselves are not consumed as food; enzymes are used over and over again by the organism to provide energy for the cell. The cell cannot function without these important units which change organic compounds into usable energy—yet the cell, as if obeying an inner compulsion, produces its own enzymes.

There are numerous types of enzymes, each with a specific duty to perform (one type breaks down starches, another protein, another carbohydrates, still another fats, etc.). Enzymes are nonliving according to biologists, yet they are an integral link in both the direct and indirect (through organic food) absorption and utilization of solar energy. Enzymes are much like miniature "suns" distributing energy. Enzymes are destroyed by excessive heat (or we might say that they are diffused or dispersed by heat, like the atoms in a nuclear explosion). Enzymes are capable of producing "sparks" of light under certain conditions, and the action of light upon enzymes instantly produces more electrical activity. As depositories for light/energy particles, enzymes bring molecules together, inducing and increasing chemical reactions. Energy is released through the removal of electrons, which can be displaced by concentration of light upon a surface.

Cells are miniature solar systems. There is a constant stream of light from the sun to each planet; on a cellular level, the electrons' own "sun-nucleus" in turn sends the light/energy to the enzymes through "connections" or "force flows." The whole secret to life is the absorption of light/energy, its proper distribution in a balanced manner, and the expansion of the organism! Adepts of the system accomplish these vital goals by establishing a force flow (a stream of positively charged electrons) to the sun. This is done through the practice of the kinds of techniques the Project has discovered. Animal life is dependent upon sunlight, just as plant life is. We know from our studies that all organisms, whether planets or atoms, are completely dependent upon the exchange of light/energy.

Energy is governed by cycles, and living organisms are governed by energy cycles. All life is occupied with the utilization of energy. All energy is basically light! Since all light emanates from the sun, it is evident that all life on the planet is dependent upon the sun for its supply of light/energy. This light/energy is not sterile—on the contrary, it has intelligence potential! If all living organisms react to light/energy and are dependent upon it for existence, then we must accept that: (1) organisms are intelligent—or at least have the capacity to respond to intelligence, and (2) light/energy is a carrier of intelligence.

Protoplasm, like any living species, has its own particular set of light/energy particles and is subject to solar energy cycles. Since energy, as a stimulus, carries a form of communicable knowledge, we must accept the existence of some form of intelligence even on the cellular level. When exposed to light radiation, protoplasm reacts—it reacts to the command of light! Information is conveyed and understood by cell life in much the same way radio waves are transmitted to receivers. For radiation to be effective, the organism must be capable of receiving it and utilizing it; otherwise, the organism cannot and will not react to the stimulus. Although all protoplasm is sensitive to light, protoplasm will receive, or absorb, only that portion of light/energy necessary for its survival (just as a mole loses its eyesight through lack of use of light, protoplasm degenerates and loses its ability to utilize light even when it is receiving it). Any reaction to a stimulus depends upon an organism's ability to utilize the stimulus and not upon the stimulus itself. All living things are only as complex as their ability to utilize solar energy.

Like the cell, protoplasm is constantly in the process of regenerating itself. Although it is composed of very basic materials, its ability to utilize light/energy makes it most unusual and essential to all forms of life. All energy comes from the sun. This energy is stored in different types of compounds (carbohydrates, fats, proteins) and then transmuted into usable form by the cell, which creates a type of nuclear reaction within itself. The cell is an electrical unit working with light/energy to maintain an electrical organism. The very existence of the organism depends upon the cell's ability to change electro/energy atoms derived from outside sources into smaller and less complicated particles that the organism as a whole can assimilate. The apparent difference among all forms of matter, living and nonliving, is due only to the arrangement and charges of the atoms composing the internal structures of the molecules of the various substances. All things from rock to man are composed of these atoms; the differences between substances lie in the number of atoms and—far more important—the makeup of each atom's nucleus, which determines the type of atom and its charge of light/energy.

All matter is composed of clusters of atoms called molecules, each of which has its own particular arrangement of atoms. In addition to other unknown particles or forces, atoms have a nucleus of positively charged protons and/or neutral neutrons, and around the nucleus whirl negatively charged electrons. The whole is enclosed in an electromagnetic field of minute forms of light/energy particles (diagram 6).

The purpose, at this point, is to stress the importance of man regaining the lost ability to photosynthesize light/energy. This ability permits man to attain a most extraordinary state. Once the "spark of life" begins to appear on the cellular level and around the electrical field, man changes from a completely heterotrophic being into an autotrophic being, elevated above the level of the degenerated normal. To fully achieve this transformation, we must unlock the secret of the cell's generative and regenerative periods.

The various wave motions, known as radiation or electromagnetic waves, contain quanta capable of doing work. In an endothermic reaction, energy is absorbed; in an exothermic reaction, energy is released. In a nuclear reaction, enormous amounts of energy are released from matter; a transformation takes place in which matter is converted into energy.

The transformation/conversion of matter/energy is governed by various laws or universal principles; there are different principles involved in each case of conversion. For example, one kilogram of coal burned by chemical combustion would give off about 8.5 kilowatt-hours of energy in the form of light and heat. On the other hand, if one kilogram of coal were converted entirely into energy through nuclear fission, several billion kilowatt-hours of nuclear energy would be released. Here we see the same material in two different reactions involving two different processes of conversion. Fusion (as opposed to fission) is a process by which our sun (as well as the sun/stars of the universe) obtains energy. Our research has shown that this absorption of energy results in the formation of a nucleus with a higher mass number—a nucleus capable of releasing enormous amounts of energy. In the Project's system, the human organism is trained to convert solar energy to specific work.

The ancient sun priests of pre-Columbian America were masters of solar techniques; they were far more advanced than natural science supposes today. But somewhere along the line they went astray.

We of the Project must not allow ourselves to commit this error, whatever it was.

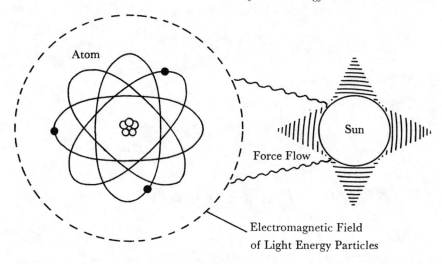

DIAGRAM 6

Putting aside the transcripts, I looked at my watch, which indicated that it was well past six o'clock in the evening.

A moment later I heard the muffled bell of my telephone.

"Sorry to bother you," said Sylvia, "but it's after six. Elena is coming to dinner. Better come up now." After hanging up, I shuffled notes together and stacked them in a neat pile in the center of the main desk. I typed a quick note to myself so I'd know where to begin writing the next morning. I picked up my heavy wool coat, slung it over my shoulder, and left the study. I spent five minutes saying goodnight to the staff, then hurried down the corridor, took an elevator to the lobby, walked to the apartment section of the complex and rode another elevator to the fifteenth floor.

A few moments later I entered the high-rise apartment Sylvia and I had shared since coming to the States. We had been married three years.

15

Fusion of Heaven and Earth

Project Center, Reno, Nevada

December 15, 1973 (P.M.)—Sylvia met me at the door and kissed me on the cheek. "Elena's here," she whispered, as I returned her kiss and looked into her beautiful, deep brown eyes.

Elena Baugh was sitting in a comfortable chair with a glass of red wine in her hand, looking out the picture window at the lights of Reno. I greeted her warmly and sat down opposite her.

"How's the editing?"

"Fine," she said.

Elena was in her late forties. She had been assisting me as technical editor of the Project for over a year. Canadian by birth, but of pure Romanian descent, she wore her black hair in a high chignon. Her black wool sweater, open at the shoulders, covered a white turtleneck. From a heavy silver chain around her neck hung a large Funchal cross. Elena was an intellectual with a bent for research. She was married to a teacher from San Francisco. I liked working with her; she was quiet, thorough and intense. Sophisticated yet restrained, she often gave the impression of severity, yet I found her to be a gentle soul. She spent about half her time at the Project center, commuting to San Francisco on weekends.

Sylvia brought me a glass of wine and joined me on the sofa.

"It's nice of you to dine with us this evening," she said to Elena, smiling. "What are you up to this time?" she asked. She was referring to a research paper of mine that Elena had been helping with. Although Sylvia always typed the final manuscript papers and so would know soon enough, she was curious to know something about it before that time. We often spent evenings speaking of research with members of the Project.

"Lots of things," I said. I enjoyed teasing Sylvia about her curiosity.

"Like what?"

"Well, we are investigating the idea of man's being. For example, is the mind the product of the brain? And what does the mind have to do with the spirit, that higher consciousness that appears to be separate from the human organism?"

"Isn't the mind distinct from the spirit?" Sylvia asked.

"Theoretically, yes," I said, "but from a practical point of view we have to prove that the brain doesn't account for the mind and, even more important, that man's being is more than physical—that there is a spiritual entity separate from the physical mind-body."

"That idea has been discussed by poets and philosophers since time immemorial," replied Sylvia.

"But where is the proof of their words?" interjected Elena.

"What man imagines is reality," said Sylvia.

"Not from a scientific point of view," said Elena.

"Indeed," I replied, sipping my wine. "Poets and philosophers have theorized, but never offered proofs. Words are cheap, as the saying goes, no matter how enlightening. Natural scientists have attempted to prove that the human mind is an enlightened faculty, the product of the spirit. So far, only opinions, simple arguments and lofty ideals have been provided. Neither science nor philosophy—nor poetry—has explained the mind and the spirit. But one fact stands out."

"What is that?" asked Sylvia.

"If the mind is the product of the brain, then it dies with the human organism. If the mind is eternal, as we believe it to be—if it survives death—then it must be nourished and sustained by energies beyond those of the physical body and the physical universe as we know it. That is certain. One thing the poets have given us is a very strong argument in favor of the unseen nature of man."

"What is that?" asked Elena.

"The lofty dreams and wonderings of human minds," I said, "as captured by the ink and pen of creative poets, do not appear to originate from the physical brain. They point to some celestial abode, to the realm of the psyche, or the eternal mind of the spirit we call consciousness—that which separates man from the animals, permitting creativity and projection into other dimensions beyond the limitations of the physical world. That man can speculate on the origins of the universe and on the nature of man indicates that man's mind has direct connections with some higher realm. We can assume this realm to be a spiritual realm, something eternal beyond the physical world. After all, man's origins eventually have to be traced to some pre-existent world beyond the physical. The brain, being a definite product of the physical world, can occupy no space in the realm of the nonphysical spiritual world."

Elena smiled and said, "We have discovered that our thinking processes, the actions of mind, draw little energy from the physical body—the brain, that is. The intake of solar energy with its X factor has shown that the mind's ability to learn is unlimited— learning need not be restricted to programmed academic teachings imposed by institutions of learning which are dominated by natural science and a physical view of reality. By drawing on this higher energy from the sun and beyond, our mind and our consciousness cease to be dependent upon physical energy per se. In a sense, we could say that the Project's techniques have taught us the meaning of immortality. Pure energy is supplied to the mind from an outside source."

"Absolutely," I said, "and this energy has inherent IF potential. It is cosmic information coming into our mind and consciousness directly from the source—the cosmos where it all began. Imagine, we don't need books to discover the secrets of nature and origins. Information comes streaming in from the universe. Remember, the first cause in the creation of the world was the 'word,' or the logos, which emerged from the mouth of God. The philosophers have always taught that this 'word' is the true nutrient of the spiritual part of man. No physical food, no matter how stimulating, can ever feed man's immortal consciousness—if it could, how would his consciousness be fed after it was deprived of the physical environment? We can see that consciousness leaves the body upon death and continues to be fed by this cosmic nourishment. As it is written in the Gospel of Matthew, 'Man does not live by bread alone, but by every word that proceedeth out of the mouth of God.' We have here the very nature of the energy that generates and nourishes the mind and the spirit of man."

"Would you say, then, that we can live on this energy without eating food?" asked Sylvia.

"Only partially," I replied. "In the very beginning I was turned off by the gigantic display of cannibalism in this world in which all creatures live by eating other creatures. At first I became a vegetarian. Eventually I went to raw foods, then fruits."

"How long did that last?" inquired Elena.

"Seven years. My body wasted away to muscle and bones, but I felt wonderful. I became so sensitive I couldn't stand the negative vibrations from large cities. I sought the stillness of the open country of the high Andes, as you both know. For a long time I felt I was more light than flesh, what with the intake of energy through the solar techniques. But something changed my whole attitude."

"What was that?"

"Well, I developed amoebic dysentery, hepatitis and low blood pressure. Not enough protein or gamma globulin. I had no immunity to the fruits and vegetables grown and fertilized with human excrement. I almost died two or three times. I had the choice of eating more protein or leaving the planet. It was as simple as that. So I made my choice: I went back to chicken and fish. Compromise can be a very practical approach to man's ills. At first I thought my physical body could be nourished by the radiant energy of the sun and the spiritual energy of the transcendental sun—the sun behind the sun, as we call it. This experience taught me a valuable lesson."

"Which was . . . ?" asked Sylvia.

"That man's spiritual consciousness is separate from the physical mind and body. Both have to be sustained by the energy forms within their respective realms. So I fed my physical body on nourishing foods while I absorbed the radiant energy from the cosmos. I accepted the dual nature of man. This compromise became easier for me once I understood that everything lives, whether it is flesh or vegetable or fruit. All things have a right to life.

"I didn't like the idea of having to kill something in order to survive, but at least I knew that my spiritual nature was being sustained by an energy direct from God. For that, nothing had to be killed. This fact—that a part of me was actually being sustained by energies from outside the planet—was a powerful stimulant in itself. Since my body was going to perish anyway, along with all other living things, it seemed acceptable to go on eating. After all, we have a right to physical life, even if we know it is destined to dissolve. I accepted the idea that the physical evolved from the spiritual, the pre-existent form to which man owes his origin. That I was putting my being in contact with the source and origin gave me the strength to go on living in a meaningful way."

Sylvia addressed me when I had finished. "Gene, though I accept your idea that the physical evolved out of the spiritual, a pre-existent form, there is something I don't understand. How would you account for the scientific fact that higher faculties in man—I mean higher consciousness—developed at a relatively late date? There seems to be a contradiction."

"Only partially true. Man has three brains: the first and oldest is the brainstem, next is the cerebellum, and third is the cerebral cortex or the new brain. The old brain gives man his deep psychic memories of past events; these ancestral or genetic ties tend to limit his expansion. Like the first, the second brain ties or binds him to emotional behavior patterns built up over many thousands of generations—these are old experiences imbedded in the brain. The third has more to do with a higher intelligence and with the processing of new information through language. All three brains are separate, and the newer brains don't seem to have control over the old. It is as if man has been provided with three distinct levels of awareness that have been linked together like the pyramids within pyramids of the Aztecs—newer ones being imposed upon older ones.

"The newer brains, like the outer pyramids, are new in external appearance only, for the older ones support them. To get at the old we have to suppress the new—go inside, that is. That is how meditation works; we still the newer brain of the cortex and get back to the older ones, there to seek refuge in the world of the primitive, which, as you both know, can be a fascinating experience if you like that kind of thing.

"Drugs serve the same purpose. The old or archaic brain deals in symbolism; it is illiterate in comparison to the more intelligent or newer brain, which seeks new information and new responses. One might say the former is more instinctive, the latter more rational. But the idea that the newer brain deals with higher consciousness is only partly true. This theory substantiates the claim of the evolutionists, the natural scientists who are trying to prove that the brain is responsible for the mind."

"Would you explain further?" said Sylvia.

"Let me put it this way: if we assume that the physical organism is a product of a pre-existent spiritual ancestor, an archetypal man before the fall (the descent into matter), then the generation of materiality, life and man—and his late consciousness—is, as Teilhard de Chardin speculated, representative of a returning to, or an evolvement back to, the perfect state. Man, a degenerate being, is struggling to return to what he was originally.

"With the development of higher faculties in his physical being (such as the late brain), he became able to process greater amounts of energy, more refined energy. And since, as our research has shown, it is the higher brain that processes solar energy, evolved man thus became more aware of his potential. This means that a more complex physical being is actually seeking to merge with, or at least become conscious of, the original form—the nonmaterial spiritual entity from which he had his origin.

"So the theory of evolution is only partially true, because it is not a matter of evolvement from the simple to the more complex, but from complex to simple to complex. Man is accomplishing this, or so it appears, through development of a more highly evolved nervous system with a greater brain capacity. The next step will be a transmutation into a more ethereal being, a more spiritual being whose grosser physical attributes will atrophy and wither away as his evolved nervous system learns to utilize cosmic solar energy. The final analysis will show man to be a higher entity than his physical senses reveal.

"Man will thus transcend his own gross physical makeup when he learns to capture more solar energy and to process the information within that energy by means of more sophisticated receptors within his more highly refined nervous system. This will result in a new and expanded meaning of life. Life and living will be speeded up; the individual will process more information in one day than has been processed by all the humans over thousands of generations who have struggled to return to the archetypal state where man was in possession of his so-called bright nature—that state of light akin to the nuclear fusion that takes place in the sun. In view of this, our evolution as a species is just beginning."

"Of course," said Elena, "what you are saying is far beyond anything even imagined by natural scientists today."

"Why should the natural scientists be the highest authority?" I queried. "Life and death have to do with the spirit. Decidedly, this is beyond the realm of science—even beyond the realm of religion as we know it. Something new will come out of all this, to be sure. We are only at the beginning of understanding the significance of the system we are applying. If the system puts us in contact with the energy of the spirit responsible for all life on the planet, then this will lead to a new religion of light—a kind of religion we cannot imagine, a religion of life that will give birth to man."

"I wonder what will happen when the details of what we are doing leak out," said Sylvia. "Won't people abuse the knowledge?"

"Why should they?" I answered. "What we are discovering is universal, the property of everyone. There are men who still believe that mysticism and science are matters for the privileged few. But this idea is changing, because mystical and scientific research will eventually affect all areas of society. Sunlight influences all living things—everyone has a right to know how the planet is being affected.

"The truth of our work beats within the cell of every living thing. It can no more be hidden than can sunlight. It is public. No individual or institution has sole right to it. We are dealing with cosmic thought. Like light, it shines on living things, carrying information as it goes. It isn't something that can just be put in a book and sold or distributed in an ordinary manner. It is something that has to be shared, experienced. It is open to everyone, but no one can purchase it; therefore it is important that the Project be well organized and that the research be meaningful, controlled and regulated by productive goals."

"What kind of organization are you speaking about?" asked Elena.

"Good question. The period of time we have in which to alter the environment is short. If the negative processes that are forming in the sun are allowed to continue to form, the result could be the total annihilation of the planet. Therefore organization is important so that information about our work can be disseminated to the world. Our object is to teach people to utilize the cosmic information carried by sunlight in order to evolve into a new and more highly complex variation of the species that will go on to inherit a place in the solar system."

"How would this inheritance come about?" asked Sylvia.

"As you know, man can become extraterrestrial by means of the light destined to transform him. We have learned that we can project ourselves into the sun using solar energy. Once we have done so, we will leave our traces there, and then go outward into the system at large."

"Please explain," Elena said.

"As man learns to specialize in absorbing solar radiation and receiving cosmic information, he will automatically become part of the whole. He will transcend his physical being and gain access to cosmic knowledge—stored information far beyond anything that can be learned on this planet. The cumulative effect of all this information from within solar energy will be to give this new breed of man—futuristic man—access to the information locked up in the stars. With this knowledge, death will be overcome, for man will no longer be earthbound, or even individualistic, as we presently know individuality.

"As man learns how to handle more energy, he will seek more. The same applies to information. This is the way an expanding or developing brain learns to process more information; it stores energy, expands, and then moves into a higher level of awareness or consciousness. This has been the pattern of *homo sapiens*—we are born with the ability to seek information and new forms of energy, to organize them, and consequently to grow. Just as the human brain learned to use language—which distinguishes man from other animals—it will learn to process and store ever increasing amounts of information and energy. With the absorption of solar energy, the brain and the rest of the nervous system will develop into a higher, more refined organ.

"After all, each of us has already experienced the first effects of application of the techniques. Our craniums have grown somewhat; my own has grown a full hat-size larger. The enlargement of the cortex—and the presence of additional gray matter which it signifies—seems to indicate that we are the first of a new variation in the species. With good organization we might very well become the creators of a new and universal civilization—a civilization in which superior brain power and understanding will make national boundaries, creeds and racial barriers a thing of the past."

Leaning forward, I looked deep into their eyes in an attempt to make my ideas felt within the depths of their beings.

"We can fulfill the dream of the old mystics—a new man with one foot in the sun, an X variation. Think of it, a great new experiment that has never been attempted on a global scale before."

"You're suggesting that man can be fused with heaven?" wondered Sylvia.

"You've heard me say that Pythagoras taught that man is a heavenly race; that his intellectual faculties elevate him above animals that live a short life and then die; that he is more noble of birth, and gifted, a creature of great intelligence with a will to maintain a divine relationship with God; and further, that without this contact with the divine he is above all souls miserable and empty.

"Pythagoras recognized centuries before Christ that man was made both in the image of the world and in the image of God, and that these two natures were in conflict with one another. He believed that man survived as an immortal soul after the death of the body; that he returned to the original state from whence he had his origin.

"The mystical religions, such as the one founded by Pythagoras, were advanced systems that taught man how to rise above his earthly nature in order to participate in a spiritual nature. In short, they were systems that used spiritual laws as well as physical laws, enabling the individual to generate greater beingness. In the ancient world in general, information or knowledge of the spirit was valued highly, especially when revealed by gifted prophets or superhuman individuals who were in direct contact with the realm of the spirit. The material world rejects such knowledge; indeed, the modern world is highly suspicious of any revealed religion, even though it is through the information on natural laws provided by gifted scientists and thinkers that we are influenced to change our attitudes and eventually reshape and rebuild our world.

"Mysticism has never rejected the world—it has always tended to fuse earthly man with spiritual man. Consciousness can never be the product of physical law alone; it has an independent life that arises from a source outside the cause-and-effect principles of physics or biology. No matter how much information we get from books, there is still within the human mind and spirit other stored knowledge that has its roots deep in the past—in that pre-existent world spoken of by mystics. If we can put our rational minds and our spiritual consciousness in contact with that pre-existent knowledge and learn how to use it, we will be on the road to attaining complete knowledge of reality. Once we have achieved that, earth will have fused with heaven."

Elena presented another question: "Let me see if I understand you correctly. You are saying it is possible to reach heaven by means of the rational mind and physical laws?"

I offered a furtive smile. "Yes."

"How?"

"Only by taking his fate into his own hands can man possibly evolve. He must approach this evolution with the physical equipment presently in his possession."

"What do you mean?"

"Simply this—biologically speaking, man ceased to evolve a good many thousands of generations ago. He is in possession of the new brain that evolution is supposed to have given him. But nature hasn't provided man with the necessary information on how to use it properly. Man has to do that himself. With proper use, the higher brain will continue to evolve, although now its development is at a standstill. Its growth will be dependent upon the use of the sun's energies. That's the first step.

"More than half the many millions of nerve fibers that connect the brain with other parts of the body go directly to the eyes. We know from our research that the eyes feed the brain with some ninety percent of its information. Furthermore, we have learned that information carried by sunlight can be processed by thinking. Here is incontrovertible proof that our physical senses are in contact with interstellar intelligences—interstellar information outside the realm of the earth. Is this not a kind of fusion with heaven?"

"I see," Elena said pensively. "You are speaking of techniques that manipulate biological evolution; direct evolution by the mind of man, not by nature."

"That's right."

"It's really the first step in leaving the planet," said Elena. "Not physically, but consciously. Mental exploration of the universe."

"That's about it," I replied. "The human race must evolve if it is to survive. Years ago man's intellect outpaced his lower nature, his instincts and the physical environment. I'm afraid it's time for man to transcend the boundaries of the world, to begin to commune with other worlds—and especially to participate in his higher spiritual nature, which is presently endeavoring to pull man away from the limitations of his physical environment. The primal energy of the spirit does not come from the world, but from the boundless energy of the cosmos. The spirit is not fixed in space and time; it is seeking freedom from the confines of earth."

"Well," said Sylvia with a smile, "it certainly cannot take the body with it any more than it does at the time of death."

"No," I said, "but there's no reason why the body has to remain forever in its present form. Perhaps through mutation it will evolve into some higher, transparent state—perhaps a light nature."

"That's a very interesting theory," said Elena. "I wonder if it's really possible."

"That's what our research intends to prove or disprove," I replied.

The discussion continued through dinner and long into the night.

After Elena had excused herself and Sylvia had gone to bed, I took the elevator down to the study to retrieve my notes, then returned to the library, as I often did in the quiet hours of the early morning, to think and write. The talk had given me an idea and had clarified many others, and I wanted to record them before they slipped away.

16

Energy Fields

Project Center, Reno, Nevada

December 16, 1973 (A.M.)—It was 5 A.M. when I finished writing my notes and the first light of the pre-dawn was just breaking. I opened and closed my eyes several times to shake off sleepiness, yawned, stretched my arms and took several deep breaths. Then I arranged the several typewritten pages, stacked them in a neat pile on the table and began to read.

TRANSCRIPTS

January 9, 1974

The radiation or energy fields around the human organism have been observed by the many sensitives attached to the Project, as well as myself, by means of our supersensitive or hypersensitive eyesight. These physical observations have also been supported by our experiments in radiation-energy-field photography.

To date we have detected three radiant energy fields surrounding the physical organism. The first is very near the skin and appears to be a dark color (its true color is a fluorescent red). The second extends about three inches from the body; the third extends, on the average, six inches from the body. The first field is simply the radiation of body heat, i.e., infrared. The second and third fields are inner and outer edges, respectively, of eight distinct energy fields oscillating within this mixed range. The predominant color of the

164

edge closest to the body and of the outer edge have been observed to change continually as one force center (and therefore the color field of that particular center) dominates the others.

This color phenomenon is characterized by the continual change in dominant color brought about by the person turning toward different points of the compass or moving to different geographic locations. Thus no single color dominates the total field for any great length of time. In general, the energy field around the human organism appears violet or bluish, but fluctuates for various reasons.

Individual energy fields may be discerned at various parts of the organism, such as the hands, elbows, shoulders, breasts, hips, knees, feet. Diseased areas give off distinctly separate radiation, usually in the form of infrared. It is interesting to note that the human physical organism is composed of chemicals, predominantly water, held together in a state that is more representative of a liquid than of a solid.

The energy fields enveloping the physical organism may be, not the product of the body's chemical components, but rather separate electromagnetic bodies with independent nervous systems that react to radiation. This relationship would make the human organism as much an electrical as a chemical phenomenon. Therefore, we can no longer regard the physical chemical organism as more "real" than the non-physical electrical organism. On the contrary, we must in fact consider the visible or physical organism as secondary to the invisible electromagnetic or cosmic/solar organism. (Here is strong support for the old metaphysical view that the human complex is more electrical than chemical, and more "spiritual" than physical.) There is every reason to believe that the energy fields are the source of life and may have the potential of surviving the death of the physical organism. The metaphysical question of immortality is bound up with these fields.

Man is a photo-complex. Photosensitization of the energy fields and the ionization of the physical organism through the irradiation of sunlight has certain therapeutic benefits. The net result is an expanded state of being through development of the psychic attributes. Metabolism is regulated by the endocrine glands, which control the chemical processes governing the generation of new cells and the destruction of old ones. To a high degree the endocrines are responsible for the continual health, youthfulness, long life, and states of behavior of the organism. While traditional science adequately describes the process of metabolism and the function of the endocrines, we must accept the possibility that these glands are governed by forces outside the human organism: solar rhythms.

States of health, youthfulness and longevity may be governed by built-in clock systems determined by factors inherited from our parents; however, the ability of an individual to alter endocrine regulation through certain techniques is something new and unsuspected.

Although the fields are interrelated with the physical organism, they are representative of a more refined cosmic body which requires electromagnetic (not chemical) nourishment directly from the source of all life, the sun. The energy fields, I suspect, would therefore affect the biophysical organism.

Prolongation of human life has attracted the attention of both specialist and layman in recent years. Medical science has suggested human life may be extended to 150 years or more with the help of certain injections and transplants of human and artificial organs. There has even been speculation that the human race may become physically "immortal." Although medical science has increased life expectancy through the use of drugs and surgery (and we can expect this trend to continue) there are certain limits. Human life is too complex to be restricted to the physical organism; its psychic attributes must be taken into consideration.

Emotional strain and stress, anxiety, worry and fear contribute to premature death as much as any physical cause. Pollution of our environment, crowded cities, an inhuman technological age of materialism, economic insecurity and other social problems all contribute to these causes. If man is to live longer, be happier, healthier, and lead a meaningful life, he must develop or awaken himself to greater states of reality, which might increase his life span.

The absorption of cosmic/solar energy into the human nervous system and energy fields has a revitalizing quality. However, since energy is the carrier of certain intelligence factors, any absorption of energy must involve exposure of the organism to these factors. Without proper understanding and application, the advantages of bringing life energy (which may regenerate the life process) into the organism can be overcome or negated by the development of the Y-factor, a destructive force counter to the constructive X-factor. While vital energy flows through the nerves and rejuvenates the cells, it could also have tremendous impact on the psyche, because it is a carrier of intelligence factors.

We know from studies that the nervous energy flowing through the nerves is related to and shares a common rhythm with solar energy. Old age begins when the organism fails to supply this energy and certain information in the required amounts. This usually happens after the age of forty, at which time the growth of the organism has come to a standstill. This slowing down appears to be a biological process locked into our hereditary makeup. With the intake of solar energy via the system of Project techniques, the organism is regenerated on the electromagnetic level, as distinct from chemical regeneration from food and oxygen intake. With the absorption of solar energy, the energy fields become activated. The endocrines seem to be influenced by the energy via the pituitary and pineal glands, and in turn influence the physical organism. The intake of cosmic intelligence factors could represent a shock to the entire psychophysical organism, for the entity in question is brought into contact with psychophysical forces with which it is not familiar. This leads me to believe that caution will have to be exercised later on. It would appear that the sun serves as a bridge between the physical and non-physical universes on the macrocosmic level of the solar system, and that the body atoms link the physical and non-physical on the microcosmic level.

The human physical organism is a mass of pulsating energy, a radiant body of factors. Thus, when the human organism contacts an unlimited energy source, such as the sun, the potential for intelligence becomes considerably heightened.

The nervous system of the physical organism can be acted upon by frequency patterns carried by energy stimuli. The psychological processes can also be affected through the nervous system or the force centers (diagram 7) by means of the IF (intelligence factors) potential carried by light energy. The diagram shows, in black, the eight force centers of the psychic body and depicts the physical body enveloped by an energy field or fields. The force centers are "contact points" through which IF acts upon the various psychophysical attributes. The four solar force centers (in white) are the catalysts through which higher energy frequencies flow and affect the light body (dotted lines). Matter or form, either physical or spiritual, is essential to any living organism. The force centers are to the psychic or electrical bodies what the nerve plexuses are to the physical body: channels of energy. The sun of our solar system serves as a catalyst or force center on the macrocosmic level through which energy IF from higher worlds pass to earth.

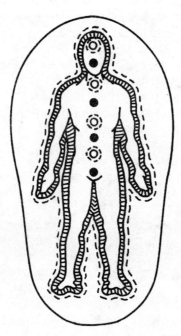

DIAGRAM 7

On the microcosmic level the atom is the link between light-energy quanta and cells. Here we see that the energy exchange occurs internally and externally, both on the cosmic and human levels of existence, and that suns and atomic particles are fundamentally the same thing, i.e., force centers for energy exchange between the physical and spiritual worlds (non-physical worlds).

Two years ago one of our associates, Henry Monteith, an engineering physicist from the University of New Mexico in Albuquerque, conducting research in radiation-field photography, developed a good camera for us, using the techniques of the Russian experimenters Semyon and Valentina Kirlian. By means of this simple device we have been able to capture on photographic film the light emanations around the fingertips and other parts of the human organism.

We have, like the Kirlians and other researchers, discovered enormous differences in otherwise invisible energy-field states among individuals. These photographs demonstrate that the state of mind and the emotions (diagrams 8, 9, 10, & 11) can and do affect the emission of energies from the human body. Diagram 8 shows the

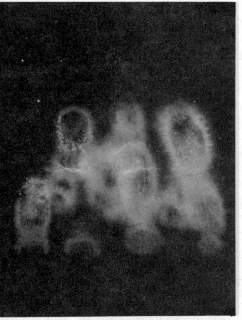

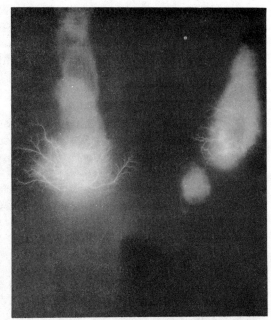

DIAGRAM 8

DIAGRAM 9

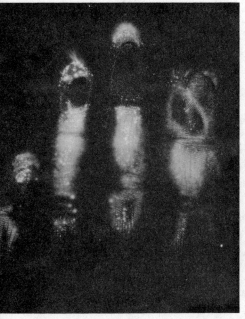

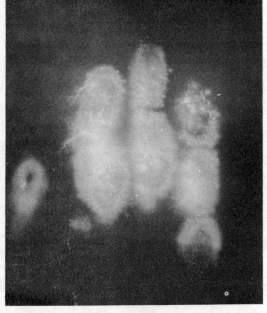

DIAGRAM 10

DIAGRAM 11

fingers of the right hand of a subject in a state of indifference. Diagram 9 shows the same right hand a few minutes later, after the subject was asked to concentrate on a mental problem in a given way (experiment 387-A, 8/8/72). The photographs indicate that energy emissions can be changed by mental states. Diagram 10 (experiment 432-A, 9/13/72), shows the right hand of another subject in a state of repose; diagram 11 is the same hand showing, like that in diagram 9, the presence of electrical activity produced by asking the subject to concentrate on the sun and imagine that sunlight was streaming into the brain and nervous system. In both cases the change of mental states produced alterations in the electro-photographs. This indicates that mental control does affect the fields or emissions of the fingertips.

We had speculated that the sparks or electrical emissions (if indeed they are electrical; for instance, the emissions may be part of the aura or non-physical energy fields of a person) might be produced by a spillover of the applied high voltage, but rejected this possibility because the sparks or bright emissions were always associated with altered states of mind.

I shoved the papers to one side and jotted down several more thoughts in the journal. My mind returned to the conversation of the night before about man's place in the framework of terrestrial systems and the projection of his mind into the sun. To me the condition of the sun was no longer a theoretical concept but a simple fact of survival. Man does have the power to alter the earth, either for better or worse. I could see the need for each individual to become informed of that fact. If everyone did not eventually participate in the bettering of the world environment, then the benefits of the discoveries of the Project would be lost. It was imperative that man free himself from the old hypotheses and view himself as a more directly related descendant of the sun.

But how best to transmit this information? New ideas often take time before they are accepted. The world did not have time.

I was thinking about this question when fatigue swept over me just before the new sun rose. I rested my head on the back of the chair, letting my mind drift as I often did when sleepy. The last thing I thought of before falling asleep was that the nature of life on the planet, of man and the sun, was not a matter for science or technology.

17

Time/Space Entities

Project Center, Reno, Nevada

December 16, 1973 (A.M.)—A little more than fifteen minutes had passed since I had fallen asleep, when the morning sun broke over the barren peaks to the east, sending shafts of light through the picture window. My eyelids trembled from the light, and as they did I experienced a flashing dream of walking in a tunnel, its walls encrusted with brilliant gemstones.

Blinking under the influence of the strong illumination, I was slow to regain full consciousness. When my eyes had accommodated to the light, I was struck by the image of a golden form standing between me and the sun. At first I thought I was dreaming. Squinting my eyes into a frown, I tried to make out the form more clearly. It was then I saw that it was a solar being, standing before me real as life. The resplendent figure stood motionless, crystalline, a silent guest from another world. Its diamond-bright eyes held me in a penetrating gaze, and I thought for a moment it was going to speak to me—then it vanished from sight.

I sat still for a long time looking at the sunrise, wondering about the entity from another world. All great world religions possess their angels, but for the most part, these remain locked within the pages of scripture, the private property of ancient prophets. If angels really existed, I thought, and appeared to so many holy men in times past, why do they not appear to modern men? Is it because scientific knowledge has replaced religious faith and in some way dulled the psychic senses?

I remembered the reports of Marcos Garcia, a Catholic friar who had gained access to the inner Kingdom of Vilcabamba shortly after the Spanish conquest of Peru. A simple priest, he had been given permission to establish a mission close to the Inca's palace at Vitcos and had first-hand experience with the ceremonies conducted by the sun priests at the temple. Solar beings were actually observed standing on the altar, apparently brought down by secret rites.

It was said that the priests, who were heard to repeat a rhythmic arrangement of Quechua syllables, communicated with these luminaries at certain times. I recognized that these rites were in many ways similar to the Egyptian ceremonies and to those of the Hindus, Zoroastrians, Mithrites and other ancient cults, but that in Peru and Mexico, the technique had attained the status of a divine science.

The Mayan sun priests maintained communication between men and angelic beings from the sun, if the reports of authoritative writers were to be accepted. Mantras consisting of selected words spoken in a certain manner were believed to have been partially responsible for this occurrence, though the temple sites themselves, their orientation to the cardinal points, and secret solar techniques all contributed to the apparitions. My mind went back to something I had read in an old scroll relating a Mayan priest's description of a solar figure. It was said to look very like a golden statue: exactly how my solar entity appeared that morning.

My own exploration into the Vilcabamba country, during which I had discovered the lost city of the Incas, old Vilcabamba itself, was the result of several years of exhaustive research of old chronicles, manuscripts and books in libraries and monasteries. The principal deity of the Incas at Vilcabamba was an idol named "Punchao," meaning the first rays of the sun over the horizon. This golden image of the sun was a disk surrounded by a series of golden medallions, whose mirror surfaces reflected the rays of the sun. In the center of the disk was a golden figure with a heart made of dough set in a golden chalice.

Two important facts struck me. The image was a replica of the sun and contained a golden figure resembling a solar deity. Second, the disk was used in the ceremonies at sunrise, reflecting the rays of the rising sun onto the faces of the worshippers who beheld its radiant surface, chanting secret mantras and throwing kisses to the sun. I knew heightened awareness could be induced by contemplating a brilliant surface, such as a golden sun image with its dancing patterns of mirrors reflecting a thousand little suns. Solar figures, angelic hosts, were purportedly manifested during these ceremonies, which was of singular interest to me, because I had experienced a similar apparition that very morning.

I wondered if I had seen an Inca deity at dawn, the image of Punchao, who had been observed so many times by the Incas. It was an intriguing speculation.

After a quick shave, shower and change of clothing, I went for a walk along the river, returning to the apartment at 7:45 A.M.

Sylvia greeted me with orange juice, boiled eggs and coffee. I said little during the meal. Accustomed to my thoughtful moods, Sylvia studied my face until I had finished eating. She poured me a second cup of fresh coffee, made in the Peruvian way. A strong essence was made by soaking freshly ground coffee in cold water eight to ten hours and then filtering it. Sylvia poured the proper amount of the essence into the bottom of my cup, added some heavy cream and filled it with hot water.

"What are you thinking about?" she asked, putting her long, slim fingers on my left hand. I had always loved the touch of her hand. It could work miracles on me, even when I didn't feel like speaking.

After I told her about the apparition, we talked about the possibility of inducing similar forms at will. After all, I argued, the Inca and Maya priests seemed to be able to do that. I talked for a good half-hour on forming brain images in a darkened room by blinking strobe lights on a subject's eyelids. I saw no reason why the same thing couldn't be duplicated in outdoor sunlight and with the eyes open.

For weeks afterward I conducted a series of experiments, hoping to discover how the Incas and other sun priests could summon solar entities of the kind I had experienced so often.

18

Brain Images

Project Center, Reno, Nevada

June 17, 1974, 10 A.M.—Some thirty members of the Project were gathered in the conference room. Word had gotten around that I was conducting experiments with golden mirrors. There was some speculation that the mirrors were ancient artifacts taken from treasure sites in the Inca ruins.

Most of the group had been exposed to earlier experiments with an electronic stroboscope calibrated to send out several brilliant flashes of light each second. Each of these people had sat for hours in a dark room, letting flicker light fall on their eyelids. The flashes of light evoked transient paroxysmal discharges in the visual area of the cortex for some, but for most, they produced vivid illusions of geometric designs in an assortment of shapes and colors—pulsating mosaics, checkerboards of deep blacks and brilliant whites, sunwheels, whirling spirals, stars, galaxies and assorted designs in colors so rich and vibrant they defied description.

Such illusions and hallucinations had fascinated everyone who had participated in the experiments, but non-visual experiences—the sensation of being detached from the body, or flying through space, projected forward in time, emotions of delight, fear, pleasure, and similar states—were more startling.

Some had observed faces and non-material forms, immaterial beings who stared back out of the darkness and the flashing light. In all cases the subjects developed a need to gaze, as if the sensations produced by the strobe lights had become a new means of communication with another world of stimuli.

The experiments had stopped as suddenly as they had begun. I explained that they should avoid the use of mechanical instruments as a means to self-knowledge. Such instruments were tools, nothing more, to help reveal to each the existence of higher dimensions that could be perceived by means of the brain and its sensory system. I stressed that light was the key to opening the door of the brain to new horizons and that no matter how intriguing the experiments might prove to be, the future of the species was more than an experiment.

Now my colleagues were gathered in the conference room to listen to my presentation, the first in a series of symposia. I strode into the room and went straight to the speaker's platform. Everyone else was seated at a large oval table. A dozen sheets of white paper, a pencil and a glass of water had been provided for each. I looked at each person, nodded, then carefully arranged my speech on the lectern and began speaking:

"The flicker tests have resulted in remarkable findings, especially when the brilliant flashes from the electronic stroboscope were made to correspond with so-called brain rhythms.

"Brain waves are classified into four basic rhythms. The first of these excites low-amplitude beta frequency, which pulses at 14 to 30 cycles per second. Beta is associated with a conscious state of awareness. The next frequency is the well-known higher-amplitude alpha rhythm which is present in a relaxed state. Its rate is 8 to 13 cycles per second, averaging about 10. As you all know, the alpha rhythm has attracted much popular attention and has also been exploited commercially in the form of brain-wave helmets or recorders and so-called alpha-development techniques. We will return to alpha later on.

"The third frequency is known as theta, or spindles, and is still slower rhythm, averaging approximately 4 to 7 c.p. s. It is generally recorded in sleeping subjects. The fourth rhythm, delta, is of very large amplitude and low wavelength, usually 1 to 3 c.p.s. It is characteristic of deep sleep and is also associated with injury, disease, degeneration and death.

"The activity of an organ is always associated with a change or development of electrical currents. Let's examine the effects and the causes of brain rhythms. Beta patterns are apparent in the active waking state. Alpha patterns will appear when the eyes are closed. They are characteristic of an awake but inattentive brain. Even with the subject's eyes closed, the alpha pattern may fade if the subject's attention is engaged by a sudden sound or the touch of a hand. Alpha rhythms appear when the subject becomes drowsy. This brings us to an interesting point.

"Electroencephalographic tests on students of meditative techniques and on Zen monks have shown that alpha patterns were present in all subjects, but especially in those who had practiced meditation for 20 years or more. In some cases alpha disappeared and was replaced by theta rhythms. Because both these rhythms are associated with states of drowsiness and sleep, they are not conducive to higher states of consciousness, where faster patterns have been recorded. For example, when a subject looks at a bright light, alpha rhythms disappear completely and are replaced by intense patterns.

"While meditative states like those achieved in Yoga and Zen extend certain beneficial physiological effects, such as restorative powers, decreased mental tension, and better mobilization of body resources, sleep provides the same benefits. It would appear that meditation, or going inward, is a withdrawal from bodily participation in the rational world, a kind of therapy and escape from events. Let's examine the evidence: the cycle of an alpha pattern is produced by a synchronized oscillation of numerous cortical neurons or nerve masses that are not then performing any useful function. Alpha patterns appear when the eyes are closed and drowsiness takes over the senses.

"Just prior to deep sleep, a faster brain rhythm, similar to the waking state, appears. It is similar to beta, but mixed. During this state, dreams and visions often occur. In states of light sleep, a subject is able to learn externally presented material. Eye movements are also associated with the dream state. It has been noted that the brain rhythms speed up and dreams occur when the eyes move under the lids, indicating that slow brain rhythms, such as alpha, theta and delta, are not present during dreams, visions, problem solving and higher states of consciousness.

"At first glance, the relatively still brain, with its slow rhythms, seems to indicate that the unconscious mind or psyche is better able to function, and to a certain degree this is true. Meditation states increase mental awareness, as any trained student of Zen or Yoga will testify. However, submerging an individual in water for long periods or isolating someone from any outside stimulus allows entirely new personal perceptions, which are as real as dreams or visions, to be experienced. These sensations are comparable to those experienced by mystics.

"Our comparisons show the difference in what the System is striving to achieve with its techniques. They teach us that the psychophysical attributes are interrelated and that an omega state, during which the brain rhythms are flooded with light energy and functioning on a high level of awareness, permits an associate to participate in perceptual or psychic experiences as students of meditation do. The techniques of the System speed up brain rhythms so the mind shares the experiences of higher consciousness. Unity of perceptual consciousness and X-consciousness is the goal. Thus the ego of the everyday mind/ brain is able to handle the ultra-dimensional experience of higher consciousness. In this way we prevent the unconscious or psyche from overpowering the conscious mind or ego.

"Again in the System we emphasize that the sensory faculties are employed, whereas the eastern systems reject the senses as a means to higher knowledge. Our statements are not based on a superficial knowledge of the better-known systems. Many adepts of the Project have practiced the older systems under the guidance of master teachers and even practiced techniques that are never given to western students. Our comparisons are only intended as an analysis, not as a criticism.

"An intake of electromagnetic energy can speed up the brain rhythms and does afford the nervous system and electrical fields an added supply of energy potential. It has been scientifically established that the currents that pass over the brain and those discharged by nerve masses or plexuses are accelerated to high-intensity pulsations when the optic centers are exposed to sunlight. Energy absorbed by the optic pathway leads to the visual or occipital regions of the brain. The optic nerve conveys impulses to the mid-brain and hind-brain. The optical thalamus is a terminal for impulses. Thus the intake of light energy through the pituitary and pineal glands increases the functional capacity of the sensory makeup. How does this come about? The physiological effects of light include electrochemical changes in the organism. However, with the speed-up of electrical currents in the brain, plexuses and other parts of the nervous system, our responses are increased.

"There are psychological effects on the cognitive processes through which reasoning, thinking and creative potential are expanded. Vision is the dominant sense, and when the eyes are exposed to sunlight, the brain becomes fully attentive and intense electrical activity floods the hind part of the occipital lobes, spreading to other regions of the cerebral hemispheres if the exposure is kept up. High-frequency currents pass over the cortex at up to 250 cycles per second. This electrical activity cannot be detected by electrodes on the skin. The brain currents associated with the solar-eye techniques are very rapid and are known as omega patterns in the Project. Even an increase of 5, 10 or 15 cycles per second, such as from alpha to beta, would give a person a tremendous survival advantage in everyday life, would increase awareness and improve decision making. The potential of an adept of the Project who works with high-frequency brain patterns is remarkable. While the speed of these omega rhythms has not been accurately measured, they are the fastest activity which the nervous system is capable of handling.

"The interaction between consciousness and the brain is a matter for philosophers, so we will not concern ourselves with the physiological details of which parts of the brain and the rest of the nervous system are involved in conscious life. Even brain rhythms are of secondary importance. Physiologists claim that only a fraction of the sensory input to the cerebral cortex is ever consciously used. While the retina of the human eye transforms light into neural energy, only a small amount ever reaches focal awareness. However, energy input is never wasted, because the nervous system can and does register data that are not always consciously detected.

"Visual perceptions involve far more than the physical properties of electromagnetic radiations, which may take the form of visible light. Signals transmitted from the eye to the brain are modified by sensory experience and memory. Information stored in the brain conditions incoming signals. In this way the physical properties of light are transformed into mental properties. But for this phenomenon, life as we know it would be nonexistent. Energy is the substance that activates the mind.

"We have learned that energy is a carrier of information. IF potential can be perceived by a receiver just as a radio receives signals and transforms them into recognizable sounds. How much information is conveyed depends upon the listener. Whereas mind transforms physical properties into mental properties, consciousness does the same thing with ultra-energy IF; that is, IF is transformed into conscious events. It is by means of a developed consciousness that man is able to communicate with ultra-dimensional worlds. How are we able to develop consciousness, and how is communication maintained with higher worlds of reality? That is the basic problem confronting each of us.

"Energy IF does not necessarily yield information. IF is coded information that must be interpreted by the receiver. Because we think in symbols, it seems logical to assume that higher consciousness works with some kind of visual symbology. IF can be accepted as the universal language of consciousness. It is apparent that you associates must learn this language, because it is the first step to the development of consciousness.

"The sun is the source of energy IF. There IF is transmitted and encoded. Consciousness then receives IF and decodes it. The goal of each associate is consciously to understand the message. While we are all individuals, we do experience very similar dreams, visions, hallucinations, mental images and mandalas, as the strobe experiments demonstrate. These images are all perceived by the sense of vision, as opposed to the other senses, which does not necessarily restrict them to the sensory level. Archetypal symbology can also be an asensory or spiritual experience. The Oriental mystics have long been familiar with the archetypal symbols perceived by the senses during inner states of self-transcendence. Western students of Eastern mysticism, neophytes in the strictest sense of the word, view such symbols with wonder and awe. Western philosophers and psychologists cannot explain them. The symbols appear to be devoid of meaning and beyond logical understanding, and indeed they are when approached by the rational mind. So let us examine the symbols, familiarization with which is a prerequisite to understanding the code of spiritual IF.

"Certain visual effects cannot be described as either physical or psychological. Take, for example, phosphenes, which are generated by pressure or electrical activity on the retina. While withdrawal from all light, such as entering a light-tight room, cuts off all inputs to the cortex, the impression of illumination is still experienced within the visual centers: fields of color, splashes of starlike specks and geometrical designs appear. This phenomenon is strengthened if the eyes are moved or if pressure is applied to the eyes.

"Neural transmissions account for 95 percent of our information about the outside world. The transformation of physical light energy into neural images or signals occurs at the retina. Light quanta or energy packets falling on the retina may be measured as a pressure, very slight by any physical standard. We have learned that the eye is able to accommodate tremendous amounts of light energy without damage, billions of times more energy than is required for visual sensation. If a person were placed in an environment where there were no third-dimensional impressions, for example, let us say an environment where there was only light and absolutely no physical objects or things, images or symbols would be discerned.

"Phosphenes give us an example of what we expect to see. The pressure exerted by placing a finger on the eyelid would be more than that equalled by all the sunlight falling on the human eyes in a lifetime (see diagram). However, the experiment does provoke the images and symbols registered on the retina by light energy and duly retained in the brain. We have suggested that the brain of man may have been an outgrowth of the eyes. If this is true, then the importance to us of light and perception of the external world is apparent. Light-sensitive protozoa without eyes or brains react to light. The human foetus, prior to development of the

brain, has been observed to react in a similar manner. This strengthens our hypothesis that man is a product of a spiritual form that existed before the evolution of the physical mind/body and that physical light energy is interspersed with ultra-dimensional energy from higher worlds."

At this statement I snapped my fingers. "Which brings us to our first experiment." An assistant turned off the lights. "We will first allow our eyes to adjust to the darkness, then we will gently press the eyeballs with our fingertips, very carefully so as not to injure the eyes. When this has been done, you will begin to discern designs similar to those experienced with the strobe-light experiments. When I have finished speaking, we will experiment together. It is interesting that brainlike patterns will materialize as if from nowhere. If the pressure is stopped and the eyes are moved about, bright sunbursts of purple will be observed. By increasing the pressure on the eyeballs, changing patterns will continue to be manifested. Violets, purples and blues mixed with silver-white light will be the dominating colors, against a jet-black background. Gold, yellows, oranges and greens, among other colors, will be observed. The whole magnificent world reported by religious mystics will suddenly appear to you researchers in all its colorful details.

"As the fingers are moved about the eyeballs, different designs will appear. They constitute an ever-changing pattern of geometric designs. These primary phosphenes will be replaced by more complicated designs, as greater pressure is applied over a larger area. Primary phosphenes include glowing circles, squares, triangles, diamonds, rectangles, concentric circles, stars, crosses, spirals and dots set against checkerboard backgrounds of white and black. More complex images may appear, such as great whirling sunbursts; mixed geometric patterns; human forms that may include golden, diamond-eyed faces, hands and fantastic figures, such as sun priests or priestesses; natural forms such as animals, flowers, birds, and others. The catalogue is varied, and I suggest you research associates compile a sketchbook of properly classified images. Now let us begin."

For fifteen minutes those in attendance conducted the experiment as explained. Afterward the lights were turned on. Naturally, the sudden appearance of the light caused everyone to blink. With a shuffling of feet, coughing and moving about, the researchers began the task of translating the visual images into two-dimensional drawings on paper. When this was completed, after about twenty minutes, the drawings were picked up and placed in a file for later reference. I began to speak again.

"The greater part of the input stimulus in the cortex is coded in cryptic symbology. Even the brain functions in symbols which perform below the level of sense awareness. While it may appear that this input is wasted energy, that is not necessarily so. It has been estimated by researchers that the retina can transform a million bits of information per second. While much of this information or sense data is not used by the perceptors, it is stored away in memory banks in the brain, as in a giant computer, and is always there for processing.

"Phosphenes are an example of what happens to energy input that is not used in ordinary conscious visual perception. These images explain, in part, the form this unused energy can take. The question is, how may we understand and learn from these symbols or images? Let's return to a study of the symbols to help answer that question. Pressure on the eyeballs produces different phosphene designs, depending upon where and for how long pressure has been applied. The middle fingers pressing on the inner corners of the eyes produces a luminous field. If pressure is then applied outward towards the ears, this field changes to different patterns of light which may become a zigzag checkerboard background with scintillating designs superimposed on it. Pressure of the index fingers at different points on the eyeball will result in the appearance of a series of geometric designs.

"Designs vary according to the individual. However, phosphenes are common to everyone. A Peruvian of the Andean Altiplano or a Tibetan of the Himalayan uplands will share the same phosphene patterns as a Bedouin of the Sahara or a commuter in New York City, though there will be some variations. There are historic and cultural conditionings that dictate a limitation of symbols. An associate of the System, though, through an expanded consciousness, will experience them all—and many others that lie dormant in the psyche of the unawakened.

"We see evidence of phosphene designs on the walls of ancient temples, usually in the form of pictographs, petroglyphs, hieroglyphics, ideograms, cave drawings, textile designs and pottery art, among others. The motifs of ancient Mexico and Peru are particularly rich in these symbols, which appear to have been observed in very ancient times, for we find their traces in the oldest cultures. The designs are not original with any one culture, but are shared by all.

"Phosphenes may be observed in positive (light) and negative (dark) aspect. Afterimages are also perceived. While looking at a bright sky and keeping the eyelids open, gently apply pressure with the tip of one finger. A dark geometric image will appear, usually a circle superimposed over the light sky. When the eyes are closed, the image will be light superimposed over a dark background. You may also note that your rate of breathing can affect phosphenes. Once images are formed, increased breathing or holding the breath for a minute or so will alter the symbols and/or the background. Many observers have noted alterations from tapping the head with the knuckles, applying pressure at one or more points, especially at the neck or the temples. After sitting in a dark room for 15 minutes or more, or immediately upon awakening in a dark room, you may produce phosphenes by moving the eyes from side to side or forcefully crossing them so pressure is exerted.

"The beam of a bright flashlight played over the eyelids will also result in a variation of luminous or scintillating designs. It is interesting to note that the phosphenes produced naturally by pressure are similar to those observed by subjects under the influence of hallucinogenic drugs. Stimulation of phosphenes just before you fall asleep often results in vivid dreams of picturesque mandalas. These are complex designs of mixed geometric, floral, animal, architectural, human and artificial forms of psychophysical symbology. Mandalas are caused by a triggering of the psychic attributes. They have symbolic meanings. They may include any of the designs described above, as well as images of the inner workings of the physiological organism, that is, brain tissue, blood vessels, nerve systems, and so on. The psychological workings may also be represented. These may include still more symbolic designs, with a great variety of color and forms interpreting the various levels of consciousness. Because these symbols are ultra-dimensional and continually shifting, as different images and symbols appear, no drawing or sketch can duplicate them.

"Astronauts traveling in outer space have reported seeing, with their eyes closed, flashes of light, phosphenelike images and geometric designs. Physicists experimenting in laboratories with nitrogen nuclei traveling at a speed near light as it passes to the retinas have reported these same images. Associates, absorbing higher energy levels directly from the sun, also report similar images, designs, or archetypal symbols. From these experiments, it would appear that these flashes of light are universal and shared by humanity.

"From earliest times, symbols, sometimes called mandalas in Oriental schools, have played an important part in the development of the adept, almost to the point of becoming holy objects. Eastern card symbols carried by the member of an order, such as pictures of saints, held a sacred place in ritual.

"Since all phenomena received by the senses are symbolic or in the shape of an image, knowledge of brain images is vital to the researcher. This is particularly true of the solar adept working with sunlight, because light assumes certain wave patterns. These patterns are frequency ranges and represent a universal language that can be understood by the adept. Before we go any further, it would be a good idea to have a clear understanding of just how important these symbols are.

"Visual thinking is a much earlier form of mental activity than its verbal counterpart. Before man learned to communicate by means of the spoken word, means of communication must have existed. The eyes were a development of light, and their development took place at a very early point in our evolution down the scale of physical existence from a higher dimensional creature. All languages, both oral and written, are symbolic. Any earlier form of communication that involved eyesight was probably based on primordial images or symbols that had a cosmic origin. This may explain why man thinks in imagery. We have discovered that electromagnetic waves contain IF, which demonstrates that light energy can be transformed into mental activity. Matter can dissolve into patterns of energy concentration and back again. Whatever form matter, energy or IF may take in the physical universe, it is capable of producing an effect. This indicates that everything in existence, even inanimate objects, is in a state of suspended consciousness. In other words, everything is mind. A developed consciousness can affect atoms and stars.

"The human organism has been compared to a feedback scanning system which hunts for information. When the device is at rest and there is no pattern for it to scan, it will produce oscillations similar to alpha rhythms. Once the pattern is found, the alpha rhythm disappears. Here is a condition analogous to opening and closing the eyes. When the eyes are looking for something, alpha waves disappear. When the eyes are closed, alpha waves reappear. If the mind is at rest and the eyes are not scanning for anything in particular, alpha waves are present. While scanning for information, the brain is dominated by beta or even higher-frequency waves, as recorded by an electroencephalograph. Delta rhythms dominate in deep sleep. Theta, or spindles, are present in regular sleep. Alpha corresponds to a relaxed state. We do not dream in beta, theta or alpha. Dreams are accompanied by eye motion and faster brain rhythms, indicating that even in sleep the human organism is scanning for information as though in the beta, or excited, state. These findings suggest that faster brain rhythms are related to higher states of consciousness, as we have mentioned previously. The research associate should seek out the radiant light-energy quanta in the sun. The very act speeds up the brain rhythms to the omega rate. With the intake of light energy, IF consciousness is activated. The result is the generation of the light body and of greater awareness. In the Project we refer to this as the logos-state, a state which has great potential for functioning on high-frequency levels.

"Once the associate absorbs solar energy, a two-way communication link is established. The adept experiences four distinct stages in the process. The first is the imprinting phase. During this stage the initiate identifies with the sun. Being programmed from birth to respond to light-energy IF factors, the actual intake of the external stimuli via the visual area of the brain, neural impulses activate memory banks probably triggered by symbols. The associate may experience numerous memory recalls of past and future events, depending upon the exposure time.

"The second stage, or identification phase, is a period when the intake of solar energy and IF lessens the attachment of the person to the ordinary sensory world. While the individual may live an active everyday life in the third-dimensional world of events, his or her attachment to the sun becomes so strong that a new personality takes over. This third stage is known as the self-actualization phase, in which the energy IF begins to take hold, the brain waves are speeded up and the electrical or energy fields become charged with radiant energy. This higher-frequency potential allows the associate greater understanding of IF. This dynamic process leads to the fourth and final state, the transformation phase. Consciousness becomes activated, and the adept now functions as a higher being. All inhibitions are overcome, the unconscious levels are not only activated, but also linked with the conscious state.

"As opposed to simply receiving information or responding to stimuli, as in a passive state, the transformed individual becomes a center of cosmic influence, that is, a living sun radiating energy IF to the world at large. The average person has no concept of the tremendous potential power of a transformed person who is identified with the cosmic whole and thus functioning as an

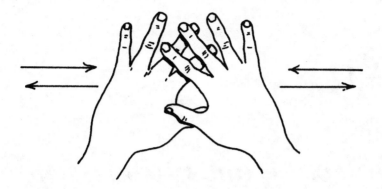

ultra-dimensional being in two sets of dimensions at the same time. The abilities of such a person can be known only to another who has attained the identical state. As we have so often repeated, the transformed state is a dynamic process which has to be experienced to be understood.

"I recommend that each of you use the sun as a light source in a new series of flicker tests. Since you will not be relying on the calibrated flicker of the electronic stroboscope, you will have to use the fingers of your hands like this, placing your hands between your eyes and the sun."

I stepped away from the table and, placing my hands in front of my face, moved them back and forth rapidly. After doing that I said, "This is the thatch technique. The speed of the hand movements determines the rate of flicker. Experience is the best teacher. The object of the technique is to allow sunlight to fall upon the eyelids, as you did in the stroboscope techniques. By working your hands back and forth as I demonstrated, you can regulate the flicker speed. It is not difficult to adjust the rate of flicker. Each of you knows from your notes which speed or brain rhythm, that is, beta, alpha, theta, or delta, produces the best symbols. As you learn to adjust the rhythm, you will discover for yourself that alpha or beta gives the best results. You should keep notes recording your experiences. While capturing the brain images with paper and pencil is difficult, do your best so that we may compare your experiences with those of other associates, as we have done with the phosphene experiments."

19

Objects from Outer/Inner Space

Project Center, Reno, Nevada

June 17, 1974, 2 P.M.—After lunch the team met again in the conference room, most arriving early, which gave them time to discuss results of the techniques described in the morning session. Some of the discussion was theoretical, but for those who had gone to the solarium or to the grounds across the river and actually applied the techniques, the discussion also involved practical experience. The results were varied, but the associates agreed that whatever each had experienced, it had been dramatic and unexpected.

In the midst of the discussion, I walked to the lectern, opened a blue leather folder containing the second half of the lecture, and began to review my notes. Soon I was ready to begin.

"Energy is the giver of life—transcending all our formulas and equations. In going to the source of all energy, the sun, you have been able to project yourselves into the universe, thus participating in energy forms having their origins in galaxies or star clusters millions of light years away. Energy may require millions of years to span the great distances between other galaxies and our own solar system, but IF factors, being born of consciousness, are not limited to the speed of light. When one's personal consciousness is linked to the impersonal consciousness of the universe, these time barriers can be shortened or overcome. We see, then, that energy and consciousness are intimately related and that time is relative and not always what it seems; furthermore, that man is intimately related to the universe. Energy can be related to time. Energy can also be related to information. Let's investigate this idea further through experiment.

"By absorbing sunlight into your organisms, you not only have a greater incidence of energy, but greater amounts of time and information. In other words, the intake of solar energy speeds up the force fields, which alters the time continuum. As we know from our studies, greater IF is then made available. Many associates wonder why masters of antiquity were able to defy the known laws of the universe by performing miracles, walking on water, foretelling the future, healing the ill, raising the dead, transmuting metals and the like. The fact is that they possessed extraordinary amounts of energy and linked themselves with the intelligence of the universe. That this brought them into a higher continuum and gave them a certain measure of control was not their principal objective; even Jesus and the Apostles limited their performances, because mastery over physical phenomena—PK or PSI—was not their goal. They were interested in higher consciousness and participating in ultra-dimensional existence, which always has been and still is the motivating force behind the power of the master.

"Let's demonstrate an example of the basic mechanics behind the overcoming of physical laws. We caution you research associates that this is an experiment, not a technique. Take an ordinary wristwatch or pocket watch with a sweep second hand. It must be your personal timepiece, fully magnetized with your own force field. Allow it to run down by not winding it. After a few days, pick it up and tap it gently against your palm: pick up the watch with your right hand and tap it against your left palm. Since a watch is an instrument with little friction, it should run for several seconds or minutes more. Now we are ready for the first phase of the experiment.

"Lay the watch on a flat desk or table. Now place your hands over the timepiece, about three or four inches above, and move them in a circular motion, counterclockwise. You are forming a vortex or gravitational field around the watch. Rotating your hands smoothly, one above the other, for about four or five minutes will result in a partial vacuum in the center of the circle, drawing atoms towards the cavity. Thus we have gravity and inertia in a field of space around mass or matter, the watch. Like this." I moved my hands in a circular motion (see diagram).

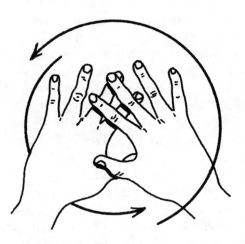

"This field will soon be charged with energy: a gravitational field is a major form of energy. The watch, being within the energy or force field of the operator, has additional energy available in the smaller field being formed. Stare intently at the watch and imagine the field is being charged with IF, which would cause the sweep second hand to move. The hand may or may not actually move. Do not be discouraged if you do not succeed the first time. If all the requirements are met, the hand will move!

"Now gently pick up the timepiece and hold it between your hands. Press gently. The sweep second hand should move; it is advisable to mark the position of the hand before attempting the experiment. If the hand fails to move, repeat the experiment. If the second attempt fails, rub your hands briskly together, like this." I rubbed my hands to demonstrate (see diagram).

"Now pick up the watch. The second hand should move. As with all experiments, practice and patience, plus determination,

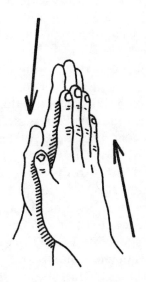

dictate the results. Most experimenters are surprised to see the hand move forward. Once it does move, if even a fraction of a second, you will be able to move it again, possibly for a longer period of time. Remember that it is not the heat of the hand or the movement of the hand that is moving the second hand, but the energy and the IF potential. Some adepts are able to move the second hand without actually touching the watch. Indeed, some are even able to move the entire timepiece. But I do not encourage this practice, because it requires unnecessary amounts of energy taken from the force field of the individual and the experiment is only a means to an end, designed to show that energy, time and consciousness are interrelated.

"We should also note that the nature of generated thought patterns is important in making the clock mechanism work. Aesthetic, emotional and exciting thoughts have a more positive effect than more rational ones, for the emotional and drive centers are involved. Thus, creative or imaginative thoughts accompanied by visual symbols have more of an influence than will, commands or intellectual involvement. What has the hand movement of the timepiece demonstrated? That space, energy, mass, inertia and gravity are somehow part of the same continuum. But what about time? How is it identified with consciousness and energy?

"I demonstrated how a gravitational field charged with IF affects mass by causing a watch mechanism to move forward. In a previous lecture I mentioned that a watch will often slow down. Are the two phenomena related? Not really. The fact is we have two opposing ends, two poles, and in generating a gravitational field around an object, time is condensed. Take, for example, a rocket ship traveling near the speed of light, seeking a star a million light-years away. Upon its arrival, apparently only a few years will have passed. How is this possible? Because the rocket is moving and generating energy. The speeding spacecraft gains time because of its velocity. The same law applies to a solar adept. With a higher-speed force field, time reckoning is altered. Time not only passes more slowly, but one discovers through experience that this slowdown permits one to bridge the time difference of events, to bring the future into the present.

"The human organism, with its electrical or energy fields, gives off energy, like a star. There are billions of excited electrons in the organism, radiating energy in all directions. Electric fields envelop the organism as if generated by a rotating sphere similar to the galaxies, suns and planets. This energy field may be compared to a magnetic field. It is not the result of motion in the chemical-atomic structure of the physical organism, nor is it a by-product of the chemical constituents, which indicates that the electrical nature of man is not secondary to the chemical. The electrical nature or higher light-energy nature sustains the physical organism, a hypothesis brought forward over four decades ago by Harold Saxton Burr and F. C. Northrop. Their experimental findings, titled 'Electro-Dynamic Theory of Life,' suggested that the electrical field is as universal in living systems as their chemical-atomic components.

"The electrical or energy field is polarized into positive and negative poles, much the same as the magnetic fields of the sun and planets. Unlike the planets, but like the sun, it can change polarity: turn into its own enantiomorph; that is, it becomes a mirror image of its former self. A negatively energized field disburses energy. A positive field conserves energy. Like the color spectrum, the field's colors radiate from deepest blue to brilliant red, with the other colors in between. Any change of the organism, such as illness or other breakdown, is first registered in the electrical field before becoming apparent in the biological organism, which can be discerned by observing the color fields or color bodies. The predominant force centers affect the organism and the fields, which means that the electrical potential of an individual is interrelated with the biological potential: the electrical structure is interrelated with the chemical structure. Electrical potential is linked with the sun, the planets and all physical manifestations of energy, including cosmic energy.

"In addition to the electrical fields, there is a higher, primary force field. It is colorless, but charged with non-physical energy. It is observed as a sphere surrounding the physical organism and the force fields. This 'light-body' is linked with ultra-dimensional levels and operates with higher energy levels—although not physical, they are interwoven with it. While there are three basic levels of a person's being, it is essential that he be viewed as a whole, with all parts interrelated and forming the unified person.

"Assuming that the physical organism and the energy fields are outgrowths of a higher primary body, the light-body or cosmic body, we are forced to accept ultra-dimensional levels of existence going beyond the restricted three-dimensional world of the material universe. This means man is ultra-dimensional, that he exists on different levels of being, each governed by the laws of that particular dimension. Our studies have already shown that man is a descendant of higher life forms, of light beings. So he is immortal, and although man has degenerated to third-dimensional life, he is not restricted to that world; only his physical being is subject to restriction. Once he activates his primary body, becomes conscious of it, he steps into higher worlds of consciousness.

"Man is thus a complex, existing continuously in space in the whole of cosmic generation, and consequently persisting in time. He is an immortal being, universally present in all dimensions according to their process and region and stage of development. While it appears he exists only in the present time of the third dimension, he is actually linked with the whole of generated existence at all points of generation and degeneration from the lowest to the highest, from the most remote regions of space with its sparse clumps of inanimate matter, to the very Godhead itself, the source of all things. Evolving through dimensional existence in cycles of expansion and contraction, man appears in the third dimension through his parents as a mutation of higher being and form which is under the influence of cosmic intelligence factors which do not allow him to gain full knowledge of his true identity. In spite of this, he has been evolving forever and will continue to do so in different forms.

"While it would appear that man is scattered to the four quarters of the universe, he is in reality unified into a whole. He is not, however, conscious of this. It is beyond the faculties of the third-dimensional mentality to grasp that he is linked with the whole of generated life at all points at the same time.

"The so-called light-body or cosmic body is made of an invisible light, the light of another dimension. It is the same light-body of Jesus, the golden body of Buddha and the sun body of the Viracocha of the Americas. This body is immortal, and once a state of cosmic consciousness is achieved, one becomes aware of this divine, unearthly origin. Knowledge of this immortal, ultra-dimensional consciousness body turns man's attention away from the limitations of third-dimensional life to a higher life. That's why our program emphasizes the proper use of any developed attributes and de-emphasizes worldy application.

"We can see, then, that man is a pre-existent being, rooted in a world beyond the material universe. The greater part of man exists in other dimensions, beyond the space-time of the physical universe.

"The light-body, unlike the physical organism and energy fields, is not at a fixed or focused point in the universe. While it appears as a light-body to the trained eye, it cannot be classified as to size or restricted to any one point in the material universe. Its appearance as a light-body is only a manifestation of energy arising from another dimension. Like the sun, a focal point of energy coming from beyond the material universe, the light-body is the gateway to other worlds of force which are still a mystery. The sun is viewed as a brilliant ball of light by the eyes. Were it not for these organs, the sun would have an entirely different appearance. These organs cannot reach beyond the focal point observed, since they are products of that very point of energy. The mind cannot penetrate to the sources of the material universe, since it is a product of the material-energy forms of the material universe. It is only by means of consciousness that we are able to perceive the light-body existing in a higher fifth dimension, and this dimension has access to all points of generated life.

"The techniques permit the research associate to transcend the limitations of physical sense perception. Absorption of solar energy through the eyes by means of our techniques and thence into the biological levels of the brain and nervous system results in stimulation of the metabolic processes. Since the quanta of energy involved in these processes are in the visible spectrum, the organism can take on a bio-luminescence which radiates energy like the sun. The energy fields are also involved and often are referred to as the 'human aura' which is observed by the actualized individual or the sensitive. We have stated that the light-body, which is activated via the X-factor, is the product of an invisible light and is not necessarily confined to any given point as the physical organism is, though it is also continuous in the time and space of the material universe. While the greater light of an actualized person can be discerned by another, it is part of a higher dimension. Therefore solar energy does not actually activate the light-body or cosmic body, though solar energy is involved in the process.

"We have established the existence of a visible light, the sun, and of an invisible light, a non-physical light, which originates beyond the physical sun, yet is manifested through it. While it appears to be a paradox that physical energy is the stepping stone to spiritual energy and thence to consciousness, it is so. We can better understand this when we realize that man is not simply a physical being, that he has his origins in a higher, invisible world of energy forces charged with spiritual IF consciousness. The fifth dimension is not to be found in the celestial heavens or in the sun. A spaceship could not hope to journey to it. It is, as we have pointed out, part of a higher world beyond the material universe. If we imagine that we are traveling outward in space at the speed of light, we might think we are nearing another dimension or world. This is not the case, any more than we could expect to find another dimension if we journeyed inward at the speed of light. Ultra-dimensions are not to be found in outer or inner space. Take, for example, a tree, of which we see the outward form—trunk, branches, limbs, leaves. It has an outer field of energy not sensed by visual perception. Its internal world is beneath the ground, a complex of deep-growing roots. There exists a force field here, too. The life of the tree is not to be found in either of the two. The tree grew from a small seed, when there was no outer or inner world. A life force made it grow into visible form, utilizing natural elements of soil and water, which contained the necessary chemicals, and sunlight. It is the same with our spiritual nature and spiritual dimensions.

"What is not understood is that anything with which man is not familiar escapes his consciousness. The phosphene and strobe experiments have familiarized each of you with the symbology of brain images and to some degree revealed to you that forms and images exist outside the sensory stimulation of normal sight. Perhaps some of you have begun to realize more than ever that there is a world of existence beyond the range of the normal five senses. These images and forms have not as yet conveyed any useful information, mostly because we have not as yet learned how to understand the messages they may be intended to convey. We have lost the ability to understand and use such images and symbols, as we have lost the meaning of the Mayan glyphs and the Inca quipu cords. We must try to regain this lost ability, for it is logical that any image beyond the ordinary range of the normal senses has meaning. We have only to interpret it, not according to our understanding of the external world, but to the internal horizon of stimulation. We must accept, first, that not only physical things exist in the universe and, secondly, that non-physical things have a reality status. If these things, objects or in this case images are to have any meaning, we must seek to have some experience with them, for it is through experience with objects that we are able to give them practical meaning.

"We must first eliminate the idea that these images or objects are simply geometric designs and therefore nonliving. It could very well be that they are intelligent living organisms, possibly beings like ourselves—but more complex than we are.

"The sun priests of the Americas, chiefly among the Incas and Mayas, were masters of utilizing sunlight reflected off small golden mirrors, much as we have done with the electronic strobo-scope. While the average person, unfamiliar with the secret prac-tices of the sun priests and what they were doing with sunlight, believes them to have been pagan sun worshipers, those members of the Project who have received oral instructions about uses of the sun and golden mirrors or crystals know better. The solar priests possessed a highly sophisticated technology that put them in contact with energies or beings beyond the physical world and, it would seem at this time, even gave them knowledge of the language of these beings—which was symbolic, that is, a language of symbols different from alphabetical ones—ideograms.

"For example, suppose that we were to reconstruct the sacred Punchao—the golden image used by the Inca sun priests at Vil-cabamba, which was eventually taken from them by the Spaniards and melted down for its contents—and that we were to use it as did the priests. We would learn that it was a device for reflecting the sun's image with a multitude of little parabolic reflectors made of gold that, like the stroboscope, brought forth images of light beings—and in some cases brought these beings of light down to earth to stand on the altar. Now I ask you, how can any intelligent and rational human being accept such a concept?

"Let me assure you that our experiments have shown that such a phenomenal experience is possible and can be demonstrated to sensitives." This statement brought some reaction from the mem-bers, some of whom turned and looked at one another with astonishment on their faces.

"The question is," I said, "are these images or beings real, or are they fantasy? Are dreams, visions or apparitions real or fantasy? What about unidentified flying objects? Are they real or fantasy? This is the central question that must be answered or at least understood. Let me read a text taken from the Encyclopaedia Britannica, quoted from a statement by A. Garrett, an esteemed professor at the University of Coimbra, who was present at Fatima, Portugal, on October 13, 1917, along with some 70,000 other witnesses, who had gathered out of curiosity at the reports of three children who had experienced a vision of a lady promis-ing to return at certain dates.

Punchao

" 'The sun, a few moments before, had pierced the thick clouds that held it hidden, so that it shone clear and strongly. . . . It looked like a burnished wheel cut out of mother-of-pearl. . . . This disk spun dizzily around . . . it whirled round upon itself with mad rapidity . . . (Then the) sun, preserving the celerity of its rotation, detached itself from the firmament, and advanced, blood red, towards the earth, threatening to crush us with the weight of its vast and fiery mass.'

"This episode is similar in many ways to two incidents recorded by the eminent psychologist Carl Jung in his controversial book, *Ein Moderner Mythus, von Dingen, die am Himmel gesehen werden,* published in 1958, and published a year later in English under the title *Flying Saucers.* The first incident was taken from the 1561 Nuremberg Broadsheet and relates the story of a 'very frightful spectacle' observed by 'numerous men and women' at sunrise on April 14, 1561. These people saw 'globes of a blood-red, bluish, or black color, or plates, in large numbers near the sun, with several blood-red crosses and tubes, all being in conflict with one another, as if fighting, then they fell earthward in a flaming mass, eventually fading away leaving a great vapor.' Another broadsheet, written by Samuel Coccius, relates that on 'August 7, 1566, at sunrise, many large black globes were seen in the air, moving before the sun with great speed, and turning against each other as if fighting. Some of them became red and fiery and afterwards faded and went out.'

"It is interesting to note that these phenomena were seen across the face of the sun at sunrise, for what reason we do not know, nor do we know what caused the symbols to appear. But from these and other recorded reports we do know, or at least we accept, that symbols or images do appear across the face of the sun at certain times, often at sunrise. It would appear the Inca sun priests were able at will to produce phenomena such as solar beings through a technology of reflected light that in some way acted on the brain rhythms."

An associate raised a hand to ask a question: "Haven't drugs such as LSD-25, mushrooms and the like produced similar symbols?"

I nodded. "Yes, but it would be an error to compare the kind of symbols produced by drugs with these solar phenomena. In the first place, drugs produce hallucinations only in the person under their influence. We are speaking of a phenomenon experienced by many persons en masse, an external, not an internal, manifestation of images. Drugs cannot produce something that is not there; they do not bestow new knowledge and it would be a mistake to believe so."

"Are we to believe the globes or crosses observed by the witnesses you mention are psychic phenomena produced by the inner workings of the unconscious mind, or do they have an external material nature?" asked an associate.

"Both."

"What do you mean?"

"The power of the psyche has the ability to produce images—images that are produced in the inner space of the psychic senses, and these images have some characteristics of physical reality: they can appear in the external space of physical reality. For example, so-called flying saucers have been visually observed and also picked up on a radar screen. They vanish later, because the mind is not able to hold them in material form, just as in my own case the visions of solar beings vanished because of my inexperience."

"How do you explain this?" someone else asked.

"As we have been saying right from the start, the energy field that sustains the physical organism is part of another dimension. We have here a panpsychism. All physical reality is the result of some psychic or mental projection. Physical reality and psychic phenomena are interrelated. There is continual exchange, more apparent to some than to others, which appears as images, recollections, memories, glimpses of the future or of other-dimensional life that cannot be explained. To give an example, the sun priests developed a technology of communication with other dimensions. This explains why the Incas believed themselves to be children of the sun. It was from the sun and from solar beings that they derived their knowledge. They made unconscious thoughts or ideas become conscious ones through symbols; they made the invisible visible—by their own will and determination. They took their destiny into their own hands—and by so doing they gave their minds an added dimension by extending them into other worlds.

"Evidently this knowledge helped the Incas conquer a large part of South America and bring many millions of people under the influence of their solar religion, although I understand they did not teach their solar technology to the masses. All dictatorships, no matter how benevolent originally, eventually become destructive by their efforts to weaken the development of the individuals under their control, to keep them concerned with material existence and to keep them ignorant of their spiritual heritage. To enslave a people and hide the truth of their access to other worlds is to invite quick and sudden collapse of an empire. The same could be said of spiritual realities, which, by stressing materialism, force mankind to devote nearly all of its energies just to eke out a living. Man and his world are sustained by basically spiritual forces. To deny that is to deny human beings the source of their strength, of their origins—sheer suicide for an individual or for a nation. It is imperative that we of the Project make every effort to share our knowledge with others and that we elevate the teachings that have come into our possession, or at least elevate our understanding of them, to heights never before realized."

Another question came from the floor. "May we have the particulars of the technique of the Inca mirror and of its technology?"

"That will be the subject of our next symposium," I said. "For the time being, please apply the techniques as given. When we meet again we will summarize. Thank you for your kind attention."

With these words the meeting closed.

20

Light Alchemy

Project Center, Reno, Nevada

October 19, 1974—A group of researchers sat in the conference room, allowing the light from the stroboscope to fall upon their closed eyelids. Except for the flicker from the strobe, the room was in total darkness. The associates had been involved in the experiment for over an hour now and their brains whirled with sparks of light, symbols and strange sensations produced by the varying frequency of the strong light. It was to be our final experiment with the stroboscope.

Each had read the brief technical report on brain waves prior to coming into the room.

> *When subjected to the slow delta rhythm (1 to 3 cycles per second) often dominant in epileptics, in persons suffering brain damage or mental illness, in infants and in others during sleep produced by light flashes from the stroboscope, some researchers were unable to function properly, if at all, because of the changes in the cortical neurons. Visual stimulation on the theta rhythms (4 to 7 cycles per second) can result in states of anxiety and frustration and even anger (especially if the subject has been subjected to irritating conditions, disappointments or overwork). Researchers have reported annoyance or mild headaches from both delta and theta flicker rates. If prolonged, these frequencies have a most disturbing effect and researchers will usually discontinue them. If they are continued, most experience these fre-*

202

quencies as a pulling sensation in the solar plexus, or as a dull pain in the cerebellum area. Theta is a disagreeable stimulus and is not a normal part of brain rhythms in adults. People who have been deeply hurt by another person, by insult or injury, show theta rhythms. Emotional stress also results in this rhythm flooding the brain. Even the removal of a pleasant sensation will result in theta rhythms.

A bad mood follows, with the subject showing crankiness and ill temper. When submitted to long exposure to theta flicker, subjects have reported being overcome by moods of guilt or sadness, without any apparent reason. The alpha flicker, the most dominant rhythm in normal adults (8 to 13 cycles per second), is closely associated with the opening and closing of the eyes.

Some experimenters believe alpha rhythms are the electrical manifestation of muscle tremor in the eyes, and that people with good vision do not have alpha rhythm, which suggests that this rhythm is a sign of possible disease. This may be only partially true. Alpha frequencies are usually predominant in personality types who think in unimaginative perceptions rather than visual ones—alpha rhythms will remain dominant even with the eyes open in this type.

Closing the eyes permits one to think in more visual terms since open eyes bring sharp visual details, and therefore interference with thought. However, even with the subject's eyelids closed, alpha flicker from a brilliant source of light registers on the retina. Alpha flicker induces many moving patterns and symbols. This is particularly true when the frequency is 10 cycles per second.

When the flicker is speeded up to 25 cycles per second, beta frequency, the patterns take on brilliant colors and become more complex designs. Often beta rhythms are indicative of anxiety states and may be present in those under stress. They are also evident in persons who are fully alert, such as someone solving a problem.

A flicker rate of 50 per second, about double the speed of the flicker produced by a motion-picture projector, has caused spasmodic jerking of the body or even more violent states in some subjects. The flicker of a fluorescent light, 100 to 120 cycles per second, can cause nervousness in some persons. Fortunately, this last problem is rare. But the subjects' reaction to artificial flicker is most dramatic.

Flicker with a natural source of light—the sun, for example— heightens this reaction. Riding in a car under tree branches with *sunlight streaming down on the eyes in flicker action, looking at sunlight dancing upon moving water, or viewing the sun through a flicker apparatus are natural flicker experiences. However dramatic these reactions or sensations may be, there is no general rule that applies to everyone, because of variations in personality types, emotional and mental outlooks and states of mental alertness.*

Researchers familiar with exposure to sunlight have a response to brain-rhythm frequency different from ordinary people. The brain frequency experienced, i.e., delta, theta, alpha, beta or omega (250 c.p.s. or more) would determine, to a large degree, what the reaction would be. The will of the person is also important.

Experiments have shown that a reaction to flicker from natural or artificial light can be predetermined. The flashing symbols or observed patterns could carry a significant message which, though perceived in fractions of a second, might require days or even weeks to interpret, though the signal might be deciphered instantly by another, more experienced subject. Some persons experience a peculiar taste in the mouth while viewing the sun. Others may hear a buzzing or ringing sound, or they may feel a tingling or prickling sensation on the skin, indicating that light energy is spilling over from the visual areas of the brain to other portions. This also shows the interrelationship of the sensory organs.

Intake of solar energy seems to sensitize a sixth sense that influences the lower sensory makeup. These are some of the delta and theta reactions; others include confusion, fear and depression. It has been found that these rhythms are suppressed in good-tempered individuals, but may be activated by negative stimuli such as emotional stress, overwork, mental strain, insults, offenses or disagreeable surroundings. Higher frequencies may evoke sensations of timelessness, spacelessness, universality and states of heightened intelligence and inner illumination.

Personality types respond to light stimulus according to the dictates of their brain rhythms, or so it appears. Strong alpha types might find flicker rates of 10 cycles per second can cause sensations of moving images and symbols. Delta and theta persons react to corresponding flicker frequencies by displaying bad temper, critical or negative attitudes and irritation. A beta type would struggle against any delta or theta flicker reactions and try to overcome them, because the lower frequencies would result in severe headaches.

An omega type's reaction to any of the above flicker frequencies would be quite different. An alpha frequency might result in observed symbols or images, but these signals would be coded and have deeper meanings. Delta and theta flicker might give annoyance to the omega type, who would struggle against any negative reactions and overcome them. A beta flicker (or one of higher frequency, e.g., 50 to 120 c.p.s.) would also have less impact on an omega type.

While all the known brain rhythms would continue to be registered during different stages of wakefulness and sleep, as with any normal adult, a faster frequency would be evident, especially while applying solar-eye techniques.

Indeed, beta or omega rhythms would more than likely be a stimulant, depending upon the kind of light source, with a corresponding sensation of optimism. Any advanced adult operating on a fast brain rhythm, such as omega, would function as a high-speed type and his or her reactions to fast flicker frequency would be converted to energy.

With development of consciousness by intake of the X-factor, the atomic light body would be activated. Faster-frequency energy forms could easily be converted into usable energy. Being familiar with high-frequency emissions from the sun (the X-factor is just such a frequency) the research associate is better able to react to negative or lower frequencies.

Symbols can be deciphered or decoded by the advanced researcher even with the eyes closed and the mind and brain at rest (the less advanced might not detect them at all). Symbols from the sun are frequency patterns that contain messages of IF and the language of consciousness. The adept can usually "feel" the brain-rhythm rate while in the presence of another person (delta and theta types radiate a negative vibration registered as a pain in the cerebellum area or a pulling in the area of the solar plexus).

Low-frequency rhythms cause disturbances in the electrical fields of the adept, whose rhythms are functioning at a higher rate, with a resulting loss of energy. An associate will usually try to avoid these persons when possible. With perceptions far more acute than an electroencephalograph, the researcher can explore areas denied the technician, because no electrical device can match the intricate sensitivity of the human nervous system.

They had also read a short description of symbols:

We have explained that a symbol or pattern is a carrier of information (IF). Such a symbol or pattern is the physical counterpart of transmitted information. Symbols or patterns are frequencies. IF is generated from an ultra-dimensional source, encoded and directed to the physical universe. This message transmission, to have any practical value, must be decoded somewhere along the line. The human organism is tuned to respond to certain stimuli from the moment of birth.

Throughout life, information is amassed and stored in the nervous system. Only a small amount of sensory information is required for the organism to react to stimuli. However, the greater portion of transmitted energy goes far beyond the data of perceptual life, that is, beyond the five senses. Extrasensory information is also stored away, and a person may go through life without ever using it—or even knowing it is there. Once an individual becomes aware of this transmitted information, he ascends the evolutionary scale, but few ever accomplish this. Let's see how these stimuli may become activated and used.

The brain may be compared to a giant computer having thousands of millions of electrical cells and memory banks which handle information input brought in by the sense organs. The brain is programmed to respond to stimuli. Only a few cells are involved in normal input. When the eyes are exposed to sunlight, brain rhythms speed up and millions of cells discharge, as light is transformed into neural energy. The brain's reaction to these strong stimuli triggers mechanisms which ordinarily are not used. Able to handle far more energy than is used in normal vision, and with an almost infinite capacity for learning, the brain begins to process the light stimuli.

As the research associate knows from experience, vivid symbols and patterns similar to phosphenes are often perceived. While it may be moot whether the images are produced in the retina, in the brain or in the light itself, there is evidence to indicate that all three are involved. An electromagnetic wave encoded with IF is registered upon the retina and transmitted to the brain, where an image and a message are perceived as a frequency pattern by the subject. Whether the IF is decoded or not is determined by the sensitivity and advancement of the receiver. When perceived and decoded, an image or symbol is experienced.

We have stressed that transformation of self is assisted through identification with archetypal symbols. The unconscious is linked with the conscious, and the individual is made aware of ultra-dimensional reality. When the symbols are experienced, the mind may be flooded with ideas, memories and creative thoughts. The research associate uses various techniques to become acquainted with these symbols, for, as we have pointed out, it is essential for the adept to become fully conscious of these image symbols. A previous paper described the effects of blinking, on-off stimuli, the presence of light as one kind of stimuli and the absence of light as another, as discussed by Bates. The electronic stroboscope, with a capability of producing light flashes in fractions of a cycle per second, produces artificial light to stimulate the retina and brain. The techniques using the sun as a light source are much more dramatic when applied by those skilled in these techniques.

The research associate is familiar with the effects of solar-energy intake and the exhilarating states of well-being that follow it. The actual identification of IF, experiencing a message transmission, can be a transcendent sensation, particularly when accompanied by the act of stepping into another dimension (usually experienced as recall of an incident not yet lived in the present time continuum or as a flash of insight).

Time plus the three spatial dimensions is the space-time continuum. Since consciousness is a dimension in itself, the consciousness-space-time continuum is another world of reality experience. When consciousness is activated, new realities are experienced. These are thrilling to say the least, for they prove that one is not limited to three dimensions. Often vivid recollections of past events are brought forth.

The adept discovers that the effects are startling. Results vary with the individual and may be determined by mental or emotional states. The results have included (1) memory of past events; (2) perception of brilliant images or symbols; (3) impression of timelessness; (4) projection into another dimension of reality; (5) reality of future experience in another dimension of time; (6) acute awareness of surrounding environment, such as sounds, smells, presences, and so on; (7) insight and creative impressions; (8) instantaneous decisions or problem solving; (9) actualization of higher consciousness, best described as a personal experience of immortality—one becomes part of another dimension in a future time continuum, which demonstrates to the

*individual that death of the physical mind-body will not or did not
claim him or her; (10) transcendent states of being; (11) visions; (12)
self-absorbed perception of unreality or unworldliness. These and
other experiences may be perceived by the advanced research associate
while conducting the strobe experiments and the more advanced solar
techniques, which are part of a separate paper.*

The strobe light had begun at the slow delta rhythm, then
graduated up to theta, alpha, beta and on up the scale to the
higher omega. Results of each rhythm had been recorded. The
omega result had not yet been put down.

"What do you see now?" I asked a researcher sitting next to me.
I had placed a small gold mirror off to one side of his eye and
reflected the strobe light onto his eyelids.

"Checkerboards of black and white, stars, galaxies. There! I see
them! Eyes staring back at me! My God! There's hundreds of
them!" The researcher almost screamed, grabbing my arm and
squeezing it tightly above the elbow. "Keep it at that rate. I want to
see them."

I checked the dial glowing in the darkness. It was set at 250 c.p.s.
I did not move it. By the light of a penlight I examined the
controls on a small brain-wave amplifier and modulator isolator
which served as an electroencephalograph for the research team
to make sure the controls were properly set. Everything checked.
Through my earphones I had been monitoring the brain-wave
frequency beating out a steady rhythm of about thirty or forty
cycles per second.

Suddenly there was a change—a rapid increase in frequency.
What had been a steady rhythmic beat of blips I could clearly hear
had now changed to a fast purr or humming noise as the rhythm
increased, a sign the brain waves had speeded up into the omega
range. I guessed their frequency to be in the neighborhood of 200
to 250 cycles per second. Quickly, I examined the electrodes to see
that they were properly attached. I felt the yellow reference wire
secured to my associate's forehead, the white wire at the right
temple, and the violet wire at the left temple. I felt the circular
adhesive pads with my fingers and pressed softly to make certain
the electrode paste securing them was firm. Then I pressed the
earphones tightly to my ears in order to hear better.

After fifteen or twenty seconds I said, "Now look straight into the eyes nearest you and concentrate. Look deep into the eyes — try to see within them. Ignore the other eyes entirely. Try not to breathe: keep your breath very still."

"Okay," the research associate mumbled.

Thirty seconds passed. No one spoke. All eyes were focused intently on the man's illuminated, specterlike face that alternated black and white as it reflected the bright flicker of the stroboscope. The channeled brow was contracted, the jaws tightly set, the lips straight. The only sound was the soft purring of the apparatus. The EEG machine now increased to an even higher pitch, the rhythm becoming much faster than before. The exact speed would be checked on tape later. Another thirty seconds elapsed.

"What do you see now?" I asked quietly.

"A beautiful golden face," came the solemn reply, almost a whisper. "A beautiful face from another world."

After a few more seconds I turned off the stroboscope. "That's enough for now. Lights, please," I said. The subjects pressed their palms against their eyes to shut out the bright overhead lights.

For several minutes the associates listened to the description of the eyes and the golden figure observed by the researcher. Many had experienced similar visions during the strobe experiments. Others, like me, had been fortunate enough to have observed these forms during the sunlight techniques, utilizing the golden mirrors. No matter how often these forms were observed, no one tired of hearing the explanations and experiences. Many took notes.

When the researcher had finished, I positioned myself behind the lectern.

"We have, through these experiments, observed for ourselves that forms and images can be produced by light illuminating the eye. Now we can ask ourselves how these images differ from those produced in sleep while dreaming, and those produced through the use of drugs, hypnotism and similar means. We want to know whether these forms are real. Or are they simply hallucinations? I would like to read you a short passage taken from Tylor's *Early History of Mankind,* which recounts a legend of the Quiche Indians of Central America preserved by Abbé Brasseur de Bourbourg.

Now, behold, our ancients and our fathers were made lords, and had their dawn. Behold, we will relate also the rising of the sun, the moon, and the stars! Great was their joy when they saw the morning star, which came out first, with its resplendent face before the sun. At last the sun itself began to come forth. An innumerable crowd of people were there, and the dawn cast light on all these people at once. At last the face of the ground was dried by the sun: like a man the sun showed himself, and his presence warmed and dried the surface of the ground. Before the sun appeared, muddy and wet was the surface of the ground, and it was before the sun appeared, and then only the sun rose like a man. But his heat had no strength, and he did but show himself when he rose; he only remained like [an image in] a mirror; and it is not, indeed, the same sun that appears now, they say, in the stories.

"I believe the account is interesting for several reasons, one being that the sun had appeared after a long period, but, more important, the sun is compared to a human form emerging as a mirror image, suggesting that ethereal forms of the Godhead were manifested to mankind in the pale light of the sun.

"Think back to Punchao, the golden mirror of the Incas. Remember how they were able to produce, or to cause to be produced, the golden image of some celestial being or beings by letting the small reflectors catch the first light of the day. This fact cannot be put aside without serious thought, because it demonstrates the personification of the Godhead appearing out of natural elements—that is, it indicates an incarnate God or gods, which we of a scientific era reject, being more inclined towards the concept of an abstract God—a force rather than a person. What secret knowledge did the Incas possess that allowed them to accomplish this feat? We have, over the past several weeks, duplicated the technique, having observed eyes, ethereal forms and faces. That we can alter what is observed is of genuine interest. Let's pursue the matter further.

"From the most ancient times, solar priests kept the uses of polarized light a secret. In Peru, sun priests used a concave parabolic mirror of gold to direct rays of the sun when they were relighting the temple fires for the coming year. Not only mirrors, but crystals and other stones were used to alter the effects of sunlight while sacred rites and ceremonies were performed. The priests were aware of the action of polarized light and its inner secrets, later guessed at by the alchemists of Europe. While polarized light was used in many ways by the old sun priests of the Americas, both natural and polarized sunlight were primarily used for the transformation of the priests themselves. Their interest was the elevation of man above matter, as the ruler of the world. They understood the importance of bringing in energy originating outside the organism and putting it to practical use . . . methods which were hidden from the profane, or so it appears now. How did they do it?

"Man lives in a universe in which every positive action has an equal negative one. Every particle of matter has a corresponding opposite. Each visible element originates out of or is allied with an invisible one. In other words, there is a plus-and-minus potential in matter. For each positively charged particle, an antiparticle with a negative charge exists. Einstein was one of the first to identify energy with matter, as in his famous equation $E=mc^2$. When matter collides with its antipotential, it is transmuted to pure energy. Elementary particles such as the photon and neutral pi meson degenerate into neutrons and radiation in a burst of light. The sun can generate energy over billions of years without decaying. That is the difference between atomic and solar fusion. The atomic-hydrogen gas of the sun differs from that of an atomic device in that the hydrogen of the sun is not heavy hydrogen. It is interesting to note that old age and the eventual death of the human organism are caused by the accumulation of heavy water. The solar adept is able to emulate the sun by keeping the heavy water, and thus heavy hydrogen, in his organism to a minimum.

"Knowledge that life forces can be enhanced through proper understanding has extremely practical advantages to solar adepts. They can emphasize the positive aspects of solar energy, which occur with left-hand polarized light. The understanding of this phenomenon helps one to grasp the secret of life itself, although we caution the research associate not to emphasize the physical aspects of solar energy over the intelligence factors it contains. The phenomenon teaches us that man changes, or is able to change, according to environmental conditions.

"A light-being person is optically active, similar to a crystal, if I may make the comparison. Living organisms, which appear to be neutral in their ability to polarize light, are actually able to twist polarized light either to the left or right, as do organic compounds of living things. Because energized force fields surrounding a solar adept are similar to the atmosphere, they react to sunlight.

"All life seems to display left-handedness, as Pasteur first discovered. All amino acids display left-handedness. The earth turns from west to east, which causes the sun to exert an asymmetrical influence, which appears to us on the earth as an east-to-west force, through the atmosphere. The earth has north and south magnetic poles.

"The solar adepts were the first to discover that elliptically polarized light, reflected from a mirrored surface, combined with the sun's east-west force, or magnetic field, resulted in a one-handed twist suitable to their own uses in temple initiations. Some researchers have postulated that it was the action of polarized sunlight on the surface of the oceans that brought forth life on the earth . . . a plausible theory, considering that basic organic molecules have a left-handed twist.

"Acknowledging that the world is a left-handed system, modern adepts were able to bring even more positive energy into their force fields, brains, and nervous systems, which tended to vitalize or energize them. The priests became a higher class—the ruling class—endowed with the knowledge of the universe and immortality. Naturally, they were looked upon as gods by the lower classes. Added energy alters the molecular structure of living tissue, as the organism is more akin to light than to matter. This fact might account for the levitation performed by some masters.

"An abundance of energy would also account for additional IF or intelligence levels attained by ancient and modern adepts. You research associates are warned that we are not speaking of worldly knowledge. Just as we regard PK, PSI, ESP and the like as meaningless physical phenomena and uses of the mind, we want to stress an even higher form of knowledge from a faculty not activated in normal persons: consciousness of a different sort of reality. One example is the ability to project oneself into a new state of existence that includes many abilities shared in common by masters of antiquity. The greatest of these is prophecy, made possible by our overcoming the time barrier.

"One of the keys to understanding the proper use of solar energy can be found in Planck's equation, $E = nhv$, giving the energy of a quantum of radiation as a constant multiple of its frequency. We would interpret this in our own system to mean that it is essential for the solar adept to increase the frequency of the force fields in order to benefit from solar-energy intake. The importance of this cannot be overemphasized. Man is linked with the cosmos through the medium of the sun. Above this, our personal level of consciousness must be linked with the impersonal or universal consciousness.

"In the science of communication theory, information is any input to the brain which reduces its state of uncertainty. In our system of cosmic communication experience, we teach you how to preselect specific information, which we call X, for the good of the individual organism. As in communication theory, any information which fails to assist the organism to make decisions is useless.

"Communication theory calls this kind of input 'noise,' like the garbled static on a radio or TV set. The nervous system hunts for information the way a scanning system does. Like any scanning device, it is programmed. It will record only that input with which it is familiar. We have learned that only a fraction of the input to the brain is ever utilized by the organism. The greater part of this input is just dissipated.

"Take electromagnetic energy, for example. A specific wavelength is experienced by most people as a particular color. An object that reflects light of a wavelength in the neighborhood of 7000 angstroms will be observed as red by most people. But to someone who is color-blind, it will be seen as green, which actually has a wavelength in the 5000- to 5700-angstrom range. Green is seen as gray by many color-blind persons. Some people see green when most people see blue. Solar adepts often distinguish colors in what normal vision perceives as white, and they sometimes experience fluorescence while looking at certain shades of standard colors. Peripheral vision, looking at an object from the side of the eye, as opposed to viewing it directly, results in more vivid colors being observed. We see, then, that everyone sees a little differently from everyone else.

"Light energy is sent as information from the retina to the brain. For example, most people can recognize different geometric designs: a circle is round; a square is different from a triangle. However, there are those who cannot distinguish any difference, particularly some primitive tribes and those suffering from congenital blindness who have been enabled to see later in life. Experiments have shown that months of learning are sometimes required before some of those with restored sight can differentiate a circle from a square or a triangle from a cube. Simple designs are all alike until the subjects learn to tell the difference between shapes. So shape, like color, is not a quality that is automatically recognizable by everyone.

"Like language, visual perception is a learned ability; this ability varies with the kind of learning one has experienced. Colors and shapes are stimuli. An organism's reaction to a stimulus depends to a great extent upon its ability to handle it, not only upon the stimulus itself. The same would apply to energy IF. Some people may react one way to a certain stimulus, others another way. Stimuli might reduce uncertainty and be useful information to one, whereas they might be wasted on another.

"We have learned that colors correspond to energy frequencies. So do shapes. Colors and shapes are vibrating energy frequencies and, as stimuli, transmit information. Colors might appear beautiful or ugly. The same applies to shapes; it all depends on the beholder. In our system of communication, vision and light are of paramount importance. Archetypal symbols, like phosphenes, are oscillating phenomena that transmit information. They are not mute designs, but radiant suns, each symbol having its own frequency. This is important because we think in frequencies. Memories are frequencies. We have only to tune to a certain frequency in order to be able to recall past events. Tuning in to archetypal symbols helps us to communicate with the future and with other dimensions and to know our ultra-dimensional selves. In order to communicate with the cosmos, we must learn how to tune in our levels of consciousness to certain frequencies, a dynamic process of self-information.

"Let's familiarize ourselves with the basics of this study. All forms of energy are manifested in patterns or symbols. Pythagoras would say everything is numbers. Plato might say everything is simple designs made complex by combination; for example, from simple triangles one can build the equilateral triangle, the rectangle, the parallelogram, the rhombus and the hexagon, which can in turn be combined to form the five Platonic solids—the tetrahedron, the cube, the octahedron, the dodecahedron and the icosahedron. Observation reveals that atoms group themselves into patterns, as do molecules. From subnuclear particles to clusters of galaxies, the whole universe is an interrelated structure of patterned energy, played upon by opposing forces. All forms of learning involve symbolic abstract patterns.

"Associates have been encouraged to experiment on themselves. Self-application of techniques is the only means of participating in cosmic phenomena and thereby increasing one's level of awareness. We are all familiar with the brilliant displays of colors and shapes experienced in phosphene stimulation. Absorption of solar energy often results in the observation of moving patterns similar to phosphenes, such as sun wheels, spinning disks, rotating spirals, flashes of starlike light, colored rays, geometric designs, and so on. These colors and shapes are usually ultra-dimensional, and though they are 'seen' the experience is more than merely visual. The oscillation of the sun, its whirling or vibrating motion and its change from brilliant white to brilliant black, is a case in point. This phenomenon is usually observed when the sun is viewed off to one side for a period of at least 30 seconds, preferably at sunrise or sunset. Figure 1 in your notes is a line drawing of the oscillating sun, but it does not depict what is

observed; only by experiencing the sensation can it be appreciated clearly. The apparent bobbling or oscillation of the sun may be partially explained by the fact that the eye changes position about every 0.1 to 0.3 seconds, 30 to 70 cycles per second, when looking at an object. Ordinary objects do not appear to move because they are not nearly as bright as the sun, which has an optical intensity of 1.5×10^8 candles per square foot. When viewed through a dark filter, the sun, like ordinary objects, does not oscillate.

"Light produces afterimages on the retina. As the eyes jump about, these afterimages blend with the actual image of the bright sun to give the viewer the sensation of a vibrating sun changing from dark to light. Any light falling on the retina will activate the cones. When the eyes move, other cones are inhibited. This results in dark and light images. The workings of eye tremors and cone on-off cycles may be tested by experiment by looking at Figure 1 for 30 seconds."

There was a slight shuffling of papers as delegates leafed through their notes to the sketch.

"While viewing the center sun, the rays will appear to form into a pattern, usually a cross or star-ray effect, and colors may be seen at the edges. Rays may also appear to oscillate and bend. The eye will not follow smoothly along the lines of the circle, but will move in jerking movements, which result in changing patterns on the retina. The same effect may be produced by moving the sketch with the hands. After staring at the drawing for a minute or so, if you direct your gaze at a blank sheet of white paper, two clusters of grainy patterns will appear, followed by a ring of black surrounded by a white circle. This afterimage will slowly fade.

"All these effects are known to vary according to emotional state, cardiac rate, and brain-wave and breathing rhythms, which are influenced by the mental state or general health of the organism. Remember that images in the retina are transferred to the visual section of the brain at the back of the head. These images, which last about a tenth of a second, are superimposed on one another. There are some 147,000 cones per square millimeter in the center of the fovea centralis, the point of sharpest vision, each capable of transmitting an image to the cortex as the retina continuously moves about, stimulating different cones. Hun-

RIGHT—Project "X" writer and technical editor Elena Baugh and Anna Quintana of Guatemala chat during seminar in Mexico in 1973.

BELOW—Members of Project "X" during one of the more leisurely moments at Anthropological Museum, Mexico City.

Ellen Seaman (right), who has transcribed over a million words on Project "X," with Rita Segal, also a member of the Project, at Tula.

The *Karin-Elke* at anchor on a tributary of the Amazon.

Project "X" Photo

ABOVE—Author and fellow-explorer Carl C. Landegger, who assisted on the search for vestiges of the Amazons, examining potsherds picked up in the course of the explorations.

RIGHT—Landegger studies pictographs on cliff site near Monte Alegre, Brazil.

ABOVE—Canoemen of Amazon Expedition at cataracts above Curua, Brazil.

RIGHT—Landegger and author discuss whether to go on by land or return to ship at anchor farther down the river. *Project "X" Photo*

BELOW—Pictograph representing the sun was found on a boulder near the Amazon, in Brazil. Such evidence suggests that the sun played a prominent part in the spiritual life of the people who occupied the area in ancient times.

RIGHT—Pictograph of a human figure with solar crown found near the glyph shown below left, facing page. In this unusual combination of human and astral bodies, the symbol for the sun replaces the head.

CENTER—Dwelling of the Uaicas Indians of the Sierra Parima region, in northwestern Brazil, near Venezuela. As the expedition airplane passed over, the Indians ran out from the hut, which was believed to measure about one hundred feet in diameter. The explorers were not able to land in the isolated area.

BELOW—Forested cliffs believed to be the Yacamiaba heights, where the Amazon warriors made their home.

James C. Geoghegan, research associate of Project "X," discusses findings with the author at the center in Reno, Nevada.

The author checks transcripts with his wife, Sylvia, and with editor Elena Baugh, at the Project Center in Reno.   *Photos by Bud Fisher*

At the Pyramid of the Moon at Teotihuacan, Mexico, the author lectures to members of Project "X." The larger Pyramid of the Sun stands in the background.

Photos by John Walker

Members of the Project head toward the Pyramid of the Sun, at whose summit they will conduct experiments.

At Lake Tahoe, members of the Project listen to author's lecture on the research being conducted.

Photos by John Walker

dreds of jerking-eye movements, involving many thousands of rods and cones, are made while looking at an object. Vision is a search for information and therefore is a scanning system. The two retinas transmit to the brain two major images, composed of numerous individual images. These two images blend into a single image or stereogram, imprinted on the brain. The whole process is a flicker system, in which different images combine in the cortex to make patterns of registered information. This flicker system appears to be regulated by rhythms much like brain waves.

"Where there is energy frequency, there is information. Any collection of rays or waves emitted by any source must be perceived as a pattern. This is significant, because it shows any energy pattern is a physical manifestation of transmitted intelligence or information, that is, it contains a message. It has only to be received and registered to be translated. Frequency patterns can be detected by scientific instruments, in fact, that's what a radio or a TV set does. Radio telescopes also pick up garbled emissions, which are not intelligible, from the sun and other stellar bodies. Frequency patterns of consciousness from higher dimensions, usually experienced as archetypal symbols, can be detected and translated by advanced research associates.

"Curiously enough, vision is not a photographic process, with outside objects transmitted to the brain as a camera captures pictures. Indeed, millions of cones, nerves and brain cells are involved in a process that registers images and then involves the nervous system. In other words, these images impress the mind with information.

"The Incas were able to make contact with images in a manner virtually unknown to modern man—and by so doing, they expanded their awareness of the cosmos. They used an alchemy of light to transform ordinary sunlight into gold—golden images that personified sunlight, and, we can speculate, gave the Incas a knowledge of things unseen.

"Each of you must become familiar with the uses of light in all forms, especially sunlight, and expand your knowledge of its true form. For the time being, continue with your experiments."

The meeting was adjourned.

21

Cosmic/Solar Energy Intelligence Factors

Project Center, Reno, Nevada

December 17, 1974—The stack of manuscript paper—the result of eight weeks' writing—loomed before me. I thought what I had written revealed a lot less than I had wanted to say. It was becoming more difficult to express with the written word the many ideas and thoughts that seemed to emerge from within my new-found consciousness.

Writing on an electric typewriter had become tedious, clumsy and time-consuming. Speaking into a tape recorder was no less an effort, because the spoken word did not really lend itself to what I wanted to explain. Language, the words and the grammar by which men understand one another, seemed inadequate, too, because the alphabet provided no effective means of describing objects that consisted mainly of sounds. I longed for an electronic instrument, perhaps a computer, that could be linked up to my nervous system and my energy fields—or to wherever the seat of consciousness might reside—that could record the information as it flowed out of my reservoir of creative thought and organize the ideas into a syntax of intelligible words and sentences. Then a print-out could be studied. But even such an invention would not guarantee that my ideas could be conveyed by language in the usual sense of the word.

Perhaps a pictorial series of ideograms or symbols more suitable to enlightened minds trained in such a system could be devised. I envisioned something like chemical formulas or mathematical equations or the sacred characters of the Egyptian and Mayan hieroglyphics—not in the archaic or traditional sense of secrecy—but new images that could be charged with energy and information from the higher consciousness levels (just as are the psychic images of dreams). The images might be transmitted to and impressed upon the mind through the eyes, much as members of the Project were doing by means of sunlight, and through the appearance of living images charged with information.

The idea of a new cosmic language captured my attention. Certainly language is energy—and energy is information. The human mind has an insatiable appetite for energy and information—they are the mind's food. The mind stores energy and information, uses it as it becomes available or draws upon reserves. Knowledge is a kind of energy, the raw material from which it is made: man grows and develops on information.

The connection between energy and information was a concept I understood well. I knew all life on the planet had evolved from sunlight. The light and other energy streaming forth from the sun held atoms and molecules together and organized matter into living things that responded to the cosmic order of the sun's information and to the intelligence factors packed into its radiation. Man, the supreme being on the planet, evolved out of sunlight no less than did the lower forms of life and is dependent upon these lower forms for oxygen and food.

It seemed natural to me that man would eventually concentrate upon the sun and learn how to obtain energy and information directly from it. This was the task to which I had devoted twenty years of my adult life. Experience had taught me that finding the answer to the quest would require direct involvement. Other forms of human knowledge could be shared through merely reading scientific papers and books and listening to lectures. Like eating, absorbing sunlight into the nervous system and learning how to process cosmic information was an undertaking that had to be participated in by each person if the benefits were to be experienced.

Access to cosmic knowledge or information outside the realm of earthly knowledge is realized by interstellar communication with the sun, the source of all life on our planet. Only the human organism is designed to receive solar information through the eyes and nervous system in a way that can further the evolution of the species.

My theory was that through the medium of sunlight and through the human mind a total knowledge of the universe could be realized. Perhaps God would speak to man not through sacred scripture or prophets, but directly, through the light of the sun. Man had only to understand the language of light in order to fathom the mysteries of creation and taste immortal life.

The developing interest of the world in solar reasearch was a subject I had often thought about. Because of the high cost of fossil fuels and the fact that petroleum and coal can not last indefinitely, direct use and control of the sun's energy will, sooner or later, be essential. It was clear to me that as man learns to increase his uses and control of the sun's energy, he will be forced to reckon with the information factors contained in that energy. At first this idea was just a theory, but my research had proven that energy intelligence factors (IF) had to be considered from a practical point of view. As the creative force of the universe, sunlight would prove to involve more than was generally believed, if only because the sun was man's doorway to the universe . . . and once opened, the flood of incoming light would bring the natural sciences into direct contact with the realm of the spirit.

The marriage of science with religion would not be far away, because the application of sunlight in concentrated form by means of solar generators would expose man to a high level of solar intelligence factors. All organic fuels, and even man's food, are the products of sunlight and the photochemical combination of carbon dioxide, water and minerals through photosynthesis, an ability that has been lost by man and animals. All living things exist because of their ability to consume, in one form or another, electrons as they are excited by solar photons. To what degree life processes are regulated by the organizing intelligence within this solar energy remains to be discovered, or at least to be better understood. With the advent of a solar age in which man increasingly turns his attention to the uses of solar energy, these IF factors should bring about changes in man's attitudes.

Years before, I had learned of the intelligence factors within sunlight and how to control them, or at least how to make them respond to my mind. One example was an experiment in which I filled a crystal container with equal amounts of sea water and rain water. I decided on a quartz crystal container because of its ability to polarize sunlight. By focusing sunlight directly on the container with a circular parabolic mirror the contents were heated to 98°F. After dropping in several crystals of iodine and bits of kelp, I noted that the polarized sunlight caused a stream of tiny luminescent objects to rise to the top of the container in a spiral-like motion, reaching for the sun. One day, I found that the tiny bits reacted to my stare, twisting from one side to the other. I discovered I could, by mental projection, reverse their action, changing the right-hand spiral to a left-hand spiral. The crystal-like bits appeared to be responding to my mind, but I had no explanation for the phenomenon.

This experiment explained in some measure the error of Pasteur, who attempted to induce asymmetry by growing crystals between powerful magnets. He was unable to create any kind of handedness in this experiment. Later, he grew plants in sunlight reflected by mirrors which created the effect of reversing the normal path of the sun from east to west. Again the experiment showed no handedness effects. Pasteur had observed that molecules have either left-handed or right-handed twists, and he sought by this experiment to cause the plants to grow substances that would twist light in an opposite direction by reversing the effect of the falling sunlight. He had not known that certain intelligence factors were involved that directed, for example, the pattern of left-handedness in the amino acids of all living tissue.

Fascinated by my experiment, I spent weeks observing sunlight and its effect on different solutions in water. To me, the container of water was a model of the earth's primeval oceans, in which sunlight found a favorable environment of ammonia, methane and hydrogen that was able to respond to the living intelligence factors contained within its radiations. The experiment had demonstrated the possibility of living organisms having evolved spontaneously through the action of powerful ultraviolet radiation passing through an oxygen-free atmosphere and acting upon simple hydrocarbon molecules in the primordial waters, thereby transforming the primitive organic substances, beginning with amino acids, the building blocks of protein, to more complex molecules, such as nucleic acids.

However, my interest went beyond the chemical composition as it was affected by polarized sunlight. I was engrossed in the intelligence or information factors, the organizing agency of sunlight, and how they may have caused life to emerge from the basic elements. Though the test conditions were far from those present when there was no living thing on earth, and although the test itself was less than scientific, it demonstrated to me the possibility that life had an extraterrestrial origin that began with the action of sunlight upon the inorganic elements on earth.

Solar intelligence factors might offer an explanation of how man developed his large brain capacity in a quick evolutionary spurt that thrust him almost overnight, geologically speaking, from a primitive state to a state of extraordinary civilization. Most scientists believe that spurt took place around 15,000 or so years ago after almost a million years of human evolution. Sunlight imposed on the nervous system from an unexpected burst of radiation might explain the cause. While many species died out, man learned somehow to adapt to the increased solar radiation, thus mutating into a favorable variation in the species. Man became a new solar creation.

The possibility of a sudden explosion or burst of solar radiation would help explain the presence of celestial phenomena, the ancient UFOs, mentioned in myths and legends, as well as the appearance of solar beings. This influence on the planet from an outside agency gives some credence to the age-old concept of spontaneous generation spoken of by Aristotle. It would also account for the rapid and unexplained growth of man's brain capacity and his accomplishments in the civilized arts of agriculture, building, language and science, and especially in the creation of religions involving the sun and the stars. Above all, it hinted that the emergence of life from a simple to a complex state could not have been one of chance, but instead was created as an act of a purposeful cosmic/solar intelligence.

It seemed logical to me that modern man should turn to the sun. In his eternal search for truth, man has always struggled towards the light. He has evolved scientifically and technically to the point where he has prepared his mind for the concept that he must eventually leave the planet and explore the stars, which is the natural result of an ever-increasing population that could outpace food supplies within fifty years. By direct use of solar energy and a proper understanding of the creative intelligence within it, mankind may be able to develop ways of nourishing itself directly from sunlight and, above all, to create a new light body that will be more akin to intelligence than to matter. When man has achieved this metamorphosis, he will have attained immortality and merged with the Godhead.

It took me a half-hour to read my paper. I was satisfied that it was the best I could write for the moment, so I turned my attention to a new project. I would return to the Amazon to continue my investigations of El Dorado and the legendary women warriors. I typed a letter to my old friend, Carl C. Landegger. Although Landegger was not a member of the Project, he took a keen interest in anthropology and jungle travel and had indicated his Brazilian company would consider sponsoring a new expedition should I want to organize one.

Fourth Transition

FORM

22

The Golden Man

Bogota, Colombia

June 23, 1975—Two beds in my hotel room were covered with notes and maps which I had been using to plan the expedition that would depart in a month for the lowlands of Brazil.

The slow pace of the planning was frustrating, but I had two weeks to assemble everything. Poor telephone communication with the interior was irritating, too, and to make things worse, I was having trouble finding good men who would risk their lives in the vast Amazon jungles, for the tribes had been stirred up by road builders and prospectors.

Exploring was definitely losing some of its fascination. However, because I was an explorer and the opportunity had presented itself, I had agreed to organize another El Dorado/ Amazons Expedition. I had spent years trying to fathom the whereabouts of the legendary El Dorado and the cities of the fabled Amazons. But now I was increasingly preoccupied with learning about the secret sciences of the ancient peoples who had occupied the high and low jungles of South America, rather than with finding the remains of their cities and temples.

I no longer was convinced that the effort expended in looking for the vestiges of cultures was worth the energy and money required. Nor was I even sure that physical remains would reveal more than I already knew. Indeed, I was certain that El Dorado, the Golden Man, was more than a historical figure. At the same time, I doubted seriously that the "city of gold" which El Dorado was believed to have built had ever existed. I was sure, however, that the historical El Dorado had existed at one time as a figure of great dimensions, a man who had been known to many civilizations in the Americas: the Viracocha or Thunupa of old Peru, the Bochica of Colombia, the Quetzalcoatl of Mexico, the Kukulcan of Yucatan, and the El Dorado of Amazonia —one who was more than human if the stories about him were to be believed. The great figure was purported to be a wise and aged man who carried on his back a large cross made of indestructible material, and who preached a high religion. He claimed to be a child of the sun and supposedly had a body without bones. He was a radiant being of light, shining like powdered gold, who took the name the Golden Man. He taught that in order to prevent the sun from going out and casting the earth in darkness, men must transform themselves into light by merging with the sun. By doing so they could understand the Creator. He taught that men were nothing more than monkeys who could not rise above their superstitions until they took on the nature of light.

Perhaps this Golden Man had encouraged the building of cities, temples and great pyramids like the many old "cities of the gods" I had found that were reputed to have been sacred colleges where priests and priestesses learned the arts and sciences of higher teachings and learned to become celestial beings. At these ancient shrines, dedicated souls practiced the secret doctrines that enabled them to light the divine spark of their consciousness and unite themselves with the Godhead. The path was difficult, but in the end the initiates became immortal. Sahagun had this to say about the ancients who had realized these goals:

> The ancients say that when men died they did not perish but began to live again, waking almost out of a dream, and that they turned into spirits or gods.

Stories related that the followers of the Golden Man acted out certain ceremonies, one of which required the neophyte to pass through fire, symbolizing the passage of the teacher from this world. This ceremony, which represented the transmutation of the body by fire into light, was called the fire of sacrifice; it was believed that the soul could be freed to rise heavenward only from a body whose matter was burned and transformed into immortal light. When the Golden Man passed out of the world, it was to prove that the man of matter can only be freed by dying and to reveal that the way to salvation is a process of returning to the light whence man came. His spiritual message was that matter touched by light is transformed. The divine seed within matter begins to germinate when exposed to the sun, and God is incarnated within this seed. Once the process is set in motion, this seed ascends to heaven, transformed into light. The Golden Man was said to have died in a funeral pyre, and, as some stories have it, he ascended to the sun whence he came. By so doing, he built a bridge for his disciples to follow and opened a communion between man and the divine. The Golden Man was a world illuminator. He was an image of the world, who transformed himself into light so that others might follow. It was an act of transcendence.

I had seen cremated remains of the dead at temple sites in both Mexico and Peru and evidence of ceremonial cremations in which the initiate walked into ritual fire or, in some cases, was enveloped by the powerful heat produced by parabolic mirrors. Stories were told of priests having exited from the world by such means, and I suspected many persons had disappeared from the material world by these methods, seeking to attain the sun directly. It was said that certain priests were able to withstand the intense heat and survive, stepping out of the fire as if from a shower, which was almost impossible to believe. All these tales told me that a search for El Dorado must encompass a greater understanding of light and consciousness. I could never hope to understand El Dorado from material remains alone.

Through the window I could see the afternoon sun appearing from behind the clouds. A shaft of sunlight fell across the top of my desk, where an array of devices, propelled into motion by the sun's rays, began to turn in every direction. The radiometerlike devices were crude instruments composed of disks, one side black and the other white, suspended on a needle. Exposure to sunlight or to any other source of radiant energy caused the disks to rotate on their pivotal needles.

For several minutes I watched them, attempting unsuccessfully to slow down the rotation of the disks by mental projection or simply by staring at them. The driving force of the sunlight was stronger than the energy radiated by my eyes and the mental projection they carried. If I moved an instrument out of the sunlight and waited until it stopped rotating, I could make the disk wobble by looking at it and sometimes make it turn by sheer force of my will, a tiring feat that seemed to work better when I stopped concentrating and willed the disk to move. Sometimes it worked; sometimes it didn't. But then I wasn't as keenly interested in working with the radiometer as I had once been.

For many months I had been experimenting on a series of little PSI motors of various shapes that I could cause to move by the sheer force of my eyesight. Like the radiometers, these motors were composed of disks suspended on needles. Eyesight and thought control caused the disk to turn. Picking up one of the generators, I balanced the disk on a needle and made certain the disk was still. To make the disks, I had drawn a circle about seven and a half inches in diameter on white typing paper, cut it out, and halved it. Gluing the edges together formed a cone, which I placed on a paper cylinder through which two drinking straws had been inserted near the top, forming a cross. A needle or wire of silver, gold or copper was inserted into the straws and the whole unit was balanced on a bottle or glass (see diagram).

The design had been inspired by temples, usually circular buildings with conical roofs, I had discovered during my explorations of the Chachapoyas ruins in Peru. I had made other motors shaped like pyramids and found they worked equally well. The shape of the little motors was important and dictated their response to thoughts or eyesight. Cone or pyramid shapes seemed to work best.

In experiments years before with the cones I had observed that vegetables and meats placed inside these shapes did not putrefy. Biologists at the University of Oklahoma who examined skin cells of the mummified remains of an Egyptian princess found the cells so well preserved they were capable of living, even though the body had been mummified several thousand years ago. Pyramids, when aligned to true north, apparently capture energy within their confines and act upon living tissue.

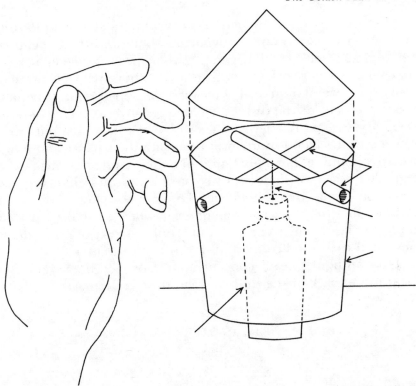

Karl Drbal, a Czechoslovakian engineer, had studied the work of M. Bovis, a French researcher who discovered that the remains of dead cats and other small animals found in the King's Chamber of the Great Pyramid of Giza were so well preserved by natural dehydration and mummification that they gave off no odor. Drbal built a replica of the pyramid and found that its shape affected the crystals on the edge of dull razor blades, aligning them to their natural sharp state. These findings suggested to me that pyramids and cones and perhaps other shapes were geometric symbols that generated wave fronts, captured energy and, in some manner not yet understood, acted upon living matter. The psychic use of energy was a concept I understood. I knew that when energized by certain frequencies of light and especially when the energizing was controlled by human consciousness, objects and living organisms luminated, that is, they absorbed energy. Once properly luminated, they could be made to respond.

After the disk on my psychic motor was perfectly still, I looked at it. After a few seconds, it wobbled about and then began to rotate clockwise. When it began to gather speed, I willed it to stop and turn counterclockwise, which it did after about twenty seconds. For several minutes I continued the experiment, changing the movement of the disk by techniques such as taking several deep breaths and filling my lungs with extra air, which put more oxygen in the blood to my brain, causing the disk to spin more rapidly; pointing the index finger of either hand at the disk—the right hand caused the disk to rotate faster—and changing the direction of the rotation at will. The fact that my mind could actually alter the disk's movement (even when it had been placed under a glass dome so air currents could not act upon it) demonstrated that mind could and did influence matter.

After an hour's heavy concentration I pushed the several devices to the back of the desk and wrote in my journal:

TRANSCRIPT

June 23, 1975

The interrelationship of matter, energy and intelligence is demonstrated by the experiments. This brings up the concept that all is mind—and to carry the thesis further, all is God, meaning that God is beyond a divine figure or Supreme Being. I have observed that mind, or human consciousness, alters the state of matter. Mind is a source of energy. Thought generates energy which carries information (IF) that acts upon living tissue and even upon inorganic substances. Moreover, objects—such as the psychic generators—can be made to respond to the will of the observer.

This brings up the question of the nature of matter. I believe matter is nothing more than some form of mind or intelligence held in a condensed state. Matter shaped into forms responds to mind control, as would be expected of organisms or organized entities. Thus, shape or form is organization, as opposed to chaos, in its most primitive condition. Form is essential to the incidence of intelligence. Any form appears to capture and hold intelligence, and its form or organization enables it to respond to other intelligence(s). So forms or images are sources of information, intelligence and meaning, as opposed to unconstructive or meaningless stimuli, which means that forms capture energy and information in a way that unorganized matter cannot. Perhaps this would explain the importance of the ceramics in primitive cultures—their forms were symbols (much as in any art form) that supplied information or meaning to the observer. Moreover, these forms could be used by knowledgeable persons, such as witch doctors, priests or curanderos, as generators—much the same as radio transmitters—to broadcast thoughts to persons or possibly to the elements, as in rainmaking and weather control. This fact might explain the enigma of the Nazca lines and those we have examined on the north coasts of Peru, as well as the varied shapes of temples and their positions on hilltops and other apparently key locations. Like the pyramids themselves, these shapes and forms were cosmic mirrors, reflecting back to the heavens, and they were also generators that sent energy beams into the universe. The priests may have believed they were able to send their thoughts to heaven by means of these energy beams.

I am convinced that the pyramids and other temple layouts could have been used by the ancients as focal points of energy which they used in a purposeful and mystic or religious way. We know the Inca sun priests were able to evoke or materialize solar beings at their temples, if we are to believe the written reports. Therefore the ideas that temples, ceramic designs, pictographs, petroglyphs and similar drawings and carvings depicted space men and that the ceremonial roads and drawings in the desert were landing fields for spaceships are limited concepts. The ancients were familiar with beings from the sun, which might be what Christians called angels, and conversed with these beings. Perhaps a better explanation would be that the ancients recognized them and fused their terrestrial cities with heavenly signs such as the galaxies. Beyond question, the ancients were in communication with solar beings, believing they would someday transcend the earth and merge with heaven—or the sun, which is a higher form of life, being energy and intelligence as opposed to matter and intelligence.

It took me half an hour to finish this writing. When I had finished, I picked up a velvet-lined box, placed it before me on the table, and took out a quartz crystal lens, which I placed to my eye. I pointed the lens toward the setting sun. Because quartz was transparent to ultraviolet radiation, I used this method to make contact with the sun—allowing my nervous system to absorb the full radiation, with its IF factors.

After twenty minutes I put away the crystal in its box and sat in a meditative state. Both my breathing and my heartbeat were slower than normal. A cool draft seemed to envelop my body, and my hands grew cold. After ten minutes I sat up and lit a candle. Slowly I placed the fingers of my left hand in the flame.

I felt no pain. It was as if my flesh had merged with the fire. After a few moments, when I began to feel the heat, I took my hand away. I blew out the candle.

While I did not have immunity to fire by any means, I did know my mind could influence the reaction of heat on the flesh, even if only for a limited period. I wondered whether it was not man's state of mind, limited by scientific and religious training, that held me in the physical state.

Again my thoughts returned to the true nature of being and the possibility of man's having two distinct forms—one material, the other energy. Now I doubted that the ultimate reality could be found in matter. Lately, I had found my brain was no longer performing as quickly as I wanted it to. My new consciousness was simply too advanced for my brain capacity. Sometimes I would command my brain to furnish me with a name or a date, only to have it fail. Its function was too dependent on proper rest and nourishment. If I overworked my tired body, the brain slowed down.

Here was a paradox: my physical mind-body was slowing down with time and age, while my light potential—my light consciousness and being—was unfolding. That newborn child, the student who had evolved out of the older man, the teacher, was outpacing the older person whom he had grown to know so well. Again my thoughts returned to the teachings of the Golden Man: the individual can bud and flower only when the conscious spirit has been freed from matter.

Of one thing I was certain: I was growing more aware of the limitations of the physical mind-body. The secrets of immortality, it was becoming all too apparent, would be found in my emerging new faculties of light generated by solar techniques and not in any physical attributes. The material mind-body was doomed to death and dissolution.

As I relaxed, watching the sun sink below the horizon, I asked myself: will it rise again tomorrow? My mind and emotions told me it would. That was the rational, logical answer to the question. But would it rise, really? I was aware that the sun could go out and fail to appear. Man, to a great extent, dictated that possibility, though most people did not know it, which told me there was more to man than was realized. The fear of the sun's not rising was physical, because the three-dimensional material body could not survive without it. But for the energy body, the light body—well, that was another story. An energy body could not die as long as there was light.

These ideas seemed to supply my tired brain with energy. I laughed to myself at the thought that my brain was like a PSI motor, driven by radiant energy and responsive to information or ideas coming from a higher intelligence. I had actually outgrown my brain, and perhaps even my body.

A transition of form was occurring, yet I was surprised how calm I felt. For the first time in my life I knew I was growing and developing a higher nature and outgrowing my physical mind-body. I accepted without any apprehension or fear the idea that I could lose my body. Indeed, I was going to lose it sooner than I imagined in the natural course of age, for death usually surprises people with its sudden appearance . . . no one is ever ready to die, really. I was tremendously excited by the transition into a higher form. Still, I wanted facts, proof, more experience with this higher form. I simply could not accept immortality on blind faith alone. Such an attitude was beyond my nature of careful deduction and analysis.

Just before falling asleep, I realized death was really not necessary. It was an old-fashioned idea. Why couldn't man generate a higher light form that was immortal? The first step would be to discover the key of doing away with the physical attributes right from the start. Why did birth have to take place in physical form? Why not as a light or solar being? That should be the goal of man on our planet: to ascend to the sun and the stars, not to wait around for the earth to die and be carried away like a dinosaur that had outlived its usefulness.

23

In the Lands of the Amazons

Boa Vista, Brazil

August 12, 1975—We had been flying in the twin-engine Beechcraft for two and a half hours, and soon we'd be forced back to Boa Vista, an hour to the east, to refuel.

Catching sight of a clearing in the dense rain forest below us, I nodded to the Brazilian bush pilot, and he pulled the plane around in a tight 180° turn, standing the plane on one wing so I could study the area with my binoculars. This maneuver had become routine. We'd scan the forests for clearings cut by Indians of this greater Parima area near the Venezuelan border at the headwaters of the Orinoco. Then we'd drop down and photograph the villages. During the past several days we had surveyed thousands of square miles of unexplored country by air, photographing dozens of Xirixanas and Uaicas Indian camps. From the building going on below, we could see the Indians of these remote interiors were flourishing.

After examining some buildings carefully through a powerful telephoto lens, I took several exposures, then put away the camera. I waved my hand, and the pilot dropped down and buzzed the camp site. Hundreds of dark-skinned Indians appeared out of the trees and stood in the clearing, watching our airplane roar overhead at 250 miles an hour. We made one more pass, then headed back to Boa Vista.

Letting my head sink into the soft headrest, I took a deep breath. The flight engineer offered cups of coffee to me and the pilot.

Sipping slowly, I reviewed the events of the past three weeks. Carl Landegger, who had flown to Santarem from Belem in the Beechcraft loaded with equipment and supplies for the expedition, was now operating out of Monte Alegre, while the other half of the crew explored for pictograph remains in the surrounding heights. From the time of my arrival, the expedition had explored a wide area, using the riverboat *Antomar* as a base of operations. We had learned about scattered glyph writings up the many Amazon tributaries and had documented them on film. We took notes on other sites that would have to wait for future expeditions, because *Antomar* broke down upriver and would have foundered if a passing boat had not taken her in tow.

At that point the expedition had taken to the air, following leads gathered during the course of the river probes. The aerial exploration, using information gathered on trips by Landegger and me in 1973 and by Dailey and me in 1971, added to our knowledge of the area by photographically documenting a mountainous region we believed could have been the home of the warlike tribe of women called the Amazons by the first Europeans, Francisco de Orellana's expedition claiming to have seen them down the Amazon river in 1540-1541.

A good case for the existence of the Amazons in America had been recounted by historian Antonio de Herrera in his *General History of Western Indies*, taken from reports of the explorers who knew the region. I had pasted clippings from the book in my journal:

> *The discourse of these Tupinambas confirmed the information, which we had heard throughout the river, of the famous Amazons, from whom it took its name, and it is not known by any other, but only by this, to all cosmographers who have treated of it up to this time. It would be very strange that, without good grounds, it should have usurped the name of the river of the Amazons, and that it should desire to become famous, with no other title than a usurped one: nor is*

it credible that this great river, possessing so much glory at hand, should only desire to glorify itself by a name to which it has no title. This is an ordinary meanness with those who, not caring to obtain the honour they desire by their own merits, acquire it by falsehood. But the proofs of the existence of the province of Amazons on this river are so numerous, and so strong, that it would be a want of common faith not to give them credit. I do not treat of the important information which, by order of the Royal Audience, was collected from the natives during many years, concerning all which the banks of this river contained; one of the principal reports being that there was a province inhabited by female warriors, who lived alone without men, with whom they associated only at certain times; that they lived in the villages, cultivating the land, and obtaining by the work of their hands all that was necessary for their support. Neither do I make mention of those reports which were received from some Indians, and particularly from an Indian woman, in the city of Pasto, who said that she had herself been in the country which was peopled by these women, and her account entirely agreed with all that had been previously reported.

I will only dwell upon that which I heard with my own ears, and carefully investigated, from the time that we entered this river. There is no saying more common than that these women inhabit a province on the river, and it is not credible that a lie could have been spread throughout so many languages, and so many nations, with such an appearance of truth. But the place where we obtained most information respecting the position of the province of these women, their customs, the Indians with whom they communicate, and the roads by which their country may be entered, was in the last village of the Tupinambas.

Thirty-seven leagues from this village, and lower down the river, on the north side, is the mouth of that of the Amazons, which is known among the natives by the name of Cunuris. This river takes the name of the first Indians who live on its banks, next to whom follow the Apantos, who speak the "lingoa geral" of Brazil. Next come the Taguaus, and the last, being those who communicate and traffic with the Amazons themselves, are the Guacgras.

These manlike women have their abodes in great forests and on lofty hills, of which the highest, which is therefore beaten by the winds with most violence, for its pride, so that it is bare and clear of vegetation, is called Yacamiaba. The Amazons are women of great valor, and they have always preserved themselves without the ordinary intercourse with men, and even when these, by agreement, come every year to their land, they receive them with arms in their hands, such as bows and arrows, which they brandish about for some time, until they are satisfied that the Indians come with peaceful intentions. They then drop their arms and go down to the canoes of their guests, where each one chooses the hammock that is nearest at hand (these being the beds in which they sleep); they then take them to their houses, and, hanging them in a place where their owners will know them, they receive the Indians as guests for a few days. After this the Indians return to their own country, repeating these visits every year at the same season. The daughters who are born from this intercourse are preserved and brought up by the Amazons themselves, as they are destined to inherit their valor, and the customs of the nation, but it is not so certain what they do with the sons. An Indian, who had gone with his father to this country when very young, stated that the boys were given to their fathers, when they returned in the following year. But others, and this account appears to be most probable, as it is most general, say that when the Amazons find that a baby is a male, they kill it. Time will discover the truth, and if these are the Amazons made famous by historians, there are treasures shut up in their territory which would enrich the whole world. The mouth of this river on which the Amazons live is in 2½° of latitude.

While there was absolutely no hard evidence to prove that a nation of female warriors ever existed in the Amazon, it was the purpose of the expedition to find it, if possible. Both Landegger and I were familiar with the chronicles on the Orellana expedition, as well as with the mythological nation of the Amazons, who were believed to have lived near the river Thermodon in Cappadocia in Central Turkey and who devoted their lives to wars and manly exercises. Legend has it that they founded an extensive empire in Asia Minor, along the shores of the Euxine Sea (the Black Sea) and the Thermodon, the latter being the site of their defeat by a Greek army.

It was said that after this the Amazons migrated beyond the Tanais (the Don River). Some writers, such as Diodorus Siculus, claim the Amazons settled in Africa. When Orellana sailed down the Amazon river, his ships were attacked by canoe-borne warriors led by women who were said to have inhabited a province on the river and who had their dwellings in the great forests at the summits of lofty peaks, the highest of which was known as Yacamiaba.

Evidently, Orellana believed in the existence of the Amazons, and so did Gaspar de Carbajal, who wrote a diary of Orellana's voyage. Both Charles de la Condamine and Baron Friedrich von Humboldt believed in the existence of the Amazons in America. While our expedition had gathered much valuable information on the various tribes that had inhabited the area at one time in history, actual documentation of the existence of the Amazons was hard to come by. However, I was convinced of their existence and believed the expedition had discovered the legendary Yacamiaba, where the Amazons supposedly had made their home. The proof might have been forthcoming if a small plane had not crashed on the landing strip near Yacamiaba, preventing access to the area for the rest of the season.

The Beechcraft came down over the flatlands near Boa Vista as the pilot made preparations to land. I thought about the enigma of the Amazons, which had brought us to the area. If they had actually existed, how had they come to America and the remote Amazon region, a land which had been named after them by the explorers who had first reported their existence? Or had it been the other way around? Perhaps the Amazons originally came from America and crossed the Atlantic. It was possible. I was convinced of the reliability of the chroniclers. They had no reason to make up such a story; and I certainly didn't agree with the rationalization of the naturalist Alfred Russel Wallace, who believed, after his voyage on the Amazon in 1848, that the Spaniards had confused young male warriors with long hair, earrings and necklaces with female warriors.

The landing gear dropped down and locked. I checked my seat belt, glanced at the instruments out of habit, then watched the concrete runway appear. The clouds gathering on the horizon told me there'd be no more flights today, which suited me, because I planned to join Landegger the next day at Monte Alegre. I hoped I could confirm that arrangement by radio that evening.

As the wheels touched down with a gentle thump, I checked the dozen or so exposed rolls of film and tucked them away in the film chest under my seat.

A week later I was back at the Project Center in Reno.

24

A New Solar Genetics

Project Center, Reno, Nevada

May 7, 1976—Nine months after I returned to Nevada I was sitting in my office speaking to Dr. Kenneth Ehler, a new member of our team.

Dr. Ehler, a man of about thirty, was a post-doctoral fellow attached to the Salk Institute. He was working on problems in chemical evolution. I had received him eagerly, because I was most interested in the research he had done in bio-organic chemistry with Albert Eschenmoser in Zurich.

"As you know," I said to Ehler, "we have been experimenting for many years with the effects of sunlight on the human body. For example, we know sunlight affects the endocrine system through the eyes. There have been articles on this subject in the past, but we of the Project feel we have carried the work much further than anyone else. We are a loose body of researchers inasmuch as we represent different fields, but we are working in a new area that goes beyond secular studies. In this, we are on our own, both scientifically and religiously.

"The work is financed by contributions from members themselves. Now, since you are a chemist and have applied our techniques, I would like to know your beliefs, from a chemical point of view, on the effects of light on the brain and other parts of the nervous system. I have discussed many of these points with geneticists and physicists, but I've never really had an explanation from a chemist of the possible effects of sunlight.

"As you know, Richard Wurtman did an article for *Scientific American* on the effects of sunlight, but in the Project we have gone a step further—we are absorbing sunlight directly through the eyes, which thereby introduces solar energy into the nervous system. According to chemists, the solar system and universe seem to be about 99 percent hydrogen and helium. Now, this is very interesting: two elements, hydrogen and oxygen, account for about 88.5 percent of the atoms of the human body, with hydrogen supplying 63 percent of the total and oxygen 25.5 percent. As a chemist you can see the tremendous relationship between the sun and the human body. The introduction of sunlight directly into the nervous system through the eyes could have profound chemical effects."

Dr. Ehler, a slim, nervous individual who always measured his words carefully, thought for a moment and then said, "We are dealing with chemical bonds, which are centers of energy in living systems. And it is known from a vast amount of literature in photochemistry that these bonds are affected by light of all kinds. You have to overcome energy barriers, and absorbing light is one way of doing so. Energy bonds vibrate at certain frequencies; if you hit a bond with light of the frequency at which the bond is vibrating, you can cause reactions that would not occur in the absence of light.

"Of course, your research is most exciting, and I lack any hard facts at this moment. The problem is that we need more facts about what actually happens chemically in the human organism when you introduce sunlight into the nervous system by means of the techniques you are teaching. I'm afraid it is not going to be easy obtaining researchers to do this kind of work—not only because of lack of funds, but because it is so radical. Most scientists will be unwilling to do this type of research because of the social and ethical problems involved. Furthermore, if a person were to indiscriminately take in sunlight, he could severely harm himself and possibly even go blind.

"I have given it quite a bit of thought. Sunlight is transduced by the eye into electrical energy, and that is what reaches the brain. It is these electrical networks that have been most thoroughly studied. And this is where the pioneering research is going on right at the moment. For example, at the Salk Institute they are trying to establish functional relationships between the behavior of animals and the electrical pathways that connect various parts of their brains.

"There does seem to be some correlation between orienting behavior and specific brain centers in the rat, although this is still being studied and nothing has been definitely established. This is just an example of some of the research that is being conducted. However, note again that the research is limited to rats. And this, of course, brings us back to the problem."

"Fortunately," I said, "our research at the Project has been done with humans."

"Yes," Ehler replied, "and that illustrates another point. You do your work within a system. And it is only by working within such a religious system that we can know we are not hurting ourselves. So there's the solution to the question most people would ask, which is, 'How do you get around the ethical and moral problem?' "

"What moral implications do you think are involved, Doctor, in taking sunlight into the brain through the eyes?"

"There are none so long as a person does this willingly."

"You have to have a sort of consent, then."

"You must have the consent of the individual."

"It goes back to determinism," I said. "We feel that there are intelligence factors—cosmic information—controlled by some kind of cosmic or universal law within the energy. Consequently, when you take the energy into your nervous system, you are taking in information governed by that superior law.

"So, the more energy you absorb, the more information you absorb, and this information does something within the organism. Now we are getting out of chemistry. But, in any case, the information appears to do something, and you have to be in harmony with it; perhaps that is what you are getting at."

"Well, the moral implications that do arise are societal—it is a societal question. Our present society is not capable of using this energy wisely, because it is ignorant of the holistic picture."

I interjected, "It would be like a yogi who used meditation to interrupt his involuntary control system by interfering with the functioning of his kidneys, for example. I had a yogi in here the other day who claimed he could drink two or three gallons of water and eliminate it all in eighteen minutes. Now, I ask you, who has the knowledge or the intelligence or the training to be able to regulate the body's involuntary functions? It would take a tremendous amount of effort and energy. If you just forgot something for a few seconds, it might result in your death.

"Similarly, cosmic energy and information do something of their own accord when taken within the system. If this natural or involuntary process is interrupted, complications may result. I am trying to stress that religion doesn't necessarily have to be dogma and theology; it can also encompass physical law from a spiritual or higher ultra-physical source. Every individual seems to be confronted with the concept of something beyond man and with the need to exercise some form of religious expression, but not necessarily in the traditional sense."

Ehler agreed. "I definitely see a higher law functioning. But we scientists are so ignorant. Most of us look on ourselves purely and simply as very complex physical organisms. In fact, some scientists would go so far as to say that all phenomena are explicable in terms of physics and chemistry. This is the concept of reductionism."

"And you don't believe or accept that?"

"I don't accept it at all. I—and many others—see that the concept of cosmic consciousness, a concept of the 'All' and God, has laws that go beyond the physical."

"Take, for example," I said, "the experience we had in Mexico, when my body glowed with light in a cave. Some followers of traditional religions might believe that to have been the result of some kind of saintliness instead of accepting that I had an abundance of energy built up as a result of our techniques; that a connection with some extraterrestrial source of energy—and possibly information—had resulted in the luminescence of a field which observers registered by means of physical sight. Some of this has to be explained by physical law."

"Yes, the problem as I see it again comes back to the fact that we need more scientists cooperating with one another to formulate meaningful experiments not only on the intellectual and physical levels, but on the psychic and spiritual levels as well."

"We do hope to be able to provide this through the Project," I said. "Scientists who are not afraid to experiment with the idea of the existence of God are beginning to show an interest in our work. Some of them do belong to a traditional religion, but are not afraid of the possibility that these experiments could show that our traditional concepts of religion are wrong—something that many scientists have already guessed or suspected. After all, we are showing that communion with God is possible, because as soon as we absorb sunlight through the eyes into the nervous system, we actually project ourselves from this planet into the sun."

"I think we can draw an analogy between our present situation and the situation twenty or thirty years ago when lysergic acid diethylamide (LSD) was discovered. We see what has happened with that. To be sure, LSD has some use clinically, but for the most part, when anyone mentions LSD, immediately the connotation is that it is 'bad' because it does have an effect on the psyche. LSD is a relatively simple chemical compound. We have, with LSD, an interrelationship between chemistry and the psyche."

"There has to be some sort of control, then," I said.

"The analogy breaks down in that with LSD you are dealing with a simple chemical compound. What we are dealing with in the Project's case are laws that we in the scientific community really don't understand yet."

"Absolutely. I agree with that. John Ott at the Environmental Health and Light Research Institute has done considerable work in the use of light and its effects on the body. But again, his research has basically been limited to the physical effects of light on the human body. We are more interested in the effects on the intellectual nature and on the psychic nature. For example, we are saying that the absorption of energy into the body through these techniques supplies information. Yet gerontologists speak of aging as loss of information. In other words, the body is unable to maintain and repair itself, so death results.

"We have been tremendously fascinated by the possibility of using these techniques to regenerate certain cells and to supply the body with information. Here again we have the idea of the fountain of youth and the possibility of human immortality—or at least the extension of the human life span. Biologists have compared the loss of information to a control factor, a destructor clock that runs down. Currently our life span is limited to 70, 80 or certainly no more than 100 years, corroborating the biblical idea of three score and ten as the life span.

"We entertain the possibility of being able to lengthen the life span by interrupting this so-called destructor clock.

"Dr. Alex Comfort, a medical biologist who is director of the research program on aging at London's University College, wrote a fascinating article on this subject. According to Dr. Comfort, the simplest way of slowing down the aging process in mammals is by calorie restriction. He seems to feel that by restricting calorie intake we can sometimes increase life spans by from twenty to forty percent. Many of us in the Project have found that we actually do consume less food as a result of practicing our techniques. In my own case, I have given up most meats and have limited myself to a light diet of chicken, seafood, vegetables, fruits and nuts. We feel that by taking in cosmic-solar energy, we are not only cutting down the calorie intake, but are actually supplying the whole human organism with additional energy with which to slow down the aging process and supply the cells with the additional information they need to do so.

"Incidentally, our experiments have also shown that the endocrines are somehow involved in the absorption of sunlight. For example, many women who have passed through menopause have actually begun menstruating again following use of our techniques. Women who have small breasts have noticed their breasts beginning to develop. In cases of baldness (not all, but some) hair has begun to return. We have noticed too that people can withstand a greater amount of sunlight and tan more quickly than they ever did before. We have also noticed that people have had greater drive, more enthusiasm, and have actually been able to increase their ability to remember."

"I can testify to that myself," said Ehler emphatically. "Since I started the program I have had many insights into my own work and many ideas for future chemistry and science projects."

"We know that the pituitary and the pineal—the whole endocrine system—are definitely affected by the absorption of sunlight," I continued. "I think this is the key to the role of the endocrine system and the aging problem."

"Yes, the pituitary is supposed to be the master gland that regulates and controls secretions of the various endocrine glands. If the pituitary is affected by sunlight, it probably can, to a certain degree, activate or regenerate some of the glands. For example, the pineal has often been likened to the third eye. There have been a lot of articles in pulp magazines about the third eye and the ability of people to see psychically with this so-called third eye, which is nothing more than the pineal. Descartes thought it was the seat of the soul. I have found myself that I have become extremely psychic. I know many things before they happen and I am able to anticipate people's actions by picking up their thoughts, something I was not able to do before I applied the system. Have you experienced anything like this?"

"I am just beginning to. Just beginning."

"Incidentally, Comfort has done some research on Hiroshima bomb survivors to see if they have aged faster than people who were not exposed to radiation. I don't really know what his research has proven, but I do know that we have found that after applying our techniques people often seem younger. Women report a nicer complexion, better skin texture; men have discovered that they respond better to exercise, that they are more agile. Many people—but not all—have actually thrown their eyeglasses away. Individuals with graying hair have reported their hair regaining its natural color. Others have reported a tremendous capacity to learn and a sudden increase in their intelligence quotient. And, again, there are those women whose menstrual cycles have returned. That brings us back to chemistry; I think we can narrow our discussion down to the endocrine system."

"Yes, I think the chemistry of the endocrine system is the key."

"There seems to be a psychic influence, too. For example, many people see things they wouldn't ordinarily see: faces, geometric designs, archetypal symbols. Some have noticed electrical stimulation in their fingers. They can shock people—it's almost as if they had static electricity. The question is, how does the energy get from the brain into the rest of the nervous system? I can understand how it gets into the pituitary and the pineal, because the pineal is affected by light. It would be a third eye in that respect."

"I can speculate," Ehler said. "A lot of work has been done in photochemistry, but, again, it has involved isolated chemicals. I have mentioned the work on chlorophyll and the implications of chemical reactions at the level of the deoxyribonucleic acid (DNA), which do lead to genetic mutations. Most of the research, though, is not done on humans—it is done on lower animals and then extrapolated. The only work that has been done on humans is with substances like vitamin D, and there is a lot of chemistry involved. I could go into all the details, but they really would bore you. What you really want to know is what chemical reactions go on in the endocrine system of humans. This is physiological chemistry, and I am really not an expert in that. I am a theoretical chemist. Most of my work has to do purely with chemicals, and not with the chemistry of the human body.

"I don't want to give the impression that nothing is known about chemistry of the endocrine system. Let me tell you what I do know about the physiological chemistry of the pituitary—how all the hormones are interrelated. They affect one another in a sort of rhythmic way. I imagine you already know that these hormonal rhythms are affected by hormonal chemicals. These chemical substances are essentially chemical bonds. They are centers of energy and can absorb energy, and they control the transfer of energy through the body. Now, we know application of the techniques affects the transmission of this energy, perhaps by triggering those chemicals in some way. That is a wide open field which we haven't even begun to look into. By applying the techniques, we are influencing the transfer of spiritual energy throughout the body.

"All we chemists really know about is the chemical energy, which exists in the bonds. The question that excites me is, as the astronomer Carl Sagan has said, 'Must we now endow the atom with consciousness?' Is there spiritual energy in those bonds? That's exciting. I just don't know."

"We have maintained from the very beginning that there is information or consciousness in energy. This ultra-dimensional consciousness, which is not necessarily part of our physical makeup, has to be spiritual."

"Perhaps that is what we are increasing—the spiritual energy.

Here is another approach. I must credit Jonas Salk with this idea. Look at the equation $E = mc^2$. You can also write it as $1/c^2 = m/E$. Another way of looking at it is to say that energy is trapped in matter. That's what we have in a chemical bond—energy trapped in matter. Chemical evolutionists would have us believe that amino acids—the bases of the nucleic acids—were formed when light hit methane, and that over eons and eons of time these evolved into what we know as life. However, this idea has not been completely proven."

"It's theory," I retorted.

"Well, it's a theory with a lot of loopholes. Only parts of it have been proven."

"Do you think that somehow the secret of life's beginning could involve the action of sunlight upon the planet and its atmosphere?"

"Yes, indeed. You see, I think one misconception we scientists have is thinking that the electromagnetic spectrum is all there is to light."

"Then you are going back to the idea of information or consciousness or intelligence in the atom?"

"I think it is the key."

"In the Project we have become convinced that energy has information, intelligence or consciousness."

"The present generation has the idea that all we are is physical matter. Darwin started that, and it was an important advance because it freed us from reliance on superstition."

"It actually went back to the Greeks."

"Yes, but now, instead of idolizing the priest in the church, we idolize the priest in the laboratory. So, again, we are back to the critical question of how to achieve a balance. We must have the spiritual and the physical in balance."

"We were talking about consciousness, information or intelligence in matter or energy. As you know, after we started applying the techniques we began to have recalls we didn't have before. We started to have ideas that didn't come from books—extraterrestrial ideas about life, and so forth.

"Did you know that evidence of new and rare plants was discovered in the ruins of London during World War II? At Hiroshima

I believe the same thing was encountered. I think that the heat and the light of those explosions caused the plants to sprout. We know there are forms of life that existed in the past that no longer exist today. What has happened to cause this? I think we can assume temperature and solar radiation were responsible.

"Man today is evolving; he is becoming more intelligent, more spatial, more ultra-dimensional (insofar as his thoughts are not confined solely to the planet). Man has already gone to the moon. We are thinking about space. We know it is only a question of time before we actually probe the sun. There must be a way, maybe chemically, of penetrating the sun's temperature barrier. There could be life in the sun—energy beings—just as there are material beings on earth. Their intelligence would be greater than ours, because they would have access to more energy. That is what we in the Project are excited about. We want to create the motivation for starting entirely new institutions of learning to work with these solar forms and solar energy. Do you think it is possible that there could be energy beings in the sun just as there are physical beings here?"

"That seems reasonable to me. But we need some way to measure these energy beings. It is going to take a break-through of some kind—maybe a new type of instrument, I don't know. Again, we need physicists in this research."

"You are part of the scientific community. Do you think our idea of starting a new scientific-religious life system outside both the academic world and traditional religion has merit?"

"There are many scientists who won't have anything to do with God, just as there are religionists who don't trust science. There will be problems in the first years of such a marriage."

"How true!"

"On the other hand, we have all these people who want to absorb energy, just like LSD, without any controls. . . . "

"None whatsoever?"

"None whatsoever!"

"We have to create a new science and go beyond the restrictions of the academic community. Religiously speaking, we have to be free to interpret God in a new way."

"It must be a slow process."

"Indeed it must. In the Project we are working with the possibility that by means of our techniques we may eventually bring about a favorable mutation in the species—a favorable variation, that is. The introduction of sunlight into the nervous system differs from photosynthesis in that there is no proof that light, or the information it carries, does any real work. By this I mean that it is generally believed that absorption of light through the eyes is only a matter of excitation—that light registering on the retina triggers electrical responses that stimulate the visual areas of the brain.

"But we have good reason to believe that with the direct intake of sunlight for controlled periods—periods that have been determined by over twenty years of actual experience—the pituitary and pineal glands can be activated to secrete chemicals that affect the genes. Eminent geneticists have agreed that, although no scientific proof has been furnished yet, it seems plausible that sunlight absorbed through our techniques could, over a long period of time, bring about genetic mutations.

"If you can produce chemical reactions in the endocrine system by the intake of drugs, I presume you could do the same thing by the intake of solar energy."

"You need to have a large number of specialists working with you—a whole community of them."

"Generally speaking, we feel that the intake of IF's can alter the genetic code, possibly by outcrossing the homozygous strain."

"Well, with homozygosity you can bring about a new hybrid with some consistency. Wonderful progress has been made in swine breeding through these methods. However, among humans, only the Incas, the Egyptians and the kings of medieval times used homozygosity to propagate their kingdoms and their families. And it was done by interbreeding between brother and sister. Traditions and social codes would certainly prohibit this from taking place in the modern world."

"But it need not be done by intermarriage and interbreeding. The same thing could be accomplished by unrelated individuals applying the system. An X strain could be produced and passed along in this manner through the children of couples who practiced the solar techniques.

"We must accept the possibility that hormones secreted by the pituitary, and possibly by the pineal gland, activate the gene system. The secretions are triggered by the intake of solar energy. Consider this: man has evolved by means of sunlight. The eyes, brain and other parts of the nervous system are all products of light. A reaction of the eyes and nervous system with direct sunlight could be most favorable if it could be controlled. At one time much more of the sun's radiation struck the surface of the earth than now.

"It is generally believed that because the atmosphere contained less oxygen, ozone and carbon dioxide, more infrared and ultraviolet radiation could reach the earth's surface. There are two ways such conditions could have affected the origins of life. According to the first theory, simple life forms slowly came forth and manufactured oxygen, which paved the way for more complex living organisms, which eventually developed photosynthesis. The result was the emergence of life from the seas onto the land.

"The second proposition, which I am more prone to accept, suggests that there have been many epochs of varying conditions on the planet. During some periods there was more solar radiation than during others. The kind of life that inhabited the planet was determined by the level of radiation. I believe that we are presently in a new epoch of solar change, one that will result in more solar radiation. The human race is going to have to learn how to handle this increase, which is by no means limited to ultraviolet radiation, or suffer the consequences. I believe our race is threatened.

"At the Project we are teaching our members how to handle larger amounts of ultraviolet radiation safely. As the genetic code is affected by this ability, a new strain will emerge. For the first time we have a means of manipulating the secretions of the activating hormones from the pituitary and pineal for a favorable variation. After all, man has survived for millions of years, even when the earth was covered by dark clouds that blotted out much of the solar radiation. No doubt man then was a far different creature than he is today. Indeed, characteristics modern man has inherited, such as savagery, fear of darkness, and hate of both animals and his fellow man, are challenging his ability to live in an age of sunlight.

"Man has lost many abilities he once possessed. For example, he has lost the ability to handle large quantities of sunlight because he hasn't had to do so for a long time. He must learn to adapt if he is to survive the effects of harsh radiation on, ultimately, the chromosomes."

"What kind of radiation?" asked Ehler.

"Ultraviolet rays, alpha-particles, X-rays, gamma rays, cosmic rays, to name but a few," I replied. "Man will also have to learn how to handle the higher incidence of information factors carried by this radiation. After all, we cannot believe that man has evolved simply by the action of radiation alone. It is not reponsible for our intellectual faculties, psychic feelings, and spiritual aspirations. This leads me to believe that the organizing fields around man are in some way linked to a cosmic intelligence. The fields that make up what we call a light body are part of a higher dimension. Traces of this complex exist in the genes of the organism just as surely as the lower instinctive urges do.

"Our techniques have brought us face to face with these traces, and that explains why members of the Project have gradually developed spiritual feelings which are not otherwise experienced. Here we have a union between the spiritual and the material—the merging of two worlds—which suggests that man is much more than science has dared to suspect. It is in this direction that we of the Project are heading in our quest for the secrets of immortality.

"I can conceive of man one day evolving into an energy being, a being who survives on pure energy and is no longer dependent on food. We know it is only a question of time before man will be forced to vacate the planet. For one thing, it will be too small for the increasing population. When we have to leave the planet it should be as energy beings—light beings—who can survive in a universe where energy, possibly in the form of pure thought, is the dominant factor. Such a being would be immortal and could survive in worlds beyond matter. A race of these beings would not fear the death of a planet—or even that of the sun. As long as there is light anywhere in the universe, as long as there is intelligence beyond the physical universe in dimensions we cannot now conceive of, man will survive."

Ehler looked hard at me and said, "There is much to do, much more than I imagined when I first came here."

"Well, maybe you can help us to understand better from a chemical point of view just what we are working with on the human level. I'm afraid we don't have all the answers."

"No," Ehler said, "but what you do have is of vital interest to the whole world."

25

Transformation of Man into the X Variation

Project Center, Reno, Nevada

May 7, 1976 (8 P.M.)—Sylvia and I were dining at home with Elena Baugh, and the conversation turned to the Ehler interview, which the two women had listened to on a cassette recording that afternoon.

"I was having a conversation earlier today with one of the typists, Anne, who, as you both know, is a trained physicist. She doubted that sunlight could influence the brain in any way," I said.

"On what grounds did she base this assumption?" Elena asked.

"Her thinking revolved around the idea that sunlight falling on the retina is converted to electrochemical energy, and it is that energy that would affect the brain and the rest of the nervous system—if there is such an effect—and not pure sunlight."

"That may be true," Elena said, "from a limited point of view. Whether sunlight is converted or not, the source remains sunlight. Her thinking is definitely prejudiced. She should stick to her typing." Elena Baugh, a deep thinker and trained engineer, had little patience with the secular scientist who used a degree as a weapon and refused to think. "After all, the image falling upon the visual areas of the brain is still a solar image. She should know that archetypal images or symbols in themselves carry information. Whether or not the image is chemical does not alter the information. It is the source that is important. Besides, man is energy. He is nourished by energy. Therefore, he needs more or different energy to evolve into an energy being. The sun is a source of additional energy—that is required, I might add, for man to evolve. Why knock the source and try to rationalize? There's too much of that in science today."

"I quite agree," I said. "I think Anne missed the whole point, and perhaps this has to do with her training. The world is moving so fast that the specialists often get bogged down. She should recognize that the nervous system is more deeply involved with sunlight than most people imagine, because it processes information from celestial realms that does affect our lives. Our attitudes and feelings are to a great degree dominated by the sun through electrochemical responses. I am almost afraid to say it, but this applies to some of our so-called spiritual feelings as well. Anne needs to see that the techniques give us a new source of learning outside the realm of books. We learn through our eyes, brain and other parts of the nervous system by processing the information within the stimuli of light. What's more, we gain a knowledge that no book can teach us, because the processed information comes from other worlds.

"The interrelationship between spirit and matter—or mind and matter—has to be accepted. So does the fact that the energy and the information contained therein can teach man a great deal about his universe. What we have to do is get scientists away from books. I am afraid one of the reasons Anne is upset is because of her contention that since I don't have a Master's degree in physics I have no right to talk about the subject."

There was some concern in Baugh's voice. "I found Dr. Ehler's comments most interesting for their wider implications, which were not really brought out specifically in the conversation. His comments regarding lack of interest and/or funds for research in areas vital to human life—as well as his remarks on the question of ethics—touch on subjects that I hope other scientists are also considering seriously. I think it is time more of the world's intelligentsia assumed responsibilities commensurate with their power and privileged status, instead of silently obeying work contracts.

"Whether by choice or not, scientists have assumed the role of priests or world saviors; they are an extremely small percentage of the population exerting an influence far disproportionate to their number. This social development is an excellent example of the way lack of awareness of types and levels of energy bonds can backfire. These bonds are like a super nervous system of the whole universe. To ignore the existence of a symbiotic relationship on such a level is evidence of an arrogance that can best be described by the saying 'Fools rush in where angels fear to tread.' By this I don't mean to denigrate either scientists or the tremendous efforts they have made to understand the structure of matter and the laws governing it. But to concentrate energy and intelligence on only a fraction of the whole picture is to invite disaster by straining the balance, or symmetry, of a complex system. What is really puzzling and tragic is the way brilliant minds can be trapped by specialization. Seeing people fascinated, as if hypnotized, by a small part without caring to see the whole is like watching play time in an insane asylum.

"These people certainly do not lack the ability to think, so the problem must be one of misguided use of energy. The key to any problem, of course, is understanding the principles involved. Fortunately, fundamental laws are often simpler than we expect. It is only the variety of forms in matter that hides them from us and makes them seem more complicated. For example, in three-dimensional space and time, everything is related by energy bonds on different levels of magnitude. As I understand it, so far we know of four basic types of energy bonds, or interactions, that operate in physical forms from celestial bodies down to subatomic particles: gravitational, electromagnetic, weak, and strong (or hadronic)."

"How do you relate this to the influence of solar energy on the brain and the rest of the nervous system?" I asked.

"I do seem to be getting far afield, so I'll try to make my point with more art and less matter, to make a pun on Shakespeare," Elena continued. "Laws of structure and symmetry are involved in every energy bond and interaction. If neither nature nor man can achieve absolute or mathematical symmetry in his creations, then such perfection can only exist in ideas or symbols. The laws of structure or symmetry must be discovered through energy processes involving the mind, processes which take us out of the three-dimensional world of space and time.

"Repetition of a form requires an identical arrangement of parts, internally and externally: the highest level of symmetry or an archetypal symbol. If an archetype is an original idea or mold, then the effect of archetypal symbols on man begins on the non-physical psychic and/or spiritual levels, which brings us to the fields associated with all matter. The physical symmetry nature displays as a result of energy transformation is a relatively minor one. Since everything has a field capable of being affected by symbols, or by some form of energy related to the symbols, the nature of the symbols becomes extremely important.

"Now, let's get back to the idea of energy bonds and how solar energy energizes the human organism. First of all, the mere act of observing the sun and taking energy from it alters the energy bond between man and the sun. If this energy exchange involves symbols, which essentially are universal information affecting the translation of that energy into form, then man's deliberate or conscious use of these symbols can have enormous repercussions, even if only a very small quantity of physical energy is involved. I don't know any way to equate quantity of physical energy with its effect on non-physical levels.

"Mere quantity of energy changed in a reaction is not the crucial factor. For instance, the energy released in a nuclear reaction, though devastating, may not ultimately be as consequential on a universal scale as the energy directed by a knowledgeable human being to the sun. For the sun registers that energy, is affected by it, and returns it to earth (as well as sending it elsewhere), amplified billions of times over. The effective power of ideas is an example of a positive result of amplification of energy transactions by some symbiotically related partner or partners somewhere in the universe. We need only think of examples in the practical realm, such as Einstein's theory of relativity, Darwin's theory of evolution, the invention of the printing press—not to mention the ideas of artists and religious figures such as Jesus, Buddha, and Mohammed. To live and explain life only by laws of the physical universe is a dangerous kind of childish, shortsighted narcissism.

"Once we recognize the intricate balance of forces influencing man and his effect on these forces, we can learn to 'design' our lives in a new age by taking advantage of the universal energies and wisdom. Modern man has set himself the immense task of trying to prove or demonstrate all he thinks he ought to believe as truth. In the realm of matter he has certainly done wonders. Perhaps this training is necessary to prepare him for the task of proving, by demonstration, the laws of the non-physical or spiritual world. In this way, the old problems of superstition and blind faith will be eliminated, and the stage set for the next level of evolution in the new age.

"I think that if we look at certain kinds of scientific investigations we can see the beginnings of a bridge between physical and non-physical realities. For example, in psychophysical studies, eminent scholars are moving more toward the use of three-dimensional representations of all sensory processes. The ability to relate sensory experiences, or energy transactions, to three-dimensional models and wave forms seems to demonstrate the symbiosis of all phenomena through similar fundamental principles, thereby showing a link between the physical and non-physical forces man experiences. Difficulties arise when what is to be demonstrated on the non-physical level is invisible to the physical senses. What is required is a pioneering spirit, a spiritual explorer, to overcome the physical resistance of the world, to break certain energy barriers. The individual must become the experimenter, the experiment and the laboratory, all in one."

At this point Sylvia, who had been quietly listening to the conversation, said, "I am reminded of the dream of Jacob. He saw the heavens open their gates and higher beings of light, then called angels, descend to earth. I believe this is an allegory describing some form of spiritual communication with other worlds in which man speaks with beings from other dimensions, probably through some form of symbology, images or archetypal symbols in light."

"Yes," I said, "the idea of man conversing with light beings would entail a form of communication beyond the spoken word."

"I believe man should not limit his sources of knowledge to the earthly world of science—not in this solar age which we appear to be entering. And I do feel that our brains possess centers that could, with the aid of sunlight, give us greater insight into the nature of the universe," Sylvia said. "We all know that sunlight produces chemicals that open up new worlds. Whether it is the radiation itself or a chemical produced by radiation that does the work seems unimportant to me. What is important is that we gain access to other worlds. In this respect Anne has become too involved in the technicalities of the effects of solar radiation on the brain. What she does not understand is that the important thing is the actual communication and the knowledge gained by it. I often feel that technology cripples people's souls."

"Absolutely," I said. "The eyes themselves are the means of reaching into the world of stellar bodies through the sun. The eyes are connected to the sun through our techniques, and then the communication through symbology, or IF, is spontaneous. The mechanics of how the eye links man to the sun are unimportant, even though they are fascinating. And I feel that the weakness of secular science is in its technicality. It's like arguing about how many angels can stand on the point of a needle."

"Science—or, more correctly, scientists—have to accept the fact that discoverers and research workers are often not technicians, but dedicated souls using their intuitive feelings," said Sylvia. "Their discoveries concerning the nature of the universe are for all people in the world to share and to experience for themselves. These experiences can be more valid than all the science in the world."

Elena continued the conversation. "According to classical science, the act of observing events or objects does not change those events or objects. However, from the point of view of quantum mechanics, the act of observing physical events or objects does definitely influence the nature of those events or objects. In other words, we are not merely products of our environment—we are shapers or creators of our environment. The bond between us and nature, or the universe, is greater and more subtle than most people realize. Knowledge of this fact and its ramifications could be a major catalyst in the creation of a truly new age. The sooner people begin to take their destiny into their own hands and stop letting power groups, such as scientists, think for them, the better off the world will be."

"That is true," said Sylvia. "I suppose the age of innocence when men could let kings, presidents, churches, universities or scientific institutions think for them has passed. And it's about time. In the final analysis, man must control his own life. The Project techniques help man to transcend the world so that he can live in it without really being bound or limited by it. What I like about the Project's teachings is the possibility that we might bring down to earth some of the order of heaven."

"As participants in a universe with both non-matter and matter energy," said Elena, "we need to better understand the relationship between the two in order to free ourselves from the ignorance that binds us to the latter. If life forms are structured matter living in symbiotic relationships with other forms, then energy, mass, and information are inextricably connected, with information representing a kind of life force. Full utilization of such information entails a conscious use of the non-material aspect of energy, or, in other words, the conscious life in energy."

"As Stromberg pointed out," I interjected, "the consciousness of the individual has become part of a more general consciousness. The techniques we are learning put us into contact with that higher consciousness. The excitation resulting from sunlight coming into the nervous system produces a new and higher form of awareness in the individual. The information we assimilate gives us greater knowledge of ourselves and the universe through direct experience, extends our faculties, and puts us into contact with the source of life. This direct contact has opened up new dimensions of existence for us, because it has given us access to new information."

"The capacity of human beings to handle or communicate information," Elena added, "makes them the greatest energy manipulators or transformers of all living organisms on earth. So it seems important that humans be as conscious as possible of the power of their role as participants in the universe. If we wanted to characterize the main difference between modern man and his ancestors, it could well be described by the amount of information we have available and the ease and speed with which we can share it with a large portion of the population. The more closely we scrutinize living biological organisms, the more we find uniformity rather than diversity among life forms. For example, consider the marvelous way genetic uniqueness is preserved by genes within similar species, or the ability of DNA molecules to replicate and express themselves in unrelated organisms. It also seems that we share some of the most basic identical kinds of tiny organisms, called mitochondria, not only with other animals, but with insects, plants and simpler life forms.

"Symbiosis on the physical level links all living forms, from microscopic to macroscopic. The relationship of life on earth to the energy of the sun is an expanded symbiosis dependent on specific energy exchanges on various levels. Since our sun is only one star among millions in our own Milky Way—one interconnected system among the numberless galaxies that all seem to share the same elements in the realm of matter—it is conceivable that we are part of a whole system or reality, which we are capable of experiencing through the ultimate form of symbiosis: consciousness. If we call the whole reality God, our insatiable search for information becomes the search for God. With that goal in mind, we move from physics to metaphysics or religion, man's most abiding concern.

"If evolution of the human mind is a result of influences outside the human body, then we can use the mind as a springboard to greater consciousness of non-material dimensions once we know the principles involved and learn how to apply them. The complex path from the initial step, the conversion of light energy into animated organic matter, to the final step, man's use of light energy for intellectual and creative purposes, has been mapped by the physical sciences. There has been, for the most part, a gradual and logical increase in complexity of form compatible with environmental conditions. However, the evidence does suggest that over the past six hundred million years, the gradual development was punctuated by several bursts of activity; these can be associated with the development of ATP (adenosine triphosphate), an increase in the oxygen level, and—perhaps—fluctuations in the oxygen/carbon dioxide level due to events such as ice ages.

"The most recent burst in the evolutionary development of

man (possibly caused by a sudden change in solar radiation) was an increase in the amount of brain-related tissue, which provided him with a new, more highly developed sensory integration system. This system gives him a greater capacity to decode and integrate information received in the form of visual stimuli, which, in turn, permits greater participation in three-dimensional space and time. Man's current fascination or infatuation with his physical world may be explained by the relatively recent expansion of his capacity to process and transmit stimuli.

"The human organism has evolved into a form capable of organizing energy stimuli into extremely subtle mental images and language. This has allowed us to construct levels of reality we can consciously share with others of the same species, as well as with living organisms of other species, and even with so-called inanimate matter. Communication with the latter is generally carried out by 'unusual' individuals, such as 'sensitives' or psychics, who can communicate with plants, perform PK, predict future events, heal, generate matter from non-material energy, and even live for abnormally long periods of time without the benefit of food other than sunlight.

"If our physical reality is that which our brain and the rest of our nervous system—an evolving intelligence—have constructed out of non-physical energy originating in the sun, then physical reality is only a fraction of the whole reality, the full interplay of energy and matter."

"I believe we have to accept that man is presently experiencing great changes in his world and that, in order to survive them, he must evolve into a species able to handle larger dosages of sunlight, especially ultraviolet radiation," I said. "Our work at the Project is preparing man for these changes.

"We know the sun is continuing to change. We had a good example of this in August, 1972, when a tremendous eruption on the face of the sun increased its temperature and sent out an abnormal amount of radiation. The violent flare activity and the resulting magnetic storms suggest that the sun is becoming unstable and is undergoing radiation changes that will affect the whole solar system. We have every reason to suspect that just as the heat from bomb explosions in World War II generated new plants not previously known in the British Isles, the human race may be transformed by mutation into a new species—or a variation, anyway. It can be favorable or unfavorable.

"Ancient texts, like Ovid's *Metamorphoses*, are filled with accounts of periods when the sun sent out enormous amounts of solar and cosmic radiation that produced new and strange forms and shapes. We have to consider that larger amounts of radiation, including ultraviolet rays, are reaching the surface of our planet. There is evidence to suggest that the ozone layer of the biosphere, which normally screens out ultraviolet radiation, is being destroyed by pollutants. This new sun of ours, the X-sun, is producing an X-radiation that will produce an X-species. Rather than wait for the possible extinction of our species, we of the Project are attempting to engineer a favorable variation, the X-variation, to produce a highly developed organism capable of absorbing radiation in large amounts. We are doing this by gradually increasing our immunity to solar radiation, the incidence of which is increasing and will continue to increase.

"Highly evolved species have become extinct in the past because they had no defense against changing climatic conditions. The new environment will contain heavy dosages of radiation, and man in his present state could not be expected to survive long. If my predictions are correct, the radiation will be more intense than anyone has dared to predict. I am basing my prediction on my research of ancient texts and on my own feelings. I am reminded of a passage in the last book of the Old Testament (Malachi, Chapter 4, verses 1–3) which describes a last and final solar age in which God shall assist the surviving people.

For behold the day cometh, that shall burn as an oven; and all the proud, yea, and all that do wickedly, shall be stubble: and the day that cometh shall burn them up, saith the Lord of hosts, that it shall leave them neither root nor branch. But unto you that fear my name shall the Sun of Righteousness arise with healing in its beams; and ye shall go forth, and grow up as calves of the stall. And ye shall tread down the wicked; for they shall be ashes under the soles of your feet in the day that I shall do this, saith the Lord of hosts.

"To me the translation is simple enough: God's new sun, a kind of Messianic sun, will bring about the final age of the world by means of solar heat and radiation. A godly race will survive, and the old race will be burned up. I firmly believe in the possibility of man's evolving into a solar being able to live on solar energy alone. This will be the beginning of man's journey to the stars."

Elena looked at me and said, "We will need to demonstrate all this to the critics. Without proof they won't accept it."

"I suppose survival would be demonstration enough," I said.

"But we can't stand by and let the world discover this for itself when it's too late," said Sylvia in a concerned voice, her brow furrowed.

"No, we can't," I said. "We need to prove our discoveries to a skeptical world."

"I for one believe the world will accept our findings," Elena said. "Humans are a hardy stock. We've been around for millions of years, and I have a feeling we'll be around for millions more. We will be listened to."

"We will have to be," I said. "Human survival depends upon it."

BIBLIOGRAPHY

BOOKS

Acosta, Jose de. THE NATURAL AND MORAL HISTORIES OF THE EAST AND WEST INDIES. 2nd ed. Mexico City: Fondo de Cultura Economica, 1962.

Alcala, Ermilo Solis, trans. CODICE PEREZ. Merida, 1949.

Babbitt, Edwin D. THE PRINCIPLES OF LIGHT AND COLOR. University Books, 1967.

Barnett, Lincoln. THE UNIVERSE AND DR. EINSTEIN. Harper & Row, 1948.

Bates, W. D., M.D. BETTER EYESIGHT WITHOUT GLASSES. Pyramid Books, 1965.

Bernal, Ignacio. THE NATIONAL MUSEUM OF ANTHROPOLOGY, MEXICO. Abrams, 1968.

Blewett, Duncan B. THE FRONTIERS OF BEING. Award Books, 1969.

Burr, Harold Saxton. BLUEPRINT FOR IMMORTALITY: THE ELECTRIC PATTERNS OF LIFE. London: Neville Spearman, Ltd., 1972.

Caso, Alfonso. THE AZTECS: PEOPLE OF THE SUN. Translated by Lowell Dunham. University of Oklahoma Press, 1958.

CODEX BORGIANUS, 3 vols. Commentary by Eduard Siler. Mexico City: Fondo de Cultura Economica, 1963.

Crile, George Washington. THE BIPOLAR THEORY OF LIVING PROCESSES. Macmillan, 1926.

Daniels, Farrington. DIRECT USE OF THE SUN'S ENERGY. Ballantine Books, 1964.

Darwin, Charles. THE ORIGIN OF SPECIES. Collier Books, 1974.

___. THE VOYAGE OF THE BEAGLE. Bantam Books, 1972.

Diaz del Castillo, Bernal. THE CONQUEST OF NEW SPAIN. Trans. by J. M. Cohen. Penguin Books, 1963.

Dibble, Charles E., ed. CODICE XOLOTL. Mexico City: Universidad Nacional, 1951.

Donnelly, Ignatius. RAGNAROK: THE DESTRUCTION OF ATLANTIS. Steiner Books (Multimedia), 1974.

Du Plessis, Jean. THE ELECTRONIC REACTIONS OF ABRAMS. Chicago: Blanche and Jeanne R. Abrams Memorial Foundation, 1922.

Eccles, John C. FACING REALITY: PHILOSOPHICAL ADVENTURES BY A BRAIN SCIENTIST. Springer-Verlag: New York, 1970.

Edmundson, Rev. Dr. George, trans. and ed. JOURNAL OF THE TRAVELS AND LABOURS OF FATHER SAMUEL FRITZ IN THE RIVER OF THE AMAZONS BETWEEN 1686 AND 1723. Translated from the Evora MS, London: Cambridge University Press, 1922.

Einstein, Albert. RELATIVITY, THE SPECIAL AND GENERAL THEORY. Henry Holt & Co., 1920.

——, and Infeld, Leopold. THE EVOLUTION OF PHYSICS. Simon and Schuster, 1961.

Ephrussi, B. HYBRIDIZATION OF SOMATIC CELLS. Princeton University Press, 1972.

Fechner, Gustav Theodor. NANNA ODER ÜBER DAS SEELENLEBEN DER PFLANZEN. Leipzig: Verlag von Leopold Voss, 1921.

Frauenfelder, Hans, and Henley, Ernest M. SUBATOMIC PHYSICS. Prentice-Hall, 1974.

Gamow, George. A STAR CALLED THE SUN. Viking Press, 1964.

Gardner, Martin. THE AMBIDEXTROUS UNIVERSE. Penguin Books, 1964.

Hawkes, Jacquetta. MAN AND THE SUN. Random House, 1962.

Jastrow, Robert, and Cameron, A. G. W., eds. ORIGIN OF THE SOLAR SYSTEM. Academic Press, 1963.

Jerison, Harry J. EVOLUTION OF THE BRAIN AND INTELLIGENCE. Academic Press, 1973.

Jung, C. G. THE ARCHETYPES AND THE COLLECTIVE UNCONSCIOUS. Pantheon Books, 1959.

——. FLYING SAUCERS: A MODERN MYTH OF THINGS SEEN IN THE SKIES. Translated by R. F. C. Hull. Signet Books, 1969.

——. MAN AND HIS SYMBOLS. London: Aldus Books, 1964.

Koestler, Arthur. THE GHOST IN THE MACHINE. Hutchinson of London, 1967.

Koshland, D. E., Jr. "The Molecular Basis For Enzyme Regulation," in THE ENZYMES, Vol. 1. Academic Press, 1970.

Kozyrev, N. A. POSSIBILITY OF EXPERIMENTAL STUDY OF THE PROPERTIES OF TIME. Joint Publication Research Service, Arlington, Va., JPRS-45238, May 1968.

Lund, E. J. BIOELECTRIC FIELDS AND GROWTH. University of Texas Press, 1945.

Martha, Karel; Musil, Jan; and Tuha, Hana. ELECTROMAGNETIC FIELDS AND THE LIFE ENVIRONMENT. San Francisco Press, 1971.

Medina, Jose Torbino. DISCOVERY OF THE AMAZON RIVER, According to the Account of Friar Gaspar de Carvajal. Seville: Press of E. Rasco, Bustos Tavera, 1.

Menzel, Donald H. OUR SUN. Harvard University Press, 1959.

Michell, John. THE VIEW OVER ATLANTIS. Ballantine Books, 1972.

Ott, John. HEALTH AND LIGHT. Devin-Adair Co., Conn., 1973.

Penfield, Wilder. THE MYSTERY OF THE MIND. Princeton University Press, 1975.

Plato. THE DIALOGUES OF PLATO, 2 vols. Trans. by B. Jowett. Random House, 1937.

Presman, A. S. ELECTROMAGNETIC FIELDS AND LIFE. Plenum, 1970.

Press, Frank, and Siever, Raymond. EARTH. W. H. Freeman and Company, 1974.

Reich, Wilhelm. THE DISCOVERY OF THE ORGONE, vols. I and II. New York: Orgone Institute Press, 1948.

Roys, Ralph L. THE BOOK OF CHILAM BALAM OF CHUMAYEL. University of Oklahoma Press, 1967.

Sagan, Carl. THE COSMIC CONNECTION: AN EXTRA-TERRESTRIAL PERSPECTIVE. Dell Publishing Co., 1975.

Sahagrin, Bernardino de. FLORENTINE CODEX: GENERAL HISTORY OF THE THINGS OF NEW SPAIN, 12 vols. Trans. by Arthur J. O. Anderson and Charles E. Dibble. Santa Fe: School of American Research, 1950–1963.

Savoy, Gene. ANTISUYO — THE SEARCH FOR THE LOST CITIES OF THE AMAZON. Simon and Schuster, 1970.

——. THE DECODED NEW TESTAMENT. Reno, Nevada: The International Community of Christ, 1974.

——. INTRODUCTION TO THE SYSTEM OF COSOLARGY. Reno, Nevada: The International Community of Christ, 1970.

——. ON THE TRAIL OF THE FEATHERED SERPENT.

Bobbs-Merrill, 1974.

——. PHYSICAL AND SPIRITUAL ENERGY IN RELATION TO THE INDIVIDUAL APPLYING THE SYSTEM OF COSOLARGY. Reno, Nevada: The International Community of Christ, 1975.

——. TIME, ENERGY AND ULTRADIMENSIONAL REALITY. Reno, Nevada: The International Community of Christ, 1976.

——. TRANSFORMATION OF MAN INTO A NEW WORLD SPECIES. Reno, Nevada: The International Community of Christ, 1972.

——. TRANSFORMATION OF MAN THROUGH ALTERED STATES OF CONSCIOUSNESS. Reno, Nevada: The International Community of Christ, 1976.

——. TRANSFORMATION OF MAN THROUGH ARCHETYPAL SYMBOLS. Reno, Nevada: The International Community of Christ, 1976.

——, and Geoghegan, James C. ESSAEI TRANSCRIPTS. Reno, Nevada: The International Community of Christ, 1975.

Sejourne, Laurette. BURNING WATER: THOUGHT AND RELIGION IN ANCIENT MEXICO. Grove Press, 1960.

Spense, Lewis. THE MYTHS OF MEXICO AND PERU. London: George G. Harrap & Company, 1913.

Stanley, Krippner, and Rubin, Daniel, eds. GALAXIES OF LIFE: THE HUMAN AURA IN ACUPUNCTURE AND KIRLIAN PHOTOGRAPHY. Interface, 1973.

Stromberg, Gustaf. MAN, MIND AND THE UNIVERSE. Science of Mind Publications, 1971.

Szent-Gyorgyi, A. BIOENERGETICS. Academic Press, 1957.

Thomas, Lewis. THE LIVES OF A CELL. Viking Press, 1974.

Troyer, Sir James George. THE GOLDEN BOUGH. Macmillan, 1972.

Vaillant, George C. AZTECS OF MEXICO. Doubleday, 1962.

Vega, Garcilaso de la. THE INCAS. Edited by Alain Gheerbrant. Avon Books, 1961.

Velikovsky, Immanuel. EARTH IN UPHEAVAL. Dell, 1955.

——. WORLDS IN COLLISION.Macmillan, 1950.

Von Hagen, Victor W. THE INCAS OF PEDRO DE CIEZA DE LEON. University of Oklahoma Press, 1959.

Wallace, Alfred Russel. A NARRATIVE OF TRAVELS OF THE AMAZON AND RIO NEGRO. London: Ward, Lock and Co., 1889.

Walter, W. Grey. THE LIVING BRAIN. Norton, 1963.

Waters, Frank. MEXICO MYSTIQUE: THE COMING SIXTH WORLD OF CONSCIOUSNESS. Sage Books, 1975.
Yariv, Amnon. QUANTUM ELECTRONICS. Wiley, 1975.

ARTICLES

Becker, R. O., "The Effect of Magnetic Fields upon the Central Nervous System," *Medical Electronics and Biological Engineering,* 1963, 1, 293–303.
——, "Electromagnetic Forces and Life Processes," *Technology Review,* Dec. 1972.
Burr, H. S., and Northrop, F. S. C., "The Electrodynamic Theory of Life," *Quarterly Review of Biology,* 1935, 10, 322–333.
Cameron, A. G. W., "The Origin and Evolution of the Solar System," *Scientific American,* vol. 233, no. 3, 1975.
Cohen, Stanley N., "The Manipulation of Genes," *Scientific American,* vol. 233, no. 1, 1975.
Freksa, Prof. Hans Friedrich, "The Realization of the Inherited Programme in the Living Cell—Genetic Information and Cellular Processes," *Universitas,* vol. 13, no. 1, 1970.
Friedan, Earl, "The Chemical Elements of Life," *Scientific American,* July 1972.
Holloway, Ralph L., "The Casts of Fossil Hominid Brains," *Scientific American,* vol. 231, no. 1, 1974.
Jacques, Hal, "Cataclysms," *Probe the Unknown,* Oct. 1973.
Jerison, Harry J., "Paleoneurology and the Evolution of the Mind," *Scientific American,* vol. 234, no. 1, 1976.
Miller, Joseph S., "The Structure of Emission Nebulas," *Scientific American,* vol. 231, no. 4, 1974.
Miller, Richard Alan; Webb, Burt; and Dickson, Darden, "A Holographic Concept of Reality," *Psychoenergetic Systems,* vol. 1. Department of Paraphysics and Parapsychology, University of Washington, Seattle, Washington, 1975; Gordon and Breach Science Publishers, Great Britain.
Murr, L. E., "Physiological Stimulation of Plants Using Delayed and Regulated Electric Field Environments," *International Journal of Biometeorology,* vol. 10, no. 2.
Parker, E. N., "The Sun," *Scientific American,* vol. 233, no. 3, 1975.
Paschoff, Jay M., "The Solar Corona," *Scientific American,* vol. 229, no. 4, 1973.

Purett, L., "Magnetic Reversals and Biological Extinctions," *Science News,* 1971, 100, 287–302.

Redfield, J. S., "Physico-Physiological Research on the Dynamics of Magnetism, Heat, Light, Electricity and Chemism, in Their Relations to Vital Force," New York, 1851.

Reichenbach, H., "The Direction of Time," Berkeley, 1956.

Sagan, Carl, "The Solar System," *Scientific American,* vol. 233, no. 3, 1975.

Siever, Raymond, "The Earth," *Scientific American,* vol. 233, no. 3, 1975.

"Some Biological Effects of the 'Laying on of Hands'," *Journal of the American Society for Psychical Research,* vol. 59, no. 2, 1965.

Willson, Robert W., "Astronomical Notes on the Maya Codices," *Peabody Museum of American Archaeology and Ethnology Papers,* vol. 6, no. 3, 1924.

Wurtman, Richard J., "The Effects of Light on the Human Body," *Scientific American,* vol. 233, no. 1, 1975.

"Zend-Avesta, Pensieri Sulle Case Del Cielo e Dell' Al Di La," Milan, *Fratelli Bocca,* 1944.

Index

Adam and Eve, 107-13, 114-15, 116, 117, 118, 119
Adam Kadmon, 80, 117
Adonis, 66
aging process, 167, 246-48
alcohol, as drug, 123
alpha rhythms, 175, 176, 177, 178, 185, 187, 203, 204, 205, 208
Amazonia, 53, 228
Amazons, 74, 88, 104, 223, 227, 237-40
America, as Old World, 5
American Indians, 132. *See also individual tribes*
Anaxagoras, 50-51, 54-55
Antonio (Indian guide), 9-10, 12-13, 14, 19
Apollo, 67, 68
Apostles, the, 189
Aquarian Age, 57-58
Araujo, Joaquim Beserra de, 82, 88, 89, 94, 104
archaeologists/archaeology, 4-5, 15, 30, 49, 75
archetypal symbology, 179-80, 183-84, 207, 214, 248, 257, 259. *See also* symbols
Aristarchus of Samos, 51
Aristotle, 52, 222
Artemis, 67
Asclepios, 68
Assyrians, 66, 67
Athens (ancient), 53, 54-55
Atlantis, 63
atomic structure, 149-50, 168

ATP (adenosine triphosphate), 263
Aztecs, 61, 63, 71, 77, 156

Babylonia, 67
Balder (solar god), 66
Bates, Henry Walter, 75
Bates, W. H., 43, 207
Baugh, Elena, 151, 152-63, 256-59, 261-63, 266
beta rhythms, 175, 176, 178, 185, 187, 203, 204, 205, 208
Bible, 62, 72, 113
    Genesis, 107
    Gospel of Matthew, 81, 115
    Malachi, 265
    Odes of Solomon, 81
Bimini, 7
black magic, 121, 124. *See also* shamanism; witchcraft
Bochica, 228
Bourbourg, Brasseur de, 209-10
Bovis, M., 231
Brahmanism, 67
brain, 144, 145, 146, 153-54, 156-57, 159-60, 161-62, 177-78, 182, 184, 195, 206, 212, 234, 242, 243-44, 252, 256, 257, 258, 261. *See also* mind
    increased size of, 160, 222, 264
brain rhythms and waves, 175-78, 186, 187, 202-05, 208, 209, 214
Bridgit the Bright, 67

Buddha, 194, 259
Buriats, 128
Burr, Harold Saxton, 192
Buyoca, 7

Cameron, A. G. W., 43
Carbajal, Gaspar de, 240
Castaneda, Carlos, 126, 130
cataclysms, 62-64, 65, 71, 72
Cayce, Edgar, 129
Celilo Indians, 76-77
cells, anatomy and physiology of,
    145-49, 206, 246
Chacha, 27
Chachapoyas, 88, 230
Chardin, Pierre Teilhard de, 6,
    157
Christ. *See* Jesus
Christianity, 66, 79, 80-81, 101,
    125, 134, 135, 233
Clement of Alexandria, 81
clocks. *See* time
Coccius, Samuel, 199
Codex Chimalpopocati, 63
Colombia (ancient), 228
Comfort, Alex, 247, 248
communication theory, 213
Condamine, Charles de la, 240
Constantine, 68
Crowley, Aleister, 124
Cuvier, Georges, 62, 63

Dailey, Bill, 45-46, 74, 75-76,
    77-78, 82, 85, 86, 89
Darwin, Charles, 31-32, 33, 62, 75,
    250, 259
death, 36, 98, 105, 106, 131-32,
    153, 158, 159, 162, 165, 166,
    176, 234, 235, 246. *See also*
    immortality
Delos (shrine), 67

delta rhythms, 175-76, 177, 185,
    187, 202-03, 204, 205, 208
Descartes, René, 248
devil, the, 115, 116
Diodorus Siculus, 239
DNA, 249, 263
Donnelly, Ignatius, 63
Drbal, Karl, 231
Du-Zu (solar god), 66

Egypt (ancient), 66, 134, 172, 219
Ehler, Kenneth, 242-55, 258, 259
Einstein, Albert, 5-6, 8-9, 55, 123,
    211, 259
El Dorado, 74, 88, 223, 227-29,
    234
El Dorado/Amazons Expedition,
    74, 104, 223, 227
electrical/electromagnetic energy
    and fields, 18, 23-24, 30, 34,
    35, 47-48, 52, 61, 72, 101, 105,
    140, 145, 150, 177, 185,
    192-93, 195, 200, 206, 212,
    213-24, 243-44, 256
endocrine system, 105, 140, 141,
    142, 165-66, 167, 242, 247-48,
    249, 252
energy. *See also* light energy; solar
    energy; spiritual energy
  body, 235, 245, 246
  as carrier of IF, 24, 179, 188, 189
  conservation of, 72, 97
  cyclical nature of, 148
  and information, 215, 219, 250,
    254, 264
  and matter, 211, 232
  sources of, 143
  and speech, 97, 264
  and time, 24, 191-92
Energy bonds, 258, 259
Environmental Health and Light

Research Institute, 246
enzymes, 147-48
Eschenmoser, Albert, 242
ESP, 47, 129, 212
Essenes, 81
evolution, 157-58, 161-62, 264, 265
eyes. *See* vision

fasting, 106, 155, 247
Fechner, Gustav Theodor, 7-8, 60-61
"Comparative Anatomy of the Angels," 8
Life After Death, 8
"First Book of Adam and Eve, The," 107-13

Garcia, Marcos, 172
Gardner, Gerald, 124-25, 126
Garrett, A., 197-98
Geoghegan, James C., 120-38
Gerbus, Michael, 99-100
God, 17, 41, 52, 53, 56, 71, 72, 78, 80, 101, 106, 107, 115, 117, 118, 119, 122, 134, 154-55, 156
gods. *See individual listings*
golden image, author's perception of, 11, 17-18, 19, 36, 40, 94, 171, 173, 209
Gonzalez, Ramon, 100
Gran Pajatán, 27, 29-30
Greeks (ancient), 53, 54-55, 67, 78, 127-28, 250
Guarana legend, 85-86

hallucinogens, 16-17, 120-22, 125-27, 128, 129, 132, 134, 136, 157, 184, 199, 209. *See also individual listings*

hara, 133
Haughton, Michael, 128
Hawkins, Harry, 46-47, 48, 50-51, 52, 54, 55-56, 57, 59, 63, 64, 70
Hebrews (ancient), 66, 68-69, 80, 134, 136
Helios, 67
Helios-Mithra, 68
Herrera, Antonio de, 237-39
Hindus, 134, 172
Hipparchus of Nicaea, 51
Hiroshima, 248, 250-51
Hitler, Adolf, 135-36
homozygosity, 252
Horus, 66
Huayna Capac, 7, 8, 79
human aura, 195
human body, composition of, 40-41, 43
Humboldt, Friedrich von, 240

IF (intelligence factors), 24, 140, 144, 154, 166, 167, 179-80, 185-86, 192, 195, 206, 207, 214, 220, 221, 232, 234, 252, 259
immortality, 98, 105, 116, 119, 165, 166, 194, 234, 235, 246, 254. *See also* death
Incas, 7, 8, 27, 77, 79, 88, 172, 173, 196, 197, 200, 201, 210, 217
India (ancient), 36, 133
Inti (sun god), 77

Jacob's ladder, 260
Jenkins, Elmer, 127, 132
Jesus, 33, 34, 44, 59, 61, 66, 68, 70, 79, 80-81, 137, 189, 194, 259
Jewish religion (ancient), 66, 68-69, 80

Joshua, 72
Julian, 68
Jung, Carl
  Flying Saucers, 199
  Man and His Symbols, 53
Jupiter, 68

Kaballah, 132
Kirlian, Semyon, 168, 170
Kirlian, Valentina, 168, 170
Koran, 113
Kukulcan, 228

Landegger, Carl C., 223, 237, 239
Lea, H. C., 125
left-handed systems, 211, 212, 221
Leon, Juan Ponce de, 7
life, origins of, 106-07, 221-22, 250
light, polarized. *See* polarized light
light beings/bodies/forms, 105,
  106-07, 113, 193, 194-95, 235,
  254, 260
light energy, 167, 204, 214
LSD, 121, 133, 199, 246

Maenads, 127-28
magic, black. *See* black magic
Maharishi Mahesh Yoga, 133
man, 170
  dual nature of, 115-19, 156, 160,
    234
  as feedback scanning organism,
    185
  imagery of, 184-85
  as source of energy, 192
  spiritual, 32-33, 34-35, 106, 107,
    155-56, 201
  ultra-dimensional nature of,
    193-94
mandalas, 184
Maoris, 136

marijuana, 123
Marx, Karl, 136
materialism, 33-34, 56-57, 58, 59,
  71, 93, 118, 161
matter, 232-33
Maué Indians, 85
Mayas, 70-71, 77, 172, 173, 196,
  197, 219. *See also* Quiche Mayas
Menzel, Donald H., 43
metabolism, 165-66, 195
metaphysics, 97, 105, 165
Mexicans (ancient), 33, 77, 79, 144,
  172, 183, 228, 229. *See also*
  Aztecs; Mayas; Quiche Mayas;
  Toltecs
mind, 153-54. *See also* brain
Mishnah of Judah, 136
Mithra, 66-67, 172
Mohammed, 259
Monteith, Henry, 168
Moros, 128
Moses, 33, 68, 72
Murray, Margaret, 124
mushrooms, magic, 121, 128, 129,
  130, 199
music, effects of, 134
mutations, 250-51, 252
mysticism, 53-54, 59, 71, 93, 97-98,
  158, 160, 161. *See also*
  metaphysics; spiritual man;
  *individual religions, gods,
  teachers*

Nahuatls, 46
Nazca lines, 233
nervous system, 144-46, 166, 167,
  176, 177-79, 195, 212, 213,
  219, 222, 242, 243, 253, 256,
  257, 258, 262, 264
Noah's flood, 62
Norse (ancient), 66

Northrop, F. C., 192

Olmos, Andres de, 69
Olympia (shrine), 67
omega rhythms, 177, 178, 204,
    205, 208
Ontaneda, Sylvia, 25-26, 27, 28,
    29, 31-36, 39, 48, 49, 53, 56,
    57, 58-59, 60, 64. *See also*
    Savoy, Sylvia Ontaneda
Opdyke, Jack, 101-03
Orellana, Francisco, 82, 239-40
Ormazd, 66
Osiris, 66
Ott, John, 246
Ovid, 265

Pan, 67
Pasteur, Louis, 221
Paul, Saint, 61, 80-81
Perkum (solar god), 67
Persia (ancient), 66-67
Peruvians (ancient), 33, 77, 144,
    172, 183, 210-11, 228, 229
Peter, Saint, 117
peyote, 17, 120, 132
Phoenicians, 79
phosphenes, 180, 182-184, 196,
    206, 215
photosynthesis, 79, 143, 253
physicists/physics, 44, 54-55, 62,
    97, 101, 161, 184, 189
Pigafetta, Antonio, 7
pineal gland, 43, 106, 140-41, 167,
    178, 247-48, 253
pituitary, 141, 167, 178, 247-48,
    249, 253
PK (psychokinesis), 47, 189, 212,
    264
Planck, Max, 213
Plato, 9, 33, 44, 52, 68, 215

Dialogues, 62
Resurrection, 101
polarized light, 210-11, 212, 222
Popul Vuh, 69-70
protoplasm, 149. *See also* cells
PSI, 47, 189, 212, 230, 235
psilocybin, 120
psychedelic drugs. *See*
    hallucinogens
psychic motors, 230, 232
Ptolemy, 51
Punchao, 172-73, 197, 210
Puranas, 67
Pyramid of Giza, 231
Pyramid of Kufu, 62
Pyramid of Quetzalcoatl, 60, 62
Pyramid of the Moon, 65, 73
Pryamid of the Sun, 45, 53
pyramids, 156-57, 233
    experiments with, 230-31
pyramids at Tollan (Mexico), 96
Pythagoras, 136, 160-61, 215

Quetzalcoatl, 33, 60, 70, 71, 228
Quiche Mayas, 69, 70-71, 209-10.
    See also Mayas
Quintana, Ana, 98

radiant energy fields, 164-65, 168,
    170
reincarnation, 99
relativity, theory of, 5-6, 8-9, 24, 34
religion, 54-56, 78, 134, 135, 137,
    158. *See also* God; *individual
    gods and religions*
Romans (ancient), 67, 68, 79, 128

Sagan, Carl, 249
Sahagun, Bernardino de, 63, 228
Salk, Jonas, 250
Salk Institute, 244

Satan, 115, 116
Savoy, Sylvia Ontaneda, 151,
    152-63, 173, 256-57, 260-62,
    266. *See also* Ontaneda, Sylvia
Seaman, Ellen, 98-99, 100-01
shamanism, 60, 121, 123, 124, 127,
    128-31, 132, 134-35, 136-37.
    See also black magic;
    witchcraft
Shamash, 67
Shirokogorof (Russian
    anthropologist), 128, 129, 130
Simon Magus, 117
Socrates, 68
solar energy, 30, 42-43, 44, 47, 53,
    72, 77-78, 92, 101, 105,
    106-07, 150, 154, 157-58, 159,
    160, 161, 166, 186-87, 195,
    197, 204, 211, 213, 220-21,
    223, 251, 252, 258, 259, 266
solar gods, 65-73. *See also individual
    listings*
solar priests, 197, 199, 200,
    208-09, 212, 229, 233. *See also
    individual cultures*
solar system, 40-41, 43, 67, 71, 72,
    75
space-time continuum, 207
Spanish conquest of South
    America, 33, 172
spiritual body, 100-02
spiritual energy, 100, 162, 249
spiritual man, 32-33, 34-35, 106,
    107, 155-56, 201
Stonehenge, 67
strobe (flicker) experiments,
    174-75, 187, 196, 197, 202-05,
    207, 208-09, 214-15
Stromberg, Gustaf, 48, 105, 262
Sufis, 134
sun, 50-51, 52, 56-57, 97, 155,

194-95, 263. *See also* solar
    energy
communication with, 75-77
earth condensed from, 43-44
effect of on body, 242-43, 246,
    247, 253, 254, 256, 257,
    259, 266
as energy catalyst, 167, 168, 211
and higher intelligence, 77-78
linking of to man, 106, 137-38,
    140, 148, 170, 188, 219
oscillation of, 72, 89-90, 118,
    140, 215
periodic instability of, 65, 71,
    264-65
responsiveness of, 72-73
staring at, 7-8, 9, 10, 12, 35,
    60-61, 79, 89-91, 114, 118,
    233-34, 243, 244
temples' orientation to, 16
worship of, 46, 65-71, 77, 80
symbols, 205, 206-08, 215, 217
Syrians (ancient), 66, 67

Talmud, 113
Tamheur (solar god), 66
Tantra, 145
telepathy, 105
Teotihuacan, 45, 46, 62, 69
    Pyramid of Quetzalcoatl, 60, 62
Tezcatlipoca, 63-64
Therapeutae, 81
theta rhythms, 175, 177, 185, 187,
    202-03, 204, 205
Thomas, Chan, 62
Thomas, Keith
    History of Witchcraft, 125
    Religion and the Decline of Magic,
    125
Thor, 67
Thunupa, 228

time
  concepts of, 98-100, 113, 122,
    123-24, 191-92
  distortion of, 131, 132-33
  experiments with, 3, 9, 11-12,
    20-25, 30, 32, 34, 35, 40, 61,
    131, 189-92
Tirios Indians, 88
Toltecs, 62, 63-69, 71
Tomich, Milenko, 46, 47, 48-49,
  50, 52, 56, 57, 59, 63, 65, 98,
  101
transcendental meditation (TM),
  133-34
Trauten (pilot), 27, 28, 29
Tungus, 128-29
Tylor, 209-10

unidentified flying objects,
  197-200, 222

Vega, Garcilaso de la, 7
Velikovsky, Immanuel, 63, 65
Vilcabamba, 172, 197
Vinci, Leonardo da, 52-53
Viracocha (religious teacher), 33,
  77, 194, 228
Viracochas (race), 27

vision, 60-61, 89, 140-44, 178-81,
  213-17, 220, 252, 256
  and afterimages, 216
  color, 42, 61, 141-42, 213-14
  peripheral, 213-14
  and shape perception, 214
  and solar energy, 42-43

Wallace, Alfred Russel, 32, 75, 240
watches. *See* time
Whipple, Fred L., 43
Whiston (theorist), 63
witchcraft, 121, 123-26. *See also*
  black magic; shamanism
Wurtman, Richard, 243

X-factor, 154, 166, 195, 205
Xipe Totec, 46
X-rays, 72, 254

Y-factor, 166
Yoga, 12, 176, 177

Zen, 176, 177
Zend Avesta, 67
Zeus, 68
Zinoz (solar god), 67
Zoroastrianism, 66-67, 172